LOVE
IS FOR
TOMORROW

To Liz,
With my love
Hope

LOVE IS FOR TOMORROW

by Hope Traver

Women's Aglow Fellowship
P.O. Box I,
Lynnwood, WA 98036 USA

Cover by Michael Hackett

Dedicated to Carol without whose thoughtful loving-kindness and expert typing this book might never have seen the light of day.

Chapter One

Margaret McAskie stood at the kitchen window and peered anxiously out into the night. Clearing a space on the frosted pane with a corner of her apron, she noted with satisfaction that the storm showed no signs of abating. The driving wind which had blown great clouds of snow before it all day had died down somewhat with the gathering darkness, but soft, fat flakes were still falling thickly. Gradually they were obscuring the familiar outline of barn and fence and tree.

Usually Margaret hated storms. They only added to the already heavy burden of chores which she had to perform before she left for school in the morning and after she returned in the afternoon; but, for once, she did not care how often she had to help her father shovel a path to the barns, nor how many times she had to wipe up the floor after him, if only the storm prevented the teacher from coming to spend her allotted time with the McAskies.

It was the village custom to board the teacher among those families who had children of school age, and the McAskie farm was the next on the list. For months Margaret had been dreading this usually much anticipated event because this year, for the first time in the village's history, the teacher was a woman and her father did not approve of women in the teaching profession. He contended that it unsexed a woman to work outside of the home, and he would not hesitate to make his feelings known to the teacher.

He had been kept, by the sudden sickness of one of his prize cows, from the town meeting at which the teacher's appointment had been approved, or the post would never have been given to a woman. The younger and more progressive element in the village had won a victory over him when his back was turned and he resented it bitterly. Angus McAskie was a God-fearing man and greatly respected by the community, but he was stern and there were not many people intrepid enough to oppose him or his decisions to his face. That the village fathers should have thus flouted his authority behind his back upset him deeply and it was his family who had been made to feel the weight of his displeasure.

The teacher was not only a woman but also young and pretty, and Margaret knew that her father would be only too willing to find fault with her on those grounds if he could discover no other. He would disapprove of her pretty clothes, her gay manner, and her dainty ways and he would not hesitate to say so. Margaret had no doubt that when he discovered that the teacher had five school dresses and wore them in rotation, he would undertake to rebuke her at family prayers by reading a passage from the Bible about vanity. Margaret cringed at the very thought.

Margaret's seatmate at school, whose family had already entertained Miss Abbott, had whispered that the teacher put kid curlers in her hair when she went to bed. Margaret shuddered to think of what her father would have to say, should such unseemly behavior come to his notice.

She sighed deeply as she finished polishing the window pane with her apron and turned back to her work. Her thoughts filled her with dismay. She adored Miss Abbott and she winced inwardly everytime she thought about her being subjected to her father's carping and criticism. He was sure to find fault with everything she said or did. Margaret had longed to tell Miss Abbott how much she personally loved her and to warn her of what to expect when she arrived at the McAskie farm, but she was too shy. Now there was nothing to do but let her come and find out how things were for herself, unless — Margaret's heart lifted at the very thought — the storm was so severe that she had to stay at the Turner's a while longer.

As Margaret filled the tea kettle from the pail at the sink she thought about the teacher's beautiful clothes. That one woman could own several pretty dresses had come as a revelation to her. Angus McAskie, who was no less famous in the village for his close-fistedness than for his godliness, allowed Margaret and her stepmother each one "Sunday-go-to-meeting" dress and one everyday dress, made of good serviceable material, in dark sensible colors. In a day when women's clothes were intricately cut and lavishly trimmed with braid, lace, or ribbon, their dresses were cut in simple lines and were completely unadorned. The only difference between Margaret's Sunday dress and her everyday dress was that the former had a simple white collar and cuffs. After two seasons' wear, her Sunday dress became her everyday dress by the simple expedient of removing the collar and cuffs. More dark, uninteresting, serviceable material was purchased under her father's strict supervision, out of which a new Sunday garment was cut. He insisted that it be fashioned upon the same lines as the old one, no matter what the prevailing mode might be. Angus McAskie always chose brown, believing it to be a color which would not show the soil, and Margaret loathed it with all her ardent young soul. It made her feel as drab as a handful of spring mud from the barnyard, and the black alpaca apron which she had to wear over her school dress to "save" it did nothing to alleviate the general somberness of her costume. She loved the gay plaids and bright colors the teacher wore. It gave her pleasure just to look at the teacher sitting like a gay bird on the small raised platform in front of the class. She sighed again as she set the kettle on the front of the stove. She knew that the storm was only a respite, but even as such, she welcomed it.

Turning away from the stove, Margaret set about her final preparations for supper. She did her work swiftly and well. It was no part of her plan to spend her life on the farm and the only way that she could see of eventually freeing herself from it was to get an education. In her heart she had determined to graduate from the local school and go on to normal school to train to be a teacher. Toward this end she bent all her energies. She did far more than her fair share of the housework so that her stepmother would have no cause to ask her father to keep her out of school. How she was going to get her father's permission to go on with her education she did not know, for he did not approve of what he called "advanced education" for a female, and he frequently aired his views on the subject. She knew that he would never be willing to give her the money for tuition even though the cracked teapot hidden behind the stove chimney was well filled, and he was known in the village to be comfortably off. She had confided her ambitions to Miss Abbott who had told her that she could arrange for her to earn her room and board, but money for books and tuition Margaret must have. Margaret had nothing she could call her own except a little lamb which a grateful neighbor had given her the previous winter for helping to nurse his wife through pneumonia.

She detested the sheep and lambs more than any of the other animals on the farm, for to her they seemed exceedingly dirty and dumb, but in spite of her feelings she tended them carefully. Her lamb was not merely a stupid, smelly creature but represented eventual freedom from the farm. She had given vent on paper to all her hopes and dreams in a composition class assignment, writing in detail how she planned to sell the lamb in the spring and use the money for her education. Miss Abbott had given her an *A* on the paper. Margaret had been doubly pleased: that she had shared her dreams with the teacher, and that she had gotten a high mark. She had hidden the slim sheaf of pages under her mattress and took it out now and again to read it. What her father would say when he learned of her intentions, she resolutely pushed into the back of her mind.

As she stepped lightly about the warm kitchen, she decided not to face that issue until it arose. Just now, she had enough to worry about with the teacher coming, and she reminded herself there was no sense in borrowing trouble. There was certain to be enough of it when Miss Abbott arrived, which she was sure to do, in due time. Margaret frowned as she opened the oven door to turn the johnny cake. Swiftly she spread the red and white checked cloth on the table and set out the simple service, placing her father's well-worn Bible at his place.

Angus McAskie expected Margaret to commit to memory a portion of Scripture daily and on Sundays, a whole chapter. He made a practice of hearing her recite her daily portion after prayers, and if she did not quote it quickly and accurately, he added ten more verses to the next day's allotment. She had a whole extra chapter to learn today because she had spilled a pail of milk on the barn floor that morning. As Margaret went from the table to the stove or the sink and back again the thought of that extra chapter filled her with rebellion and she set her small mouth in a straight line.

The teakettle began to steam and Margaret crossed the room to push it to the back of the stove. As she did so, she glanced through the open door of the small bedroom which opened off the kitchen. Her stepmother was sound asleep on the large double bed, her breath coming and going in an occasional wheeze, her small plump hands folded on her breast, a hand-quilted comfortable tucked snugly about her feet.

Matilda McAskie took full advantage of the fact that Margaret never dared to refuse to do anything she asked of her. She not only made her stepdaughter do a large share of her work but she forced her into making excuses for her when she wished to do something of which she knew Angus would not approve. She loved to drop down on the bed in the warm, back bedroom and take what she termed a "catnap," but she did not dare to indulge herself in this delightful pastime unless Margaret was in the house to warn her of her husband's approach, for in his simple and uncomplicated scheme of things, sleeping was to be done only at night. He was perfectly persuaded that the good Lord had given man the day in which to work and the night in which to rest, and any reversal of this order by any member of his family would have met with his instant and vehement disapproval, had he been aware of it. In the few years that Matilda McAskie had been his wife, she had learned to avoid his disapproval at all costs. Margaret gazed at her stepmother with contempt. It would serve her right, she thought as she returned to her work, if I let him come in and find her like that, but she did not dare to risk it and she knew Matilda knew it. If Matilda complained to her father, he would take her out of school and she would be unable to graduate in the spring. That was an eventuality she must avoid at all costs, even to protecting Matilda from Angus' wrath.

She heard her father's heavy footsteps on the porch floor, stamping the snow from his boots. He brought as little wet into the house as possible, not out of any consideration for his women folk but because he said dampness rotted the timbers of the floor. Quickly, Margaret went into the bedroom and roused her stepmother, and by the time Angus had opened the outside door, Matilda was bustling back and forth between the stove and the table with a great show of activity, her plump cheeks flushed with sleep, the whole of her small rotund person quivering with energy.

Slipping the johnny cake out of the oven, she spoke to her husband quickly before he could discover some reason for reproving her. "Sorta late in the season for such a heavy storm, ain't it, Angus?" Then to further distract his attention from herself, "That Miz Abbott dismissed school early terday. She musta thought we was goin' ter git a real blizzard!"

Angus scowled and rose to her bait. "Hmm. She must be a city woman. Anyone brung up in the country'd know it was too late ter git a big blizzard. Why, we're most half way through March. She's probly jist tryin' ter git outer some work. The town's payin' her to larn the young'uns readin', writin', and 'rithmetic, not ter be a weather prophet!"

Matilda slammed the door of the oven shut with her foot. "Well, she's probly tickled pink ter have any 'scuse ter git rid of 'em for a piece."

Angus, removing his big oiled boots in favor of well-worn carpet slippers, stopped a moment to scowl at his wife. "She's bein' paid one hundred an' fifty dollars a year ter larn the young'uns and that's a heap of money! She outer be willin' ter work fer it, seems ter me." He dragged his big chair closer to the table and reaching out a long arm turned down the wick of the lamp. He frowned at his daughter. "How many times do I have ter tell ye that kerosene don't grow on trees?"

Margaret, who knew that Matilda had lighted the lamp, said nothing. Matilda, seeing that her stepdaughter was not going to give her away, twisted her lips into a sly smile of satisfaction and folded her plump hands on the edge of the table. Angus took the hint and offered up the evening blessing.

Nothing more was said until he had had his second helping of pork and beans and his third piece of johnny cake liberally spread with molasses. Whatever else Angus McAskie economized on, it was not on the food he ate!

He put down his fork and helped himself to more beans from the big crock in front of him. "Did thet teacher say anythin' 'bout termorrer?"

Margaret hesitated, not wishing to involve her beloved teacher in further criticism. Rising quickly and going to the stove, she removed the big crockery tea pot which was brewing on one of its hot lids. Taking it to the table, she set it down hastily in front of her father. "Here's your tea, father. See if it's strong enough to suit you." She spoke swiftly but distinctly for she was always careful in her speech not to fall into the slovenly habit of slurring her words which she had come to detest in her father and stepmother. Her careful speech was one of the reasons Matilda hated her. She often complained to her husband that the girl had "high falutin' notions" and considered herself above her ma and pa.

Angus lifted the cover of the teapot and sniffed the fragrant drink, distracted for a moment from the teacher's shortcomings. "It's all right, I guess, if'n it's hot 'nuff," he admitted grudgingly.

Matilda, watching this bit of strategy on Margaret's part, frowned and wrinkled her small nose like a rabbit. She did not like her stepdaughter to make use of her own tactics in handling her husband. Passing her plate to Angus to be refilled, she renewed her attack on the teacher. "Well, I, fer one, am glad she's at the Turner's and not here. I don't want 'er sittin' round my kitchen watchin' me work, if there ain't gonna be no school!"

Margaret looked across the table at her stepmother and her heart was full of scorn. "What you mean," she thought indignantly, "is that you don't want her around long enough to find out how much of your work I have to do!" But, again, she said nothing aloud.

Angus gazed at his wife reprovingly over his steaming cup and said, "I should think ye could find somethin' ter keep her busy. T'ain't no reason she should set round and 'spect folks to pay fer it. If the selectmen took some of her pay fer every day she shirked her lawful duty, she might be a bit more cautious 'bout 'scusing school!"

Margaret bit her lip at this and lowered her head. It was worse than useless to try to make her father see reason when he was prejudiced against someone.

Matilda attacked her food vigorously, satisfaction written all over her flushed countenance and Angus poured himself a second cup of strong tea that he loved and spooned in plenty of sugar. He glanced across the table at his daughter. "I serpose there ain't no use'n you goin' ter school if there ain't gonna be nobody there to larn ye," he said resignedly. "Maggie, ye can do some piecin' on yer quilt." Angus believed with all his heart that the devil found work for idle hands to do.

Margaret, toying with the hot food on her plate, brought her slender black brows together in a frown. She hated to have her father call her Maggie because it sounded common, but she did not dare to tell him so, for she knew that if she did she would never hear the end of it. With Matilda's able assistance he would point out to her that it had been a good enough name for her mother and was good enough for her.

Margaret had loved her mother very much, but she preferred not to have to think about her in the presence of her father and his wife. The contrast between life as it was under her step-mother's regime and as it had been when her gentle mother was alive brought a lump to her throat and tears to her eyes. As she sipped her tea, she thought of a remark she had overheard that noon at the school house. She had been helping some of the younger children into their outside clothing when the teacher announced that if the storm continued there would be no school the next day. The child she had been assisting looked up at her with delight. "Oh, goody!" she exclaimed joyfully, her blue eyes sparkling with anticipation. "We have lots of fun at our house when it storms. Ma lets us pop corn and make molasses taffy and sometimes we roast apples over the coals, and when the work's done, Aunt Nellie sings to us or Pa tells us stories." Fun was a word the meaning of which Angus McAskie had never learned.

When Angus had eaten all he could hold, he pushed his chair back from the table and Margaret was free to go back to work. She stacked the dishes on the drain board of the sink and set the bread to rise. She washed and wiped the dishes, rinsed out the dish towels, then went down to the cellar for more wood and the soap stones which were used to warm the beds. These she placed on the front of the stove to heat. It was a great source of annoyance to her that her father would not let her leave them in the back of the oven all day to save an extra trip down cellar each night, but Angus contended that by so doing the stones would become too hot and would scorch the old flannel clothes in which they must be wrapped. As he frequently reminded his family, "Cloth don't grow on trees!"

Matilda had settled herself in a low rocker by the warm stove, her knitting in her hands. She made a great fuss about having to do all the family knitting so that she could avoid giving her step-daughter a hand with the dishes. Matilda hated washing dishes but she loved to knit. Socks, mittens, stocking caps, mufflers, afghans, and petticoats were produced rapidly by her plump fingers. When she finished her own knitting, she undertook to do some for her neighbor, although she was careful that her husband should not become aware of that fact.

Margaret, filling the water tank on the side of the big iron stove from the water pails on the sink, gave her a contemptuous glance in passing. It was all she dared do. Angus sat at the table, fingering his worn Bible and waiting for her to put the remains of the meal in the pantry. When the last towel had been hung behind the cellar door she drew her chair up to the table and Matilda reluctantly put down her knitting. She privately thought it very silly to have to sit with her hands idle while her husband read the Scriptures, but Angus demanded strict attention at prayers. Being a simple woman and utterly devoid of imagination, she had never learned Margaret's trick of sitting with her eyes glued on Angus' face while her thoughts roamed at will. She could only settle herself resignedly and hope that tonight's reading would be brief.

Margaret, sitting bolt upright in her chair, her hands folded demurely in her lap, had left the four walls of the kitchen far behind her. As her father's harsh voice droned monotonously on and on, she imagined herself in Stewart's Emporium picking out some material for a new dress that she really liked. She knew just what she wanted, a bright red challis. She would have Miss Atkins, the village dressmaker, make it for her, and it would be trimmed with yards and yards of narrow black velvet ribbon. She might even have a lace yoke in it like the one in Miss Abbot's dress. She wished wistfully that she had a little more bust. She had no figure at all; she was tiny and thin. Once she had overheard one of the children at school whisper to another that her older sister, who had a beau, pinned lace ruffles inside the bosom of her dress, which were so stiff with starch that they made her look just like a grown-up lady. While Matilda sat twisting her hands together and thinking how boring the passage was that Angus had chosen to read, Margaret was planning a way in which she could acquire a false front, impishly delighted that her father could not read her thoughts.

When Angus finished reading the allotted portion of Scripture, which allowed him to boast that he read the Bible through each year, he closed the book and glancing at the women of his family to make sure that they were as reverent as he thought they ought to be, he bowed his head and began to pray. He prayed for the state of the nation and the town, the church, and every member of his family by name. Above all the hard things in her life, Margaret loathed most hearing her father's nasal voice beseeching Almighty God to make her an obedient and considerate daughter and to make her grow in grace and in the knowledge of the Lord. She considered that she *was* an obedient and considerate daughter. He would soon see how obedient and considerate, she thought to herself scornfully, if he were left to Matilda's care! Margaret knew she did everything she was supposed to do and more besides. She accepted the fact that she had to work hard and endure her mean, small-minded stepmother in the bargain, but it annoyed her that she should be expected to grow in grace while doing so.

Angus, having finally finished his petitions, turned his attention to hearing Margaret recite her daily Scripture. Margaret acquitted herself brilliantly as usual, but she refused to allow herself to think of the meaning of the words she recited; she hated everything to do with God and the Bible.

As soon as Margaret finished speaking, Matilda picked up her knitting again. Angus dragged his barrel-backed rocker up to the stove and, opening the oven door, thrust inside the oven a thick, flat, block of scarred wood which he kept on hand to protect his carpet slippers from the hot grates. Then, hitching himself into a comfortable position, he thrust his big feet into the oven's comforting warmth and settled himself for the evening. Margaret was now free to commence her studying.

This was the part of her day which Margaret loved best. Her father was sure to nod over his Bible or Almanac (which was the only other reading matter he permitted himself) and finally fall asleep, so when she had completed her lessons she had time to enjoy herself in some contraband book or magazine. The teacher's arrival in town had opened up to her a delightful new source of supply. Tonight she had a copy of *Harper's New Monthly Magazine* hidden between her school books and slate. It wasn't exactly new. It bore the date June 1886, now almost two year's past, but it was new to Margaret and she was looking forward eagerly to perusing its contents.

Miss Abbott had taken to borrowing back copies of current magazines in order to keep up with her favorite pupil's thirst for knowledge. Margaret scanned the table of contents for an anticipatory moment before she turned to her studies. Long practice in doing what had to be done, no matter how disagreeable the task might be, had taught her to get necessary work out of the way as swiftly as possible, but in the back of her consciousness was the delightful assurance that when she had completed what must be done, there was a treat in store for her vivid imagination. Her eyes on her father's broad back and nodding head, she reached over and turned the wick of the lamp up a little before she settled herself to work.

The clock on the mantle struck seven as she finished her homework. She slipped the strap off her books and extracted her precious magazine. Ascertaining that her father's head was turned away from the table, she leisurely reviewed the table of contents. Her interest was caught by an article on farming called "Home Acre," which she carefully marked with a bit of paper so that she could find it if her father suddenly demanded to see what she was doing. Then she abandoned herself to a story in the magazine and in a few moments the walls of the familiar kitchen fell away and she became, in the twinkling of an eye, a beautiful blond society woman who had been overcome with an attack of sleeping sickness. She imagined herself lying, in the body of her heroine, in a casket, beautifully covered with a blanket of white roses, vainly trying to make the minister, who was conducting her funeral services, understand that she was not dead but only asleep.

Suddenly, the long, drawn-out howl of a wolf brought her back to reality with a start. Her father's heavy head came up with a jerk. Even Matilda stopped her knitting for a moment. They all listened intently. In a few seconds the howl was repeated. Angus turned to Margaret, a deep scowl on his seamed countenance. "Ye sure ye fastened the door of the sheep fold good?"

"I'm sure," she stated briefly. "I'm always careful."

Matilda who was sitting forward in her rocker appeared to be in deep thought. Suddenly, she thrust her feet into her shoes, rolled her knitting into a ball and stuck her needles through it. Rising swiftly to her feet, she crossed the floor to the cellar door. Snatching a knitted shawl from a hook by the door, she threw it over her head and shoulders and announced briefly that she was "going down celler fer some pertaters." Before anyone could move she had disappeared down the cellar stairs, closing the

17

door firmly behind her.

Margaret stood for a moment, stretching her work-weary young body. As she did, she glanced through the window and saw with alarm that someone was in the barnyard. Reaching up, she polished a small space on the frosted glass so that she could peer through. The shawled figure of her stepmother was hurrying back from the barn. "I wonder what she is doing out there?" she thought. "She hasn't got her gaiters on and she hates the wet like a cat. She must be up to some mischief, or she would have gone out through the kitchen door instead of going through the cold cellar and the cellar bulkhead."

Puzzled, Margaret resumed her seat and pretended to busy herself with her books. In a few minutes, the cellar door opened and Matilda appeared. Margaret noted that she had carefully wiped her feet and shaken the snow from her shawl. In her hand she carried a small wooden bowl of potatoes. She spoke to her husband. "I thought as how ye might relish some pertater pancakes fer breakfast, so I run down cellar to git some to put ter soak."

Angus gave a nod of satisfaction. He was extremely fond of potato pancakes, but when he asked for them his wife usually whined that "they was an awful lot of work."

Matilda went to the sink and washed the potatoes. Then, sitting down in her rocker, she kicked off her shoes once more, and placing a piece of brown paper over her apron commenced to pare them. "She must be up to something," thought Margaret. "It isn't like her to do any dirty job she can get me to do for her."

Putting the potatoes in a saucepan, Matilda sliced them thinly under her husband's watchful glance and, covering them with water, put them on the shelf of the stove to soak. As she held her hands over the stove lids to warm them, Angus addressed himself to her in rebuke. "Margaret could've just as well run down cellar for them taters. Seems as though young'uns ain't near as considerate of their folks terday as they was in our day."

Matilda smiled slyly. The shortcomings of Margaret was a topic upon which she enjoyed hearing her husband expound at length, and she never failed to egg him on once he got started, for if he were complaining against his daughter he would leave her alone. Shrugging her fat shoulders she added fuel to the fire of his dissatisfaction. "Trouble is chil'run don't obey like they used ter. Miz Atkins was tellin' at the missionary meetin' how that teacher ain't half strict enuf with 'em. She even lets 'em draw in school if they want ter, an' she ain't used the cat a' nine tails once since she come!"

At this, Angus snorted his disgust and turning to Margaret, he brought his heavy brows together in a straight line over his big nose. "Don't let me see ye git any notions to disobey inter yer head! The Good Book says, 'Children obey yer parents in the Lord, fer this is right.' "

Margaret's bitter thoughts raged in her mind, but she made no answer. How she would love to speak her mind just once, but that privilege was accorded to no one but Angus in his house.

Quiet descended once more upon the kitchen except for the ticking of the ancient clock on the mantle back of the stove and the sharp clicking of Matilda's needles. Ordinarily, Margaret would have tried to figure out what made her stepmother venture out in such a storm, but tonight she was so anxious to get back to her story that she dismissed the matter from her mind.

The next hour passed on the wings of the wind. The clock struck nine slow, sonorous strokes, causing Angus to pull his feet out of the oven to the floor with a thud. Raising his long arms over his head, he yawned prodigiously and announced flatly that it was time for bed. He took his big silver watch out of his pocket and compared it with the clock on the mantle. Satisfied that it was correct, he wound it slowly and carefully and put it back where it belonged. Angus had great respect for any and all of his possessions.

Margaret closed her books at once. Taking a soapstone off the stove and handling it with heavy crocheted potholders she slipped it into the flannel bag which had been warming over the oven door. She took a candle down from the shelf, noting with satisfaction that it was practically new; with any luck at all she might be able to read for an hour in bed without her father's realizing that she was wasting candle grease so unnecessarily. She gathered up her books in one arm, holding the lighted candle in its holder hooked through her thumb, and hugging the hot soapstone to her with the other arm, she opened the door which led to the unheated bedroom on the upper floor. She closed the door quickly behind her lest she receive a final reprimand for letting cold air into the warm kitchen.

Gone were the days when she had been permitted to wash and

undress behind the warm kitchen stove. Her own mother had seen to it that there was a basin of hot water waiting for her and that her long flannel nightclothes were pleasantly warmed on the oven door. She herself had braved the icy upper regions with the hot soapstone so that Margaret's bed was comfortable when she climbed into it, but with her death all these little comforts had ceased abruptly. Angus, who made a practice of sleeping in his long flannel underwear without benefit of washing or changing before retiring, had not insisted that Margaret follow her mother's precepts. But Margaret could not bear to retire for the night until she had bathed her slender body in warm water as her mother had taught her and dusted it softly with cornstarch. She never failed to make the extra trip back to the kitchen to procure a pitcher of hot water although Matilda made frequent biting comments about it. She dreaded disrobing in the chill of her bedroom but her flannel nightdress was a lot more comfortable than her woolen underwear, once her body had warmed it through.

Jumping into bed, she wrapped a quilt about her shoulders and snuggling down against the hot soapstone, she pulled the candle to the edge of the small table which stood beside her bed and settled herself to the first real comfort she had known all day. She was thankful that her stepmother's limited intelligence had not caused her to wonder why Margaret took her books upstairs with her each night when she only had to bring them down again in the morning.

Margaret finished her story and was about to blow out her candle when she again heard the eerie howl of a wolf. A shudder went through her and a great fear leapt into her heart. What if something should happen to her lamb? Her lamb was her passport to freedom and her one great hope for the future. She clutched the covers more closely about her thin shoulders and thought wildly that she simply couldn't bear life if the wolves got her lamb. For a moment she lay trembling with her own emotion, then slipping from the warmth of the big bed she knelt on the cold floor and, folding her hands, offered up to her father's God the first heartfelt prayer she had ever uttered. "Oh, God, keep my lamb safe." Vaguely comforted, she crawled shivering back into bed, blew out the candle, and settled herself to sleep.

Chapter Two

By morning it had become apparent that the storm was going to assume the proportions of a blizzard. The wind had risen once again and it was blowing the snow before it in great gusts, whipping savagely around the corners of the house. The fences were entirely covered yet still it snowed swiftly and thickly. By noon the drifts had crept up the windows of the first floor, blanketing them neatly, and making artificial light necessary for the rest of the day. The barn was a huge white mountain and the silo a snowy peak. The outhouse and chicken coops were completely buried. Angus fought his way to the barn in the morning but by evening the storm was so much worse that he abandoned the attempt.

The next day things were no better. Indeed, the longer the elements raged, the more intense was their fury. Angus gave up trying to reach the stock after a half hour's struggle with the wind. It filled in the path he made as rapidly as he made it, and his labors did nothing but exhaust him. He returned to the house irritated that he should be thus defeated even by an act of God and was surly the rest of the day as he considered the amount of kerosene they must burn in order to accomplish the simplest household tasks.

The third day the snow stopped falling, and Angus began to clear a path to the barn. Even though he spent the afternoon shoveling, the early winter dusk closed about him and the house before he succeeded in reaching the sheepfold. When he returned to the kitchen at last, there was a deep scowl on his florid countenance. He was obviously upset. As he pulled off his outside clothes, he muttered over his shoulder, "I can't fer the life of me see how a wolf could git inter the fold with the gate shut, and drag a lamb out with him. We'll have to strengthen the gate ter the fold as soon as this is over."

Margaret's heart leapt into her throat. She looked at her father but he wouldn't meet her eyes. He appeared to be absorbed with his boot laces. She went and stood in front of him until he was forced to look up at her. Her eyes pleaded with him to tell her the truth even as her stiff lips framed the question, "What lamb did they get?"

He answered her briefly. "Yourn. I found what was left of it in the snow bank just outside the fold. I s'pose I should be thankful the wolf didn't git none of the sheep!"

Margaret stood frozen to the floor. So that was what her stepmother had been doing at the barn the first night of the storm! She must have found and read Margaret's composition about her plans for the sale of her lamb. She had deliberately let it out of the fold so that the wolves would get it! She had never had a penny she could call her own and she did not intend that her stepdaughter should acquire any money. She could not risk the independence which some ready cash would give the girl. She was shrewd in her small, mean way and she was not willing to risk losing Margaret's help on the farm. Life would be very different for her without Margaret to bully and manipulate for her own ends. She had no intention of giving up such competent free labor. During the conversation about her lamb Matilda had made a great fuss about setting the table and rattling the pots and pans about the stove so she wouldn't have to face her stepdaughter.

Angus, disgruntled at the loss of anything which belonged to him or to his daughter — which, in his mind, was practically the same thing — told Matilda sharply to stop her racket, sat down dourly at the supper table, and motioned the others to do likewise. Somehow, Margaret got across the floor and found her chair. She had to keep her hands clenched tightly in her lap to keep back the scalding tears which crowded against her eyelids. She was determined not to give Matilda the satisfaction of seeing her weep but the effort to restrain herself made her feel physically ill. Her throat ached with the struggle and the hearty food nauseated her. A wave of dizziness engulfed her, but she fought it off by sheer effort of will. There was nothing she could do and she knew it. If she told her father her suspicions, Matilda would deny them vigorously. It would be her word against her stepmother's and Margaret knew that her father would believe Matilda because he preferred to do so. There was no justice nor mercy in the world. It would do her no good to work; there was no one to help her. Suddenly she recalled that she had asked God to protect her lamb, but He had failed her. He had denied her simple request and forsaken her when He must have known how much that lamb meant to her. Now she would never get a red dress nor an education nor anything else she really wanted. She groaned inwardly.

Going stonily through her work after supper in sullenness and despair, Margaret felt that life would never hold any hope for her again. At prayers, her father read a passage from the Bible about the Good Shepherd caring for His sheep, and a great wave of bitterness flooded the girl's soul. God had not been a good enough shepherd to keep her lamb safe for her. This God of her father's cared not at all for her, or her lamb, or her problems. If He had, He would have answered her earnest plea. She had trusted Him enough to ask Him for help, but He had refused to help her. In great bitterness of soul she took a vow which she determined to keep until the day of her death. Never again, as long as she lived, would she ask God for anything. If He would not help her, she would just have to struggle along by herself as best she could. She had given God a chance and He had refused to take it. From now on, she would go on alone, without His assistance.

That night for the first time since her mother's death, Margaret cried herself to sleep.

It was several days before the roads were opened so that the pupils could once more assemble at the schoolhouse. The storm had kept the teacher away from the McAskie farm during this period as Margaret had hoped that it would, but her deep despair over the loss of her lamb so overshadowed everything else in her life that she was unable to fully appreciate the reprieve.

The morning school opened, Margaret trudged along the road in the snowy ruts, preoccupied by her gloomy thoughts. When she finally arrived at the schoolhouse, a fire was roaring noisily in the small, round-bellied stove, and the familiar smell of steaming woolens, dust, and chalk filled the air. The teacher, dressed in one of her prettiest dresses, a crocheted fascinator thrown over her shoulders, smiled at Margaret as she entered the schoolroom and Margaret attempted to smile back, but her face felt as if it would crack and the smile got no further than her eyes. To hide her feelings she bent over and helped one of the little girls with her gaiters.

When the morning classes were finished and the children had eaten their lunches, Miss Abbott suggested that anyone who cared to might go out and play in the snow. There was a general stampede for coats, mittens, stocking caps, and leggings. The room soon cleared, but Margaret sat on in her seat too discouraged and indifferent to move. She took a book out of her desk and pretended to be studying it, her head between her hands, her elbows on the desk, but somehow she did not feel the same pleasure in studying that she had had before the wolf had gotten her lamb. Her incentive was gone. As long as she had had the lamb, there was some purpose in standing at the head of her class, but now she had a feeling that it was a waste of time and effort. Her head drooped and her long black braids tied with bits of old black shoestring dragged on the schoolroom floor. Margaret did not even notice, although she was usually most particular to keep her hair off the dusty boards.

Miss Abbott, correcting papers at the desk, watched her favorite pupil out of the corner of her eye and became gradually aware of her deep dejection. She had never heard Margaret give a worse account of her lessons than she had that morning. Inasmuch as the girl had had so much extra time for study during the storm, Miss Abbott could not understand it. Margaret had not only given a poor recital but she had been inattentive. Never before, at least since Miss Abbott had been teaching at the school, had such a thing happened. Something was wrong and it was up to her to find out what it was.

Her clear, soft voice called down the room to where Margaret was sitting. "Margaret, wouldn't you like to help me with these papers?" Margaret rose at once and moved listlessly to the teacher's desk. The usual eagerness with which she would have greeted such a suggestion was entirely lacking.

Miss Abbott pulled a chair up close to her desk and handed Margaret a small pile of papers. "I thought," she said softly, her eyes on the downcast face, "that if you would help me with these, we might have time for a chat before I have to ring the bell."

They were soon finished and Miss Abbott stacked the papers in a neat pile and turned to Margaret. "Now then," she said kindly, putting her hand over the small listless one lying on the edge of the desk. "What has happened to make you so unlike yourself? I have never heard you give such a poor recitation as you did this morning."

Stung to the very quick by the gentle rebuke, tears sprang unbidden to Margaret's eyes. "The wolves killed my lamb the first night of the storm," she blurted out. The teacher knew what the lamb had meant to Margaret and her sympathy was quick. "Oh, my dear, I *am* sorry!" The warm tone and the look of compassion were all Margaret needed. She put her dark head down on the desk and burst into violent weeping.

Miss Abbott let her cry her heart out for a few minutes, contenting herself with stroking the lustrous black hair gently. Then, with her eyes on the clock, she opened the desk drawer and drawing out a handkerchief, she tucked it in Margaret's hand. It would never do to let the younger children come in and find her dissolved in tears. The handkerchief was clean and soft and smelled of lavender. Margaret dried her eyes and blew her nose vigorously. "I'm ashamed to be such a baby," she said shamefacedly, straightening her dress and pushing back her disordered hair, "but my stepmother deliberately opened the gate of the sheepfold and let out my lamb so that the wolves would get it." The teacher was horrified and puzzled. "Why should she want to do a cruel thing like that?"

Margaret folded the handkerchief carefully and put it in her pocket so that she might take it home and launder it before she returned it to its owner. "I think she must have somehow read my composition about my plan to sell it and give you the money to keep for me so that I could go to normal school. If I went away, she would have all the housework to do and she is too lazy to be willing to run that risk, I guess."

"But, why didn't you tell your father?"

Margaret's mouth hardened. "He would never believe me. He takes Matilda's part in everything."

The village people had not failed to regale the new teacher with an account of the head of the McAskie household and his second wife; the teacher knew that the girl was probably telling the truth. Putting her arm gently about Margaret's shoulders she said kindly, "You are very unhappy at home, aren't you?"

Fresh tears welled up in Margaret's eyes at the caress, and she burst forth, "Oh, Miss Abbott, I've got to get away from the farm, I've simply got to! I — I can't stand it if I have to spend the rest of my life on a farm. I want an education and some pretty clothes and I want to see a city and learn to play the piano really well, and not have to work so hard. I want to grow up to be like you," she ended her outburst shyly.

Miss Abbott was thoughtful for a moment. "You're sure your father won't help you?" Margaret shook her dark braids vigorously. "Then I will. The battle is not yet lost, my dear. I do not know at this minute what can be done about this deplorable situation, but I know that in time something can be. There is no situation in the world so hopeless it can't be improved, providing you are willing to work and wait and plan. However, not getting your lessons is not going to help you any. I want you to promise me something. If you will guarantee to keep up your usual high standard of work, I will undertake to do all in my power to help you get to normal school. Is it a bargain?"

"Oh, yes!" exclaimed Margaret, her courage returning to her in a great swelling tide. She had absolute confidence in the teacher and she felt that what she had promised was as good as done. God might not be willing to help her, but here was someone who would.

Margaret was cleaning the parlor. It was not the day for it but Matilda had insisted that she give it a "reddin' up." The teacher was due to arrive that afternoon.

Margaret fervently hoped that her father would stay in the barn until after the teacher arrived. She did not want him to get too close a look at her modish outdoor attire. She had scarcely finished preparing dinner when the tinkling of sleigh bells drew her to the window and she saw Jim Sawyer's cutter turn into the drive. She had heard about Jim Sawyer's new cutter but had never seen it. Angus had spent all of one supper hour, discoursing upon the extravagance and folly of Jeremiah Sawyer in allowing his son to purchase such an equipage.

Throwing a shawl over her shoulders, Margaret ran out into the yard, the better to admire it. The cutter was bright red and the bells which had warned them of its approach were silver with tiny red tassels and they shone and glistened in the late afternoon sunlight. Jim, who was reputed in the village to be sweet on the teacher, helped her down. Margaret looked at Miss Abbott admiringly. She had on a coat of fashionable cut, in a deep plum color, and a hat of the same rich shade tilted jauntily over one eye. A small ball muff and a tippet to match completed her costume, and Margaret privately thought that she looked as lovely as anything in *Godey's Lady Book*, but she turned her eyes anxiously toward the barn where her father was finishing the evening chores. To her great relief there was no sign of him.

She hustled her guests into the house. Her stepmother was standing in the middle of the kitchen obviously ill at ease in the presence of such company. Jim nodded to her and the teacher introduced herself most graciously. Matilda peered at her guest with her small nearsighted eyes but merely nodded her head by way of greeting. Margaret asked Jim to carry the teacher's things to the spare room on the upper floor. She was anxious to get the teacher out of the kitchen so she could remove her outside garments as soon as possible. When Jim had brought in the last of her bags and there was no longer any reason to linger, he took his reluctant departure.

Margaret suggested that the teacher might like to unpack some of her things while she completed the supper preparations. Matilda, instead of retiring to the bedroom, settled herself in her favorite rocker; she did not intend to miss anything that went on. In a few moments, Miss Abbott re-entered the kitchen. Margaret noted with relief that she was attired in one of her simplest dresses. She did not offer to assist Margaret but drew a chair up to Matilda's rocker and engaged her in conversation about her handiwork. Margaret, watching them covertly out of the corner of her eye, saw the teacher gradually charm her stepmother. It was only ten minutes later that Matilda brought out her collection of mufflers, socks, mittens, shawls, and petticoats and spread them out before her admiring guest. When the teacher asked her hostess to teach her a particularly intricate stitch, and Margaret heard Matilda promise eagerly to do so, the girl knew that the conquest of her stepmother was an accomplished fact.

The clock struck five and Matilda, reminded that Angus might return at any moment, bundled her things together in haste. Miss Abbott then tactfully asked Matilda for the loan of one of her aprons, saying that she would like to help with the supper. Matilda was loath to have the teacher's attentions diverted from herself and her cherished handwork but glancing out of the window she saw Angus' tall figure crossing the barnyard so she made haste to accede to Miss Abbott's request.

When Angus came into the kitchen, he was both surprised and pleased to see a quietly dressed woman helping his women-folk with supper. That was as it should be. Perhaps this woman teacher was not as bad as he had imagined. She went to him at once, introducing herself and holding out a small hand for him to shake. He took it rather sheepishly. She helped him out of his heavy outside clothing and brought him his carpet slippers from beside the stove. He was unaccustomed to these little attentions at supper time, for Margaret was too busy and Matilda too lazy to give them to him. He made no comment but Margaret could tell that he was not displeased, although he offered the teacher no thanks for her little courtesies. The tightness about Margaret's heart loosened a little. Perhaps Miss Abbott's visit wasn't going to be as bad as she had anticipated.

Matilda dished up the creamed codfish and Margaret took the baked potatoes out of the oven, and they sat down at the table. The teacher bowed her head at once and folded her hands on the edge of the table. Angus eyed her dourly, wondering if she thought she was going to offer grace, but she waited patiently for him, and somewhat mollified, he returned the evening blessing. She had not removed her apron when she sat down and that pleased him; it showed that she was careful of her clothes. He did not realize that she had merely followed Matilda's and Margaret's example.

She made no attempt to talk at the table which rather surprised him. From what he had been able to gather in the village, she was something of a chatterer. He disliked chattering women; they made him think of a flock of sparrows and he considered that their talk made about as much sense. Besides, he felt that if there was anything to be said in the family circle, the head of the house was the one to say it. He had intended putting this woman in her place if she attempted to usurp his rights, but she was evidently going to save him the trouble. He faintly regretted the fact.

When the meal was finished, he noted with satisfaction that she arose at once from the table and helped Margaret to clear away the things. If he had an extra mouth to feed, the very least the possessor of that mouth could do was to contribute her services.

When the dishes were done, and the kitchen was again tidy, the teacher asked to be excused to go to her room, saying that she would only be a minute. Angus sat fiddling with his Bible, annoyed to be kept waiting and glad of a chance to criticize. When the teacher returned, it was with a Bible in her hand and his criticism died on his lips. It was only natural that she would not want to leave her Bible about the kitchen. She sat down beside Margaret and waited quietly for him to give out the evening reading. Cheated of his reprimand, he gave out the chapter in his harsh voice and commenced to read. As the teacher flipped the pages to locate the passage, Margaret's quick eye could not help but see printed in large black letters in the title page, the words, "Jeremiah Sawyer." Miss Abbott had borrowed the Bible on purpose to impress Angus! How clever she was! The girl's heart lifted.

When prayers were over and Margaret's passages heard, Miss Abbott leaned across the table and addressed her host hesitatingly, "Mr. McAskie, they tell me in the village that you are an excellent Bible student. There is a passage of Scripture which has always puzzled me. I find it very obscure and I was wondering if you would be good enough to take the time to explain its meaning to me?"

Margaret, seeing the pleased expression on her father's usually forbidding countenance, knew that the teacher's conquest of the McAskie household was complete!

Chapter Three

    The days of the teacher's visit soon settled themselves into a regular routine. When it became apparent to Margaret that Miss Abbott was amply able to take care of herself and that she had nothing to fear on her account, she relaxed and began to enjoy the weeks to which she had looked forward with such dread. As she watched Miss Abbott's clever manipulation of her father and stepmother for her own ends, her respect and admiration for her grew daily. For the duration of her stay, the teacher gave up any life or interests of her own. She started to knit a "fascinator" under Matilda's eager tutelage and sat respectful and attentive under Angus' expositions. There were no lengths to which she was not willing to go to ingratiate herself to them. She wore the same dress every day that she was there, only allowing herself a change on Sundays. The only ornament which she permitted herself was her small chatelaine watch. Even this she pinned to her dress with the face out so that the delicately chased bird with the sapphire eye did not show. Although Margaret recognized the necessity for such subterfuge and deeply appreciated the teacher's making such an effort on her behalf, she just as deeply resented the fact that it was necessary, and the hatred she already nourished in her heart for her father did not decrease. She knew that what Miss Abbott was doing, she was doing for her sake and that she had a well-defined plan in mind. That the teacher herself would in no way benefit from the carrying out of this plan made Margaret feel very humble, and in the days that followed she came close to worshiping the young woman who had so generously undertaken to help her.

The nicest part of Miss Abbott's visit from Margaret's point of view was that she elected to sleep with her instead of in the spare room. It was a great luxury for Margaret to have someone to talk to and another soapstone to warm the big feather bed. When she watched the teacher prepare for bed by washing herself with some sweet-smelling soap and dusting herself with equally sweet-smelling powder, Margaret was thankful that she had not abandoned her mother's teachings. The teacher made no bones about crimping her hair. She even asked Margaret to hold the basin so they could huddle under the covers while she twisted the strands of hair on kid curlers. Margaret watched this process with a fascinated eye. "I wish," she said wistfully, "that I dared to do that! I haven't any crimpers, but I suppose I could use rags."

The teacher took a strand of hair and dampened it in the basin. "Don't you ever do it! If my hair were as heavy as yours and as thick, I wouldn't do it myself. I have to use crimpers to give my hair some body, but your hair is a glory in itself. If you would brush it a hundred times a day, it would shine like Nellie's coat." Nellie was Jim's lively young horse. "Besides," she continued, her fingers busy with the last curl, "your father would think I put you up to it and what would happen then? If you departed so far from your usual custom as to appear at the breakfast table with your hair crimped, he would be sure to suspect me. As it is, he isn't quite sure but that my hair grew in this state, not ever having seen it in any other, but if you suddenly blossomed forth into curls he would decide that I was an abandoned woman and all that I have tried to accomplish would be undone. We can't risk that at this stage of the game, now can we?"

Margaret agreed that they could not, but her resentment against her father did not decrease because of it. The crimping of her hair would have to be pushed into the limbo of other

31

impossible and forbidden things as long as she lived under his roof.

The last night of the teacher's stay, Margaret tried to express some of the gratitude with which her heart was overflowing. Miss Abbott squeezed her hands under the covers and stopped her thanks with a giggle. "It really has been fun. I always knew that you could catch more flies with molasses than with vinegar, but I never before had such a good chance to prove it. It has been like a game and we have won the first round, my dear, so you mustn't lose heart. We'll win yet, see if we don't!"

For once in her life Margaret fell asleep in utter contentment, assured that if the teacher could make such a conquest of her father in a few short weeks, there was nothing that she could not accomplish, given time. With a friend like this at her side she did not need a God who was obviously indifferent to her welfare. She could very well get along without His help.

After Miss Abbott's departure for the Evan's farm, Margaret missed her sorely, but she went about her tasks with a will, certain for the first time that the hard work was only a temporary expedient and not a permanent factor in her life.

The orchards were a riot of color and the air was filled with their fragrance, when Miss Abbott made her first move. She had learned from the Riders that there was a meadow between the McAskie farm and theirs that Angus had long had his eye on, and she had learned from Margaret that the only thing that kept him from purchasing it was that he could not bear to cut into the hoarded store of gold kept hidden in the china teapot. Therefore, she decided to attack him in his most vulnerable spot: his pocketbook. With this in mind, she approached him with a proposition.

She had Jim Sawyer drive her out to the McAskie farmhouse on a Sunday afternoon just about the time that she knew Angus would be replete with a good Sunday dinner. She had Jim leave her around the bend in the road and she walked the rest of the way. Angus was sitting on the back porch in his shirt sleeves, for the day had become unseasonably warm. His feet were propped on the rail and he had a broom straw hanging out of the corner of his mouth. The teacher came directly to the point. She had a distant relative, Mr. Stillwell, who was a man of considerable wealth, but an invalid. He needed a secretary-companion to help him write a book, someone who could do some research for him and who could take his notes. He was willing to pay the munificent sum of twenty-five dollars a month to the right person. The teacher stressed the point that the twenty-five dollars would be quite clear, for the proposition included room and board for whomever took it.

She was fairly sure, she said hesitatingly, that he would take Margaret after her graduation from school were she, Miss Abbott, to recommend the girl, but she had come to her father before she had said anything about the matter either to her relative or to Margaret. Angus nodded approvingly at her astuteness. The teacher took courage and went on to insinuate that, although by permitting Margaret to take the position providing of course that it would be arranged, he would be deprived of her labor on the farm, yet she would be no expense whatsoever to him and twenty-five dollars a month added up to three hundred dollars a year. She saw Angus' eyes glisten as she mentioned this figure, but he only grunted and agreed to think about the proposition. As she had hoped, his acquisitiveness was stronger than his convictions, for when Miss Abbott saw to it that it reached his ears that the meadow he coveted could be purchased at a low figure, he somewhat grudgingly capitulated, on the stipulation that the money be paid to him and not to Margaret. The teacher stifled her resentment at his smallness and hid her feelings of her triumph until she told Margaret what she had done. The intense and pathetic gratitude in the girl's clear eyes as she made her announcement more than repaid her for the self control she had had to exercise. She dared not mention the fact that she had had almost as hard a time persuading her relative to consider the idea as she had had in getting Angus to agree to it! She cautioned Margaret not to mention at home the fact that Mr. Stillwell lived in the same city in which was the normal school from which she herself had graduated!

"You know, Margaret," she said, drawing little patterns on the paper under her hand as she talked, "this is only a means of getting you away from the farm. You will have to make good with Mr. Stillwell first and then perhaps something can be arranged about normal school. Your penmanship is excellent and you have a good command of words. Mr. Stillwell is a man of great culture and refinement whose life was ruined when he was thrown from a carriage and so badly crippled that he has never been able to walk since. He had only been married a short while when the accident happened and his wife has not shown him very much sympathy. She had a very meagre education and has no fondness for books and music — the only pleasures left to him — so they are not very companionable nor very happy together. He has lived too much to himself and in himself and it is for that reason that I have persuaded him to write this book. It will give him something to think about besides himself. So you see, my dear, I am not only helping you, but I am putting you in a position to help somebody else if you really try."

Margaret nodded, her heart too full for words. The teacher continued, "It is a shame that your father has to appropriate all your earnings, but that was the only condition under which I could obtain his consent to your leaving, so we can't afford to quibble over it. Perhaps something can be done about it later on. We have to take one hurdle at a time and we can be thankful that we have been able to clear this one at all. For a while I wasn't too sure we would succeed. You know," she paused to place her hand over Margaret's lying on the desk, "I shall miss my star pupil very much."

Tears did not come readily to Margaret, but her eyes were swimming as she watched the teacher pick up the bell and ring it loudly for the children to come in from the schoolyard. There seemed to be a mist before the teacher's eyes also, for she had to take a handkerchief out of the drawer and wipe them before the children came trooping noisily into the room.

Margaret was making soap. She detested the job but Matilda saw to it these days that she did as many extra tasks about the farm as she had the time and strength for. Even the fact that when this soap was ripe she would not be here to use it did not lighten her gloom. She had once thought that when she was certain she was to leave farm, she would have all the happiness that she could bear, but now she found that her happiness was tempered and adulterated by a dozen petty worries. Graduation was coming and she had been chosen to give the class oration. All the other girls in the class were to wear white dresses with colored sashes, but her father considered her drab brown Sunday dress plenty good enough for the occasion. Nor was that the worst; her classmates were to wear white slippers and the thought of her clumsy black boots in comparison with them made her shudder. She almost wished that she had not been chosen for such an honor. She would stand out like a sore thumb and being graduated at the head of her class did not compensate her for having to look so different from the rest of the girls.

She knew from experience that it was worse than useless to ask God to help her and she was ashamed to say anything about the matter to the teacher when she had done so much for her already. Her thoughts went round and round in her tired head and just like the old horse down at the tread mill, they got her nowhere. She was thinking for the thousandth time that her father was as usual the cause of the difficulty when she saw him drive into the yard. He had been to town to get the horses shod and purchase some supplies. This always put him in a bad mood and he would take out his anger on his family at the supper table. She was marking the rapidly hardening soap into exact squares with a broken handled knife when her father came into the kitchen. He eyed the soap critically, "It don't seem as smooth as last year's," he said gruffly.

Margaret, who knew that it was the best soap she had ever made, did not deign to answer him, but her small mouth tightened as she thought resentfully that he would have another song to sing when the making of the family's supply of soap was left to Matilda!

Washing his hands at the sink, he said over his shoulder, "Saw the teacher in town."

A quick dart of fear shot through Margaret. Supposing that something had come up to prevent her leaving the farm! Her heart skipped a beat, but her father's next words reassured her. "She wanted ter know would I let her give ye a dress she has — too small fer 'er. Says she only wore it once and there's lotsa wear in it yet." Clever teacher to realize that Angus McAskie could never resist getting something for nothing! "I tol 'er that I didn't hold with females dressin' up fancy, but she said as how this wasn't too fancy, so I tol 'er ye could try it on termorrow. She said as how ye might want ter shorten' it a little so it wouldn't git all dirty draggin' on the ground. Where's Matildy?"

Margaret, who in her resentment and frustration had fully intended to let her father discover her stepmother sound asleep, felt

35

such a surge of happiness over the possession of a new dress of the teacher's choosing that she changed her mind. Instead of answering her father directly, she said over her shoulder as she moved toward the bedroom, "I think there is a leak in the potato bin, father. Some of the potatoes I brought upstairs seem damp." Angus, forgetting all about Matilda, made for the cellar at once. "Oh, well," thought Margaret, excusing herself for her sudden softness of heart as she awakened her stepmother with a gentle hand. "Graduation's only a week away and after that she'll get no more catnaps!"

The dress turned out to be white and quite new. It was all that Margaret had ever dreamed of in her wildest dreams. She suspected that the teacher had had it especially made for her, for the only alteration it needed was at the neck and wrists, but she did not know how to ask without appearing unduly inquisitive. When the teacher lifted it out of its box, she was lost in admiration. She had truthfully told her father that it was simple, but such artful simplicity Margaret had never seen. It was made with a yoke, cut square and edged with a tiny ruffle. The yoke itself was tucked with a myriad of tiny tucks put in by hand. The small leg o' mutton sleeves tapered into a close fitting cuff edged with lace. The skirt was very full and so artistically gathered into the tiny waist that it gave the approved hourglass effect even to Margaret's thin, straight figure. Three lace-trimmed ruffles of graduating widths finished the skirt. Speechless with delight, Margaret admired her reflection in the pier glass in the corner of the room. She stood on tiptoes to see if the hemline would hide her ugly boots and Miss Abbott catching her eye smiled knowingly. "You don't have to worry about them; I have white slippers and stockings for you. I only hope they fit; I had to guess at the size. Here, let's try them on. We'd better not let your father see all this grandeur until you march onto the platform," she giggled. "He might insist on dying it all brown."

The graduation exercises went off smoothly enough and Margaret covered herself with glory. Her remarkable memory, trained by her father in his insistence upon the daily memorizing of Scripture stood her in good stead. For once in her life, however, she had completely forgotten her father. The excitement had brought high color to her usually pale cheeks and not the least intoxicating part of the day was to have Jim Sawyer exclaim when he saw her in her finery, "My goodness, Miss Margaret, I never realized how pretty you are!"

On the way home, Angus launched into a long tirade about the teacher's extravagance and folly in purchasing white shoes and stockings which would so easily show the soil, but Margaret, with her small feet crossed demurely, stars in her eyes, and a deep happiness in her heart, did not even hear him!

Chapter Four

As long as she lived, the memory of her first journey by train was etched indestructibly upon the retina of Margaret McAskie's mind's eye.

Miss Abbott had succeeded in persuading Margaret's father to let his daughter spend her last night at home in the village. He had consented grudgingly to the teacher's suggestion in spite of the fact that the train left early in the morning and he would be spared the trouble of hitching up and driving his daughter to town at an inconvenient time. The teacher spent their last evening together giving Margaret what instruction she could to help her to enter gracefully a world which was as different from the one she had always known as day is from night. Looking over the girl's scanty possessions, neatly packed in a shabby dark green carpetbag, Miss Abbott's heart ached for the meager quantity and shabby quality.

"You know," she said, as much to distract herself as Margaret, "I do not see why you do not put up your hair. After all you are nearly seventeen and you will soon have to come to it anyway."

Margaret, her eyes like stars with expectancy and excitement, agreed with the proposition readily enough and they spent a pleasant hour trying one hair style after another, only to decide finally that the most becoming one was simply to wind Margaret's heavy coils about her small head in a coronet. The next morning when she pinned her simple sailor hat on top of her thick mass of hair, Margaret felt herself to be quite the young lady. On the way to the station she held her head very erect, as if she expected her hair to tumble down her back at any moment!

As they stood on the wooden platform waiting for the train to pull in, the teacher pressed a two-dollar gold piece into Margaret's hand "for luck." With a cautious glance around, Margaret hastily tucked the shining disk into the bosom of her dress, apprehensive about the possession of more money than she had ever had in her life.

The trip was uneventful, but from her first glimpse of the small local train (which consisted of two wooden coaches with slippery straw seats, a baggage car, and a smoke-belching, wood-burning engine) to her final arrival in the big city terminal, all was enchantment to Margaret. Adding to her pleasure was the thought of the gold piece nestled in her bosom and of Matilda's frantic search for the lawn dresser scarf which now lay in even rows of ruffles on her once unadorned corset cover!

It was after four o'clock when the train arrived at its destination. Following the impatient crowd into the enormous waiting room, Margaret tried not to stare too obviously, but never in her wildest dreams had she ever conceived of a building so vast, and, in spite of her eagerness to leave the farm and all it represented, she felt very young and inexperienced and alone.

She went and stood under the clock where she had been instructed to wait, but nobody in all the hurrying throng paid the slightest attention to her. She held the heavy carpetbag in her hand, hesitating to put it down lest somebody pick it up and make off with it. It grew heavier and heavier and she grew hotter and hotter but no one approached her. Apprehensively she scanned the crowd. Mr. Stillwell had promised that she would be met. Surely he had not forgotten. The moments passed and the hands of the big station clock pointed to five o'clock before a little man with ridiculously bowed legs, dressed in what she was later to recognize as a coachman's livery, came rushing through the swinging doors toward her. He was out of breath when he reached her, but he doffed his tall silk hat and bowed before her with a certain dignity.

"Yer Miss McAskie, ain't yer, Miss?" he questioned her breathlessly, and at her shy nod of assent, "I'm Mr. Stillwell's Patrick."

Taking her bag, he clapped his shining hat back on his head with a flourish and led the way to the exit, opening a way for her through the crowd. With a bow he ushered her ceremoniously through the swinging doors to the street. Standing at the curb under the wooden awning which shaded it and its occupant from the glare of the late afternoon sun, was an open carriage, the like of which Margaret had never seen. Everything about it gleamed and glittered with polish or varnish. A lady of considerable size and of commanding appearance reclined on the wide back seat, a small lace parasol held at a fashionable angle over her flushed face and high pompadour of hair upon which perched a feathered hat of gigantic proportions. She made Margaret feel very shabby and countrified as she sat haughtily watching her timid approach. When Margaret reached the carriage, the lady unbent sufficiently to inquire icily, "I suppose that you are Miss McAskie?" There was a veiled sneer in the emphasis she placed upon the word *you*.

Her tone made the girl flush, but before she could frame an answer, Patrick intervened, "This here's the young ledy, mum." He placed the carpetbag on the front seat then turned to help Margaret get in beside his mistress who pushed some packages lying on the seat beside her further into the corner and spread her voluminous skirts more generously about her. Raising her lorgnette she glared at Patrick through it and said imperiously, "It is rather crowded back here, Patrick. The young woman can sit up front with you."

There was venom in the words and tone and Margaret saw the little Irishman's mobile mouth tighten ominously. For a second she thought that he was going to defy his mistress. The two glared at each other, the one haughty, the other defiant, for what seemed to Margaret, standing uneasy and forlorn on the sidewalk, an eternity. Finally Patrick snatched the bag from the front seat and slammed it angrily on the floor in the back of the carriage. Turning, he assisted Margaret in climbing up to the driver's seat. He took his time about assuring himself that she was comfortably settled and hastened not one whit when an irritated voice from the back seat demanded that they start home at once. He sauntered around the carriage and climbed up to the other side of the driver's seat in a leisurely manner, but as soon as he had the reins in his hands he forgot his lassitude. Giving the pair of perfectly matched blacks a smart crack with the whip, he started the carriage over the cobblestones at a smart pace.

Margaret, her hat clutched in her hands to keep it from blowing off, looked about her eagerly. They were proceeding at too great a rate of speed for her to see much and she was relieved when the irritated occupant of the back seat commanded the coachman to slow down. Patrick obeyed the pre-emptory command sullenly and with obvious reluctance. At the first opportunity he took a turn from the main thoroughfare to a side street. Instantly his mistress's sharp voice came over their shoulders. "Patrick, turn back to Market Street at once, I want to stop at Crosse and Treadwell's!"

Patrick, his thick red brows drawn together in a scowl, took the smart-looking whip out of its socket and flicked it over the backs of the blacks, pulling sharply on the reins as he did so. The carriage turned smartly, throwing the occupant of the rear seat hard against the side of the vehicle. Mrs. Stillwell's squeal of protest was smothered in lace and feathers as her elaborately trimmed hat lost its mooring on her high pompadour and, along with her parasol, came down about her ears. Patrick kept up the rapid pace, completely ignoring the smothered exclamations behind him until they drew up with a flourish in front of a large store whose big plate glass windows displayed such a fascinating collection of merchandise catering to feminine tastes that Margaret could not take her eyes from them.

Mrs. Stillwell straightened her disarranged hat and garments angrily. With the help of a fawning doorman who stepped quickly to the curb as they drove up, she descended with what dignity she could muster. Turning, she gave Patrick an ugly look. "I've a good mind to make Mr. Stillwell fire you for that, Patrick Mulroony."

But Patrick was in no way disturbed. He gave her back look for look and straightening his heavy shoulders answered her with a knowing grin on his red face. "I'm thinkin' he wouldn't be doin' it, mum. I been with 'm man and boy fer thirty years and he's always tol' me he couldn't do without me. What's more, if I'd had me hands on the 'orses, he wouldn't be a lyin' there helpless now!''

Mrs. Stillwell flushed an angry purple and for a moment Margaret thought she was going to strike the coachman with her raised parasol, but the doorman pacifically drew her away and much to the girl's relief the incident came to a peaceful conclusion.

Patrick airly brushed a fly off of one of the horses with the tip of his whip. "The devil take 'er," he muttered angrily. "Someday, I'll be doin' ter 'er what she done ter the marster, if it's me own neck as gits broke doin' it!"

Seeing Margaret's startled look, he apologized swiftly, "Sorry, Miss, I shouldn't 'ave lost me temper, but she sure does git me dander up. It was 'er, considerin' herself sich a good one with the 'orses as caused the accident what made 'im a cripple fer life." The sympathy on Margaret's face made him continue. "He'd bought a new light gig, and she was wantin' fer ter drive it. She fancied herself flyin' down Market Street behind a fast 'orse and everyone sayin', 'Don't that young Miz Stillwell handle that fiery 'orse like a vetern?' They'd only been married a short while and he was fair crazed with her blond hair and takin' ways, so after a while he give inter her, tho' t'was myself as begged 'im not ter. He went along jist in case anythin' happened. He wouldn't let me go tho' I begged 'm ter." Patrick took a large, red plaid handkerchief out of his pocket and mopped his red face. There was a suspicion of tears in his clear blue eyes. "It happened all right, all right. She *would* go down Market Street 'cuz that was the best place to make a show of herself, even tho' she knew as how that brute was hard to hold if a train come by, and it come, and the 'orse bolted when he saw the engin'. The marster took the reins and he was thrown out of the gig and dragged over the cobblestones, but he held onter them reins like grim death, tryin' ter save her. He did, too. She was tossed out onter the grass and not hurt a mite, but he ain't never walked since!" Unashamedly, Patrick blew his nose vigorously and returned his handkerchief to his pocket.

Margaret's gray eyes were full of horror. The teacher had spared her the worst of the story. "How dreadful for her," she said softly. "She must regret her rashness every day of her life."

Patrick straightened in his seat. "Regret, me grandmither!" he retorted angrily, and then seeing Margaret's expression, said,

42

"Beggin' yer pardon, Miss. It ain't in her ter think of nobody but herself. She'd be tickled ter death if 'im was ter die termorrow and leave all his money ter her. It's all she ever wanted of 'm anyway, and 'im as is the salt of the earth."

Margaret, embarrassed at these personal revelations concerning her employers, was silent, and the little Irishman continued bitterly. "What's more, she fancies herself with gintlemen. I drive her and I know." Not knowing just what he meant by this last remark, Margaret changed the subject by asking him about some of the sights near them. Patrick was ready enough to instruct her, delighted in her interest in a city which he had come to think of as his own, and for the next fifteen minutes he pointed out to her with his whip various points of interest. By the time the shop owner had ushered Mrs. Stillwell out of his shop to the sidewalk, the two on the driver's seat of the carriage were chatting like old friends.

The rest of the trip was completed without incident, although Margaret noticed that Patrick seemed to be inexplicably upset with his mistress when she made him stop for a few minutes by an open market so that she might chat with the plump and befeathered occupant of another elegant carriage.

They finally turned off the main thoroughfare into a small square with a park surrounded with iron railings in its center. Several children, attended by uniformed nursemaids, were rolling hoops or playing hopscotch along the graveled paths. The houses on all sides of the square were built close together, their fronts flush with the sidewalk. Number Six, Grove Park was the largest house on the square. It was set back from the street slightly by a shallow porte-cochere. Patrick drove under this roofed carriage entrance and pulled the horses to a stop. The massive oak door opened at once as if someone had been waiting for them to appear, and an elderly woman, dressed in rustling black taffeta, with a severe and forbidding countenance, her hair pulled into a hard knot at the back of her head, descended the steps and opened the carriage door. A look passed between her and her mistress which bode no good. She turned and gave Margaret as cold and mannerless a stare as she had received earlier in the afternoon from her employer's wife. It sent a chill to her heart. There was no question about it, but these two women hated her for some as yet unknown reason. Patrick did not miss this exchange of glances. As he handed the reins to a young lad who

43

had run around the corner of the house at the sound of their approach and turned to help her down, he whispered, "Them two is in cahoots. She's the housekeeper and as mean-minded as herself, to be sure. But ye mustn't give her no mind, me and the rist of the servants 'll look after yer." With which scanty comfort, he gathered up Mrs. Stillwell's bundles and Margaret's bag and motioned her to precede him into the house.

In the hall, Mrs. Stillwell paused, her plump foot on the bottom step of the stairway. She turned to the glum housekeeper and performed a belated introduction. "Parker, this is Mr. Stillwell's new secretary. Take her into the drawing room until I find out what he wants done with her. Patrick, you can put down her bag and give my packages to Parker."

Reluctantly, Patrick did as he was told and, tipping his hat to Margaret with a reassuring grin, took his departure. The girl's heavy heart lifted somewhat. She had made one friend at least in this house. Parker took the packages and stalked after her mistress, leaving Margaret standing at the foot of the graceful curving staircase. She gazed about her with delight. The hall in which she found herself was as wide and deep as a large room and ran the full length of the house from front to back. There were two beautifully carved oak doors on each wall opening into large, elaborately furnished rooms. Between the doors on each side wall were deep recesses. To the girl's amazement, she discovered that they contained life-size statues. The one on the left was headless and had enormous wings sprouting from its shoulder blades. The one opposite it was the armless figure of a beautiful woman, the lower part of whose body was draped discreetly, but whose torso was completely nude. Margaret turned away from the naked woman with a blush. She had not known that such things existed. Each statue stood on a marble-topped pedestal which had a gilded base. There was a gilded bench and two gilded chairs upholstered in rose satin damask standing against each wall, but it did not occur to Margaret to sit down. She stood where Parker had left her, quietly awaiting her return, overawed at the unaccustomed elegance of her surroundings. The floors were almost entirely covered with rich oriental rugs and complete silence filled the house.

Margaret was beginning to wonder whether Parker had forgotten all about her when she perceived the housekeeper's grim figure appear around the bend of the stairs. The woman descended slowly as if she had all the time in the world, making it amply plain that she had no intention of hurrying on Margaret's account.

When she reached the girl, she motioned her to pick up her bag and, without a word, led her into the drawing room at their left. Indicating a chair near the door, she said coldly, "Put that thing down and sit there till I send for you." There was utter contempt in her tone. For a moment she paused, her small colorless eyes on Margaret, her long-fingered, bony hand on the door knob. "It would be well for you, Miss, to remember that I am the housekeeper in this establishment and am *Miss* Parker to you at all times. The servants are all under my direction. I do not believe that you will be here very long, but while you are, don't forget that you take orders from me." Her voice left no doubt as to her hostility and dislike.

Margaret could not help wondering why the woman should dislike her so when she had so recently met her, but to distract herself from her gloomy thoughts, she looked about the room. It was unlike anything she had ever imagined. She sat studying it in astonishment, amazed that there could be so much glass and gilt in the whole world. She wondered who kept all the glass so spotless and who polished the profusion of brass and gilt. The room was very large and had a high frescoed ceiling in the center of which hung an enormous crystal chandelier. Among its myriads of crystal drops were several small frosted globes which she was to learn later were gas lights. Her chair faced an immense fireplace with a black marble mantle which supported in its center a black onyx clock, the works of which were encased in a glass dome. On either end of the mantle was an elaborate gilt and crystal candelabra. The empty grate was filled with an arrangement of bridal wreath whose sharp, pungent odor was evident even from where she sat.

She had almost reached the conclusion that she had been completely abandoned when the door opened softly and a rosy-cheeked housemaid entered the room. She curtsied shyly to Margaret and said in a soft, rich Irish voice, "The marster'll be after sendin' fer ye as soon as they tell 'im ye're here." Margaret realized that Patrick must have sent her.

The handle of the door turned and Miss Parker's forbidding countenance appeared upon the threshhold. At the sight of her, the young housemaid recoiled visibly and began to twist the edge of her clean apron in her red, work-roughened hands. The housekeeper's harsh voice cut across the room like a whip. "What are you doing here, Minnie?" she inquired, the frown deepening between her sharp eyes.

The girl hesitated a moment and then said the first thing that came into her head. "I t-thought as maybe t-the g-gas would be after n-needin' a light, Miz P-Parker," she stammered.

Miss Parker snorted through her long thin nose, "You know perfectly well that it is too early to light the gas. Besides, it is a very funny thing that you came to light the gas and forgot to bring the lighter with you! Get back to the kitchen where you belong at once and do not let me find you in this part of the house unless I expressly tell you to come here."

"Yes, m-mum," muttered the flustered Minnie, and fled.

"You," Miss Parker indicated Margaret with a flick of her hand, "follow me and bring that thing with you." Her vast contempt for Margaret's luggage was given full expression by her tones. Margaret obeyed her as meekly as Minnie had. They left the room and crossed the hall to the stairs, but they had scarcely started to mount them before the massive door just to their left opened and a big man dressed in a neatly pressed pair of black trousers and a gray cotton coat came out and thrust his flaming red head over the curved banister.

"You, Parker," he said sternly, a brogue as thick as Patrick's on his tongue. "The marster was after tellin' ye only this afternoon that ye was ter bring the young ledy ter him the minute she come in."

Parker rested her bony, blue-veined hands on the banister and glared down at him. "Mrs. Stillwell thought she had better go to her room and change before she saw him, Michael." For a fleeting moment Margaret wondered what she was supposed to change into. She had donned her one Sunday dress for the trip, and the only other garment she owned beside her everyday dress was her graduation dress. Surely that was too fancy to don the very first evening of her stay even in a house as formal as this one!

But Michael was not to be routed. It was evident that the feud between these two was intense and of long duration. He glared back at the woman above him angrily. "His orders was that she should be brought ter him at once," he said firmly, not giving an inch, "and ye know it full well!" He mounted the stairs to where Margaret stood. "Here, Missie, let me take yer grip fer ye. It's way too heavy fer a young ledy as is no bigger'n a pint o' cider." Margaret surrendered her bag to him gladly with a secret feeling that she had another ally in this friendly Irishman.

Miss Parker tossed her head and continued on her way up the stairs. "Probably to report to her mistress the turn events have taken," thought Margaret as she followed Michael's broad back through the door he courteously held ajar.

The room they entered gave her an instant sensation of repose and quiet. It ran under the stairs across the full width of the back of the house. Through the French doors standing invitingly open at its further end she caught a glimpse of a garden blazing with light and color. Michael set her bag down on a chair and led her across the room to a wheel chair in which sat a man, a light rug thrown over his knees. Even the rug and his somewhat stooped position could not hide the fact that he was very tall. His straight mouth gave his tired face a stern look, but his blue eyes were kind and he held out his hand with evident cordiality.

"So," he said in a pleasant deep voice, "you are Rosemary's star pupil." He smiled kindly as he held her hand a minute. "You hardly look old enough to go out into the world and seek your fortune." The fright which had seized upon Margaret as she had entered the room and realized that her future employer was before her, eased somewhat at the kindness in his tone and she assured him hastily, "I'm older than I look and most reliable."

Mr. Stillwell's smile broadened. "I'm sure of it. My cousin recommended you highly. Michael, please take the young lady's hat and wheel me out on the veranda. She must be very hot and tired from her long trip. I think that some lemonade would be in order and perhaps Katie can give us a few sandwiches to go with it."

Michael obeyed his master with alacrity, and Margaret, following in the slow wake of the wheel chair, felt swift tears of relief spring into her tired eyes. At least Mr. Stillwell did not hate her as did the other members of the household. Surreptitiously she wiped her eyes with her small plain handkerchief and chided herself mentally for being such a baby, but Mr. Stillwell did not appear to notice anything amiss in her conduct. He sat facing the garden and his eyes were on the flowers.

"The garden is particularly lovely this time of day with the setting sun highlighting the colors, don't you think so?" He did not seem to require an answer to his question as he continued smoothly, "We will do a lot of our work out here. Won't you take that rattan chair? I am sure you will find it comfortable and you can relax a bit while they are bringing us something to eat. This is my favorite time of day in the summertime. When the glare of the sun has passed, everything out here is so still and cool. Now, tell me about Rosemary. How is she?"

By the time he had finished talking, Margaret had recovered herself sufficiently to answer him shyly. "She is well and sent you her love. I think," she continued hesitatingly, casting about in her mind for some news about Miss Abbott which might be of interest, "she is growing quite fond of Jim Sawyer. He is her beau."

"Is he indeed?" replied her host, his blue eyes smiling at her across the small space which separated them. "And is he good enough for her?"

Remembering Jim's many kindnesses, Margaret sprang instantly to his defense. "Oh, yes! He is most considerate," she explained, sitting forward earnestly in her chair as if to convince him. "He isn't a farmer. He and his father own the bank. If she marries him she won't have to work as hard as the farm women do. The Sawyers live in town and his mother keeps a hired girl. My father thinks that he is a spendthrift, but I am sure that she can make him save his money after they are married. He is so crazy about her that he will do anything for her." She hesitated again, not knowing quite how to go on. She did not realize how much she was revealing about herself to the quiet man in the wheel chair, whose household staff numbered seven servants, by her obvious eagerness to convince him of Jim Sawyer's virtues. "I really do not think you need to be concerned about her future," she concluded rather lamely.

His eyes watched her kindly as he answered her. "I can see that. Here is Michael with some food." Michael, closely followed by Minnie, was pushing a small, wheeled rattan table across the floor toward them. Minnie set the large tray she was carrying down on the table when Michael had it properly placed and looked relieved to see Margaret seated beside her master. Smiling shyly, she served them deftly and, followed by the light-footed man servant, left them to their small repast.

Margaret, tired and thirsty, thought the wafer thin sandwiches filled with something she could not identify and the cool drink with its sprig of mint, the most delicious food she had ever eaten. Beside a large plate of sandwiches, there were crisp sugar cookies and tiny frosted cakes, and she did full justice to the little feast.

The man watched her evident enjoyment with satisfaction, but took very little himself. He was thin to the point of emaciation, but he did not seem to have much appetite. As Margaret ate he sipped his drink in companionable silence. The shadows of early evening had begun to make themselves felt in the garden before Mr. Stillwell picked up a small silver bell left within reach of his hand and rang it. It gave out a musical tinkling sound which was very pleasant. Margaret was soon to learn of her employer's extreme distaste for harsh noises. Michael appeared as if by magic and stood awaiting his master's orders. "I think we may turn Miss McAskie over to Miss Parker now, Michael. Tell her to help her get settled, and I will send for her tomorrow." He turned to Margaret. "You must be exhausted."

Michael led her into the hall where they found Miss Parker hovering about just outside the door. Michael scowled at her. "I'll be after takin' the young ledy up, Parker," he said belligerently.

But Miss Parker was not to be overruled a second time and stood her ground firmly. Snatching the carpetbag out of the man's hand, she started up the stairs with it. "You needn't bother yourself, Michael. Your place is with Mr. Stillwell, not in the rest of the house. That's my province."

They turned to the right at the head of the stairs, passed down a long hall and ascended another flight of stairs. In passing, Margaret caught a glimpse of several handsomely furnished bedrooms and one which seemed to be a sitting room. Both flights of stairs and the hall were carpeted so thickly that their footsteps did not make a sound. They passed along another hallway and came to a door set in the wall at the rear of the house. This Miss Parker opened, disclosing a flight of steep uncarpeted steps. She motioned Margaret to precede her with a wave of her hand. "Your room is the first room on the right at the head of the stairs. You will find a wash stand in your room and a toilet at the end of the hall. Be careful that you do not break the wash basin and pitcher. I'll let you know when you are wanted. You might clean up a bit; your appearance is hardly such as we are accustomed to in this house." Her tone brought a flush of resentment to the girl's pale face, but she could think of no suitable reply so she closed the door on the hostile woman with what dignity she could muster and ascended the stairs wearily.

She found her room without difficulty. It was small and close, tucked into a wing of the house, its one window overlooking a blank brick wall. The floor was completely covered with straw matting which gave the room a stuffy odor. There was a narrow white iron bed with a chipped frame, a walnut bureau with a smeared and discolored mirror, an unpainted washstand with a pitcher, basin, soap dish, and slop basin, none of which matched, and a stiff, straight-backed chair. There was no curtain at the window. By the bureau there was a gas jet and from it hung a small glass containing matches and a piece of cardboard with two black cats on it, one of which was made of sandpaper, the other, with an inscription painted on it in flaming red letters: "Don't scratch me, scratch mother."

It was quite dark now and she would have liked to light the gas, but she was afraid to experiment with it. She washed her face and hands in the tepid water she found in the pitcher, changed into her nightgown, let her hair down over her shoulders and lay down on the bed to rest. Worn out with the unwonted excitement of the long tiring day, she was soon sound asleep, Mrs. Stillwell and Miss Parker temporarily forgotten.

Chapter Five

The days which followed were exciting ones for Margaret. Mrs. Stillwell and Miss Parker were unrelenting in their animosity and did everything in their power to make her uncomfortable, but the hours that she spent with Mr. Stillwell were sheer joy and his pleasure in her company more than compensated for the numerous petty humiliations she had to endure.

Bit by bit she learned what her employer liked and what she could do to please him. She learned that in his younger days he had traveled all over the world and when she questioned him about it, she sat spellbound while he recounted his adventures to her. He was an easy and fluent talker with an excellent command of language and he made her visualize the places about which he was talking almost as clearly as though she were seeing them with her own eyes. Her eager questions stimulated him into bringing out his postcard albums and the diary he had kept through those carefree years and they went over them together, much to their mutual pleasure.

When they wearied of that, they made a pretense of doing

some work on the book he wanted to write on the city's founding fathers or he played the piano for her. She was utterly amazed at the power and strength in his long fingers and she wondered why he made no effort to propel himself in his chair but always summoned Michael when he wished to move about. His magnetic and powerful playing appealed to her no less than did his delicate touch on the keys when he was rendering a Brahm's lullaby, and when she indicated her interest in certain composers, he had Michael get down from the book shelves the stories of their lives and they went over them together. She discovered that he liked to read aloud and she encouraged him to do so frequently. They took all their meals together on the veranda, for Mrs. Stillwell did not care to eat with her husband. Her employer questioned her about her family and her life on the farm and he soon had a clearer picture than she knew of the hardships and restrictions that she had had to endure there. Gradually, as she lost her shyness in his presence she opened her heart to him and revealed her hopes and ambitions. The days which for him had dragged so interminably suddenly commenced to pass as swiftly as a weaver's shuttle.

One evening they were sitting on the veranda lingering over the remnants of a delicious meal and watching the evening shadows gather over the garden. A companionable silence had fallen between them as Minnie cleared the table and took her soft-footed departure. Patrick and his young helper were at the lower end of the garden, one with a hose which he was wielding vigorously and the other with a big watering can. They could faintly hear Patrick's rich brogue as he admonished the lad to watch what he was doing with the hose. The peace and quiet all about them laved their spirits. The man sat and watched his protege and thought how much happier the small heart-shaped face looked than when he had first seen it. Margaret, her eyes on the garden, thought of how hard she would be working were she back on the farm and gave a sigh of relief. Thoroughly sensitive to her moods, Charles Stillwell asked, "Why the mournful sigh?"

Margaret smiled and turned her eyes from the garden to her employer's face. "That sigh wasn't mournful. It was thankful. Couldn't you tell the difference?"

The invalid laughed. It was the first time Margaret had ever heard him really laugh and her heart leapt with pleasure at the sound. "No," he said, "I cannot say that my male perception goes that far. To me a sigh is a sigh."

Margaret caught up the argument eagerly. "Oh, no. There are all kinds of sighs. At least I have quite a few, but up till now they haven't often been thankful ones. When I was home, it made me sigh to think of how much work I had to do and of how little time there was to do it. I often sighed because I wanted more education and there were times, especially when my lamb was killed, that I was afraid that I would never get it. I sighed when I thought that there was no chance of my getting a graduation dress like the other girls, and I often sighed for my mother after she died, but this sigh tonight was a sigh of pure pleasure."

"Pleasure? Pleasure in what?" the man asked eagerly.

"Oh, pleasure in being able to sit down and enjoy an evening like this. Pleasure in eating a dinner I did not have to cook and," she finished shyly, "pleasure in being with you."

For a moment the man did not speak. Then, somewhat huskily, he asked, "So you do like it here with me?"

She answered him directly and simply, "It is as near heaven as I ever expect to get on this earth. For the first time since my mother died, I feel rested and relaxed and content. People may contend that mental work is as exhausting as physical, but in my opinion they do not know what they are talking about. I am quite sure that they never lived on a farm or they wouldn't say so."

"But all mental work is not good either. I have been bothered about you that you have been here nearly a month and you haven't been out once. It is not right." He could not keep the bitterness from creeping into his voice. "You shouldn't constantly be tied to a cripple like me."

It was the first time Margaret had ever heard him refer to his useless legs. She had never seen him out of his wheel chair but she knew from something Michael had let drop in an unguarded moment that he had no use of his body whatsoever from the waist down. Her heart went out to him and reaching over she placed one small hand on his arm. "I'm not tied down," she said sturdily, "I am here because I want to be and I am happier than I have ever been in my life. But," she continued eagerly, "I do not see why you could not get around more. I have been thinking about it quite a lot and I am sure that I could wheel you down into the garden if you would have some kind of a ramp built and I really do not see why we cannot take an occasional drive together. Surely Michael and Patrick between them could manage to lift you into the carriage." She stopped aghast at the look on his face as he jerked his arm away from her, and quick tears sprang into her eyes. "Oh, Mr. Stillwell, I am so sorry. I did not mean to offend you. I was only trying to help. I . . . " she stopped unable to proceed for the lump in her throat.

Her distress brought him to himself as nothing else could have done. "My dear," he said simply, reaching for her small hand and placing it back on his arm where he could feel it trembling. He cursed himself for being a fool. "I want to ask you as a favor to me, never to mention driving again." He saw by her expression that she was mentally castigating herself for reminding him of the manner in which he had lost the use of his limbs. "Well," he thought bitterly, "it is better so." How could he tell her that he could not bear the thought of having her see him carried about like a baby? It was better to let her think that it was the memory of the accident which had upset him. "However," he continued aloud, longing to bend over and wipe the tears away from her gray eyes, "your idea about a ramp is an excellent one. I will have to start wheeling myself about. The doctor has been trying to get me to do so for some time, but somehow it didn't seem worth the effort with Michael always hovering around like a hen with one chick. But, this chair and my great hulk would be much too heavy for you, so I must perforce learn to propel it myself unless we want Michael listening to every word we say." He was observing her intently and when he saw the distress leave her face, he patted her hand. "It will be nice to feel the sun on my face once more."

The ramp was finished without delay. Margaret marveled at the ease and swiftness with which plenty of money could accomplish its owner's desired ends. The ramp enabled them to spend many hours together in the garden and a little color began to creep into the invalid's face and his appetite to improve. He took a new interest in the flowers and the way the gardeners had arranged the beds. The family doctor found them there one day when he came to make his periodic call. His shrewd old eyes went over Margaret as he introduced himself with a bluff, "Well, well, is this the young lady who has succeeded in getting my patient out into the sunlight? I suppose that he did not tell you that I have tried my best for a long time to do that very thing?"

The invalid laughed, "You haven't this young lady's persuasive powers, my dear doctor. Margaret, this is Dr. Barry, who alternately bullies me and beats me at chess." Margaret extended a small hand shyly.

The doctor grinned down at her. "Pleased to meet you, young lady, even though you succeeded where I failed." His professional eye looked her up and down while he squeezed her hand in a strong grip. "You look to me as if you could do with a little fresh air and sunshine yourself. I do not believe that you are fully grown yet."

"Oh, but I am,'" Margaret hastened to assure him, "I was seventeen yesterday and I'll probably always be small. My mother was and they say I take after her."

"Well, well," said the doctor jovially, "that is an advantage to be sure. I remember when this young feller was seventeen. He fairly wore me out with his energy. He was always tearing hither and yon, mostly to parties, mind you. Speaking of parties, what do you say to having a birthday party, Charles? We shouldn't let this young lady pass the ripe old age of seventeen without taking notice of the fact, now should we? I have a free evening tomorrow, or at least I think I have, so why don't we have some music and maybe some ice cream and cake?"

The birthday party was an unqualified success. When Margaret descended the stairs at dinner time, dressed in her white graduation dress with a bunch of tiny red roses tucked in her sash and a few artfully placed among the shining braids wound around her small head, Michael was waiting for her outside the door of Mr. Stillwell's apartments with a gaily wrapped package which he extended to her. "I hope that ye'll be acceptin' this little token of me appreciation, Miss. It's that glad I am ter be having ye wid us. If ye could've seen the marster as I seen 'im not more than two days afore ye come, with his face ter the wall and refusin' ter eat or ter talk even ter me, it'd warm the cockles of yer heart to see him now, gettin' out inter the garden an' givin' a party. 'Twarn't that he was ever cross or hateful like, but jist so discouraged that I couldn't git him to notice anythin' or take to any interest. The change is all due ter you, Miss, and I do thank ye with all me heart." Upon opening the gift Margaret found a gaudily embroidered handkerchief of white silk. When she expressed her pleasure at his thoughtfulness, Michael's ruddy face beamed.

Margaret could not fail but be pleased at the big Irishman's heartfelt admiration to which her employer added. She knew that she had never looked better in her life. The unwonted excitement had brought color into her cheeks and her eyes were like stars. Her dress was stylish and becoming and the red roses twined into her braids and tucked into her belt were as lovely ornaments as anyone could wish.

The table was set for dinner out on the veranda, and by her place she found a small gray velvet jeweler's box. She could not believe her eyes. "For me?" she asked incredulously. The man across the table nodded. "So that you will never forget your seventeenth birthday or the friend who wishes you all the happiness in the world."

Margaret's fingers trembled so with excitement that she could barely press the catch and open the box, but she finally succeeded in releasing it. Inside, nestled against the velvet, was a tiny chatelaine watch. Its case was chased with lilies-of-the-valley and in each flower was set a tiny pearl. There was also a small pearl-studded pin with which to fasten the watch to the front of her gown. It was the most beautiful thing she had ever seen and for a moment she was too overcome for speech. When she could take her enchanted eyes off of it, she lifted them to her employer's. "It is the most gorgeous watch I ever saw. Do you really mean for me to keep it?"

Her pleasure more than repaid him for the trouble he had taken to look over a case of watches he had had sent up that afternoon while he had insisted that she rest. "Look inside." She pressed the stem and the case opened. On the inside of the case was engraved her name and the date. She let out a longdrawn, "Oh!"

"Put it on. I want to see how it looks."

She succeeded in fastening it to the bosom of her dress. "I don't know how to thank you."

"Then don't try. We must have our dinner so that we may get through in time for the doctor. He sent word that he couldn't get here until nine o'clock."

When the doctor arrived he had a large box of chocolates under his arm for Margaret and in his pocket some sheet music he had taken the trouble to procure. At sight of Margaret he stopped in amazement. "Well, well, our little wren has turned into a bird of paradise and I must say the change is most becoming. Do you play the piano?" At Margaret's reply, "A little," the doctor waved the music in her face. "Then try this for me; I am sure that it is much too low class for Charles' taste, but it just suits me." Margaret took the music from his hand and went to the piano. The notes were simple and she had no trouble in reading the music. It was not long before the three of them were singing heartily:

"Daisy, Daisy, give me your promise true,
I'm most crazy all for the love of you.
It won't be a stylish marriage,
I can't afford a carriage,
But, you'd look sweet, upon the seat,
Of a bicycle built for two!"

In the kitchen, one of the maids was unpacking ice and salt from around the ice cream freezer. The cook was standing over her to see that she did not let any salt get into the frozen mixture. She had a wet cloth in her hand with which to wipe the top of the freezer. She paused in the midst of her task, her eyes rolled up to the ceiling. "The saints preserve us! Can that be the marster I hear, aliftin' his voice in song? 'Tis the first time I heard 'im sing since he was hurt and him that used ter be asingin' in and out of me kitchen all the time." Unashamedly she mopped her eyes and absentmindedly blew her nose on the cloth she held in her hand.

Michael had just come into the kitchen to secure the birthday cake to take upstairs. Patrick was sitting in the cook's rocker, stroking the cat. Michael crossed the room and the two men shook hands without words. Michael also found it necessary to blow his nose before he was ready to take the refreshments upstairs.

All the servants but the housekeeper were gathered in the basement kitchen finishing the remains of the party. Patrick, who was inordinately fond of frosting, had just finished licking the knife which had been used to cut the cake. He put it down on the table as clean as his tongue could make it. "Sure, 'tis a glad day that brung the young Miss ter this house. I hope that herself," he made an ugly face, "an' that Parker don't drive her away with their shenanigans. 'Twas bad enough at first with herself makin' the young lady sit up on the box with me and ignorin' her as if she was a stone when she stopped ter pass the time o' day with that Miller woman, which shenanigan she done apurpose, mind ye, but now that the young ledy pleases the marster, there's no tellin' what the pair of them won't stoop ter!" Gloomily he sat down in the rocker and picked up the cat again.

Minnie, scraping the bottom of the freezer for the last bit of ice cream, took up his lament. "And that ain't all neither. Where do ye be thinkin' they put the young ledy?" Michael, who was bent over, polishing his already spotless shoes with an old rag, said over his shoulder, "In one of the guest rooms where the marster said she was ter go."

"Guest room, me foot," exclaimed Minnie, pleased to be the center of attention. "She's up in the attic with us maids!"

Norah, not willing to be left out of this interesting conversation, contributed her bit, " 'Tis the worst room in the lot she's got, too."

Katy, with her arms akimbo, surveyed the group, "Some thin' outer be done, and that's a fact. She's too nice a young ledy ter be treated so. 'Tis the back of me hand I'd like ter be takin' ter that Parker." The "Miss Parker" that the housekeeper insisted upon being called to her face was never accorded to her behind her back.

" 'Tis a kind heart she has, too," continued Minnie, stacking the plates. "I burned a hole in one of the tray cloths and she mended it fer me so tidy like that Parker didn't even notice it."

The cook snorted, "Yer expectin' too much. She'll see it yet. She's got eyes like a hawk, she has. Always snoopin' round me kitchen and interferin' in matters which ain't no concern of hers. I'd like ter tweak her long nose fer her, that I would. 'Tis glad I'd be ter see her fall down and break a leg and I'd be offerin' no candles fer her neither! Here," she said, passing the last of the cake to young Jimmie, Patrick's helper, "Yer might as well finish this, or she'll be arskin' all kinds of questions in the mornin'. 'Tis pleased I'd be to be tellin' her that the marster ordered a cake fer the young ledy, but it'd only make her hate her more'n she does already. That niece of hers she tried to get the marster to hire wouldn't of started him singin' and well she knows it. She's green with envy that's what she is. 'Tis more likely t'would be swearin' he'd be if the niece is anything like her hatchet-faced aunt."

Michael neatly folded the rag he was using and returned it to the shoe box. "I'll be seein' that the marster hears about this, don't yer fret. Miss Margaret won't be up in the attic long or me name ain't Michael O'Shaughnessy."

Michael was as good as his word. The results of his imparting this bit of information to his master were even quicker and more drastic than he had dreamed. When the battle was over and he had reported it below stairs, there was heartfelt rejoicing in the kitchen and the cook made a pitcher of lemonade to celebrate the victory.

Mr. Stillwell lost no time; he sent for his wife at once and asked Margaret to go out into the garden and leave them alone. The mistress of the house was dressed to go out, but he commanded her to sit down in such a tone that she obeyed him instantly, though sullenly, murmuring that she had an engagement. He eyed her balefully. "Well, you have a more important one with me, and I want you to answer several questions."

"Can't they wait until I get back?"

He frowned. "No, they cannot! They are about Miss McAskie."

She pretended not to understand. "Miss McAskie? Why I thought that you had found her quite satisfactory. Of course, I think her rather crude and her clothes are awful. But, after all, she is only a country bumpkin from a farm . . ."

He interrupted her savagely, his usual courtesy deserting him entirely. "If I ever hear another remark like that from your lips, I'll make it a point to see that your charming friends hear that your father was a bartender and your mother a drunken slattern when I met you." She paled under her poorly applied rouge.

"You wouldn't."

"Oh, wouldn't I? Just try me and see, madam. And what is more, I'll invite your charming parents here and invite your friends to meet them. How would you like to have them see your father eat with his knife and see your mother drink herself under the table?"

She fairly stuttered in her distress. "But, you haven't seen anyone or gone anywhere in years."

He glared at her, satisfied that he had drawn blood. "No, I haven't, because it made me sick to see you trying to make a lady of yourself. Your airs and graces were too much for me, my dear. But there is no reason why I should not watch you perform once more, if I wish to, although it would be hard to stomach that bunch of riffraff that you call your friends."

Tears stood in her pale blue eyes. "Oh, Charlie, how can you be so cruel?"

"So, it's 'Charlie' again, is it? Dry your tears, my love, they are entirely wasted on me. It is too late for that sort of thing. I know perfectly well that you married me for what I have of this world's goods, and that I cannot die too quickly to suit you. You are just itching to get your fat little paws on my money so that you can marry one of those good-for-nothing young wastrels with whom you consort."

He saw denial form upon her lips but cut it off by saying, "Oh, don't bother to deny it; I know where Patrick takes you and whom you see."

Her anger sputtered into a feeble spark. "Why, that miserable little Irish mick! I'll . . . "

He regarded her icily. "You'll do nothing of the sort. He is my servant and, as long as I am paying the bills, will remain so. Now answer me this. Did you make that poor child sit up on the box with Patrick and refuse to introduce her to your friends on the way home from the station?" Watching her intently, he saw her lick her dry lips, and when she did not answer at once, he barked at her, "Well, did you? Answer me!" Uncertainly she tried to find some words which would not add fuel to the fire of his wrath.

"Well, I-I had a lot of packages in back with me and it was rather crowded — and — "

Once more he interrupted her. "So crowded that you had to humiliate a poor little country girl by treating her like a servant. I suppose it never occurred to you to put the packages up front with Patrick."

She tried to defend herself with a toss of the head. "Well, she didn't seem to know the difference nor to mind much. She chatted with Patrick all the way home, just like the common, ignorant creature she is," she ended defiantly.

The man brought his fist down on the edge of his chair with a bang that made her jump. "Let me hear you speak of her again like that and I'll notify every shop in this town to stop your credit and then we'll see if you can't be made to treat a guest in your own house with common decency!"

Her plump chin went up. "I'd hardly call a paid . . ." She started to say "servant," but at the look on his face continued, "a paid employee, a guest."

"Oh, wouldn't you, indeed!" His tone was dripping with sarcasm. "She is here because I have invited her to come and in the future she is to be treated with the same consideration as if she were a guest, and don't you forget it! A real lady would not descend to such smallness and meanness as you have employed against a helpless child and as for talking with Patrick, he can carry on a more intelligent conversation than you can any day in the year, my dear."

She wiped her eyes with a wisp of linen and lace. "You never talked to me like this before she came. She must have turned you against me."

He laughed bitterly. "How true to type you are! She gives me the time, attention, and appreciation which you have always denied me and so you have to excuse your lack by turning on her because she has succeeded where you have failed."

Her anger flared to meet his. "Well, she gets paid for it!"

He was watching her through narrowed eyes as if she were a performing monkey. "And, I suppose, you are not? Who pays for all your giddy fripperies which are so often in abominable taste? Your beaux?" Then, as he saw her flush, "No, I thought not, the bills still come to me. And what do I get in return? My accident relieved you of my physical presence, much, I now realize, to your relief. What is there left? No, don't get up. I am not through with you yet. I have one more question I want answered. Why did you put that child in the worst room in the house? Now don't blame it on Parker. I know perfectly well that she does what you tell her. You hoped to make her so uncomfortable that she would leave, didn't you? Well, she is not the quitting kind. She expects to work for what she gets and she is willing to put up with a few inconveniences. She is not fat and lazy and soft like you. No, she didn't tell me about the room you gave her," as he saw an accusation form on her lips, "I learned about it in my own way. I have other ways of keeping track of your actions than through Patrick. It might be well for you to remember that in the future."

The unbelief registered on the plump features opposite him gave place to an ill-concealed fear and she bit her full lower lip to try and hide it from him. But he gave her no respite. "Now, I want you to call that cardboard cutout of a woman whom you call *Parker* and tell her that Margaret is to be moved into the yellow guest room at once!"

Frantically, she seized upon the only straw within her reach. "So, you are calling her *Margaret* now!"

He picked up an open book lying on the table beside him and slammed it down on the arm of his chair. "I'll call her by her first name or any other damn thing I please. Now, get out! Michael!" he shouted, "Show Mrs. Stillwell out. She annoys me!"

Chapter Six

Margaret, who knew nothing about what had transpired while she had been visiting with young Jimmie in the garden, could not understand why Miss Parker suddenly commanded her to move her possessions downstairs to a larger room. As she had passed back and forth to the upper regions and had glanced eagerly into the rooms she passed, the yellow bedroom had seemed to her the loveliest of them all. Its rear windows commanded a view of the garden and its side windows looked out upon the street so that it was always flooded with light and this gave it a cheerful, lived-in look. Its floor was covered from baseboard to baseboard with gold carpeting that was as soft as velvet. The draperies and slipcovers were of a gaily flowered chintz and the walls were a pale yellow. Between the two back windows stood a small desk and chair. To the girl's amazement the dressing table and desk had appointments of gold and it was a long time before she could bring herself to use them. The bed was a large fourposter and the mattress was as soft and thick as the one upstairs had been hard and thin. On either side of it was a small table on which had been placed a lamp which was just right in height for reading in bed. At the foot of the bed was a small sofa invitingly stocked with several soft plump pillows. The fireplace was of yellow marble and a comfortable rocker stood at one side of it and a low slipper chair at the other. A chest of drawers and a small sewing table completed the furnishings. There was no need of a commode, for there was a bathroom next to the roomy closet. Margaret had never seen an inside bathroom before she came to the city and she was entranced. The shining copper tub was encased in a wide rim of well-polished walnut. The washbowl was of china, stenciled in gold leaf about its upper edge and set in a great slab of yellow marble. It had, as Minnie pointed out to her with pride, solid gold faucets. For the first few days Margaret turned the faucets on and off as often as she got the chance, marvelling at having running water just by the turning of a handle.

To have such beauty and comfort suddenly put at her disposal was rather overwhelming but she enjoyed it nevertheless. She hung her few garments on the padded scented hangers and put her meagre possessions in one drawer of the tall chest, and it was not long before she was soaking her slim body in the shiny copper tub and brushing her hair in front of the dainty dressing table as a matter of course. Life suddenly became very easy. Everything was done for her. From the time her breakfast tray was brought to her in the morning until she retired at night she did not have to lift a finger. Her bed was made for her, her clothes picked up, laundered, and returned to her bureau drawers smelling of verbena; her room was aired and tidied and filled with fresh flowers daily. The easy life and relaxed routine benefited her in many ways. For the first time in her life she was happy and was not working far beyond her strength during every waking hour. She began to put on a little weight and her clear skin took on a rosy translucence that it had never known. Her black hair gleamed from the combined effect of good food and good grooming, and her clear gray eyes took on a new luster. All the natural joyousness with which she had been endowed and which the harshness of her father and the drudgery of the farm had succeeded in smothering, came to the surface and overflowed spontaneously.

The effects of well-being were no less apparent in her employer. He, too, was eating better and sleeping more without the aid of medicine. For the first time in many years, days did not stretch before him like an interminable space of time between dawn and dark, which had somehow to be lived through. He kept discovering new interests for himself and his little protege. Soon after the birthday party they were playing duets together with considerable facility, for although Margaret had not had his opportunities for practice and education, she was gifted with a good ear and possessed a natural ability to sight read musical scores. Gradually, he was instilling in her a love of good music. Often after they had spent some time together at the piano she would beg him to play for her. She had long since learned to ignore the hand lever which substituted for the foot pedals when he played. One evening he was playing Saint-Saens', "My Heart At Thy Sweet Voice," to her as she leaned against the curve of the big piano. The music was very familiar to him and his eyes were on her face. When he had finished, she said softly, "I think that must be the sweetest music in the whole world. I wish that I could play it on the violin."

He caught her comment up eagerly, glad to escape from his thoughts, "Would you really like to learn to play the violin?"

"Oh, yes! I do not know why, but I have always had a secret desire to be able to play one."

His left hand played a few bass notes carelessly. "I wish you would let me give you lessons." Then, as he saw a refusal form upon her lips, he continued eagerly, "It would give me great pleasure to have you accompany me on the violin. I have always been very fond of string music." To himself he was thinking that if her eyes and hands were busy with music and an instrument he would be able to watch her unashamed. He held his hand out to her across the piano. "Wouldn't you do that for me?"

Instantly her small hand found his. "There isn't anything that you could ask of me that I wouldn't do," she said softly.

He withdrew his hand somewhat hastily. "That's a good girl. I do like a woman who can grant a favor gracefully. Thank you, my dear." Something out of the ordinary in the tones of his voice drew her eyes to his from the garden where they had been resting, but he had broken into a Strauss waltz in order to cover his emotion and his eyes were on his rapidly moving hands.

65

The lessons were a great success. Three times a week an old German professor by the name of Gruber came to the house. Mr. Stillwell did not seem to mind having him there and insisted that the lessons be conducted in his rooms. After a few weeks the professor brought his big bass viol with him one day, because Margaret persuaded him to join them in the few simple pieces she had already been able to master. The old German was enchanted when his host invited him to bring it again some evening when Margaret was more proficient and Margaret was delighted that she had been able to bring another person into the secluded life of her benefactor.

Her employer taught her to play chess and it was not long before she was giving him a run for his money. He loved to watch the earnest heart-shaped face bent in deep concentration over the exquisitely carved chess men and he was almost as pleased as she when she succeeded in capturing one of his men or stalemating him. After she had once conquered the game she played her very best, convinced that was the right way to keep his interest alive. This delighted him, for he had long supposed that the doctor with whom he occasionally enjoyed a game let him win in sheer sympathy for his affliction. She frequently encouraged him to read aloud and although she employed the time so spent with a bit of needlework in her hands, she never let her attention stray from the story. Nor did he object to this for he loved to look up and see her near him, her dark braids bent over the fabric in her slender fingers. When he read something particularly interesting or amusing, she never failed to look up at him with a question on her lips or a laugh in her eyes. Her complete attention was always his when he wanted it and he grew to depend on it more each day.

She had not been long in that house before she came to the realization that there was going to be no religious observance of any kind. Grace was not offered at table, prayers were unheard of, and no one but the servants ever went to church. To Margaret, this was a great relief, and one hot Sunday morning, dawdling over the Sunday papers in the shade of the deep veranda, she voiced her satisfaction in a state of affairs of which she thoroughly approved. "It is so nice to be here instead of shut up in a stuffy church!"

Instantly, he was chagrined at his thoughtlessness. "I say, I am sorry! It never occurred to me that you might be accustomed to attending church. You may do the same here if you wish, you know."

She laughed, the soft little laugh that he had grown to love and watch for. "I'll never go unless you send me. I had enough of church-going at home to last me for the rest of my natural life."

Always anxious to learn anything about her that she would tell him, he asked curiously, "You did not like it?"

Her tone was vehement as she answered him, "Like it? I hated it! But my father never missed it nor allowed us to do so. I think he loved hearing the minister rave about hell and damnation."

"And you didn't?"

She thought a moment before she answered him. "I not only didn't, but I am not at all sure that I believe that there is such a place as hell. Besides, it used to frighten the little ones dreadfully. Sometimes," she went on, daringly taking her eyes off the flowers and directing her earnest gaze at his face to catch his reaction to such rashness, "I even wonder if there is a God who cares about individuals and what they do."

He did not seem in the least shocked but only smiled in his kindly manner, at her earnestness. "Well, I don't know. There is certainly some force which has brought order and beauty to the universe. One might as well call it *God* as anything else, I suppose. I agree with you, however, that if you do call it *God*, He is too abstract a being to concern Himself personally with us as individuals. To me, it has always seemed the height of self conceit to suppose that the Creator of the universe would be interested in me as a person. When one considers the universe in all its vastness, one really constitutes such an infinitesimal part of the whole that as an individual one scarcely warrants direct notice from the Almighty!"

"Then you do not believe in prayer?" Her tone was eager. If this kind and considerate man, who in the short time she had known him had become her ideal, did not believe in prayer, she did not need to worry about her lack of faith. He shook his head. "I am afraid that I do not consider myself and my puny affairs important enough to demand that God listen to my petitions. Why should He be interested in me?"

For a moment she made no answer. Then she said, "God is supposed to love you."

The long slender hands lying idly in his lap clenched themselves into a hard fist. "I am afraid," he said, his voice crisp in spite of himself, "that since my accident I find it a little difficult to believe in the love of God." Then, seeing her distressed look, "My dear, my dear, don't look like that! I did not mean to hurt you. I was only trying to answer your question."

Her lips trembled as she answered him, "I am afraid that it is I who have hurt you, but I didn't mean to. Surely you know that. I'm afraid that I was thinking only of myself when I spoke." She hesitated uncertain whether or not to continue, but the kind eyes on her face reassured her and she continued somewhat diffidently. "I believed in prayer once, and I asked God to help me by protecting my lamb. Perhaps your experience was the same as mine." She did not look at him, but at her hands clasped in her lap.

The man's eyes were very tender as he looked across the small table which separated them at the dark, bowed head. "And God didn't see fit to answer your prayer?"

She shook her dark braids. "No, He didn't and at the time it meant everything in the world to me."

"Would it help to talk about it?" There was deep concern in the kindly voice.

For a moment she looked up at him shyly. "Yes, I think it would. I had a little lamb. It was the only thing of my very own that I had ever possessed. I was planning to sell it and use the money it brought me to leave home and go to normal school. My stepmother found out what I was planning to do and the first night of the big blizzard, she let my lamb out of the fold so that the wolves got it and ate it. God evidently thought that I was too insignificant to bother with, too!"

For a moment the man did not speak. Much as he longed to comfort her, there was nothing in his own experience upon which he could draw to help her. Facile as he was with words, he could think of nothing to say at that moment. Unable to reassure her, he turned to another aspect of the situation. "But you did get away eventually."

"Yes," she defended herself quickly, "but it was the teacher and you who helped, not God!"

She had him there, so he changed the subject. "Why were you so anxious to become a teacher? You hardly seem the type to me."

Quickly she came back at him, "Do you consider Miss Abbott

the type?"

He laughed aloud at her shrewdness, "No, I cannot say that I do."

"But she makes a wonderful teacher!" Her eyes glowed in remembrance. "When I was so discouraged after the loss of my lamb, she helped me and encouraged me and inspired me to go on working. I really do not know what I should have done without her. Why, she even brought me to you and for that I shall be grateful to her all of my life!"

He was more moved than he cared to admit. He turned his eyes away from her clear glance and fumbled with the light cover with which his legs were draped and without which he never let her see him. It was his turn to be embarrassed. He cleared his throat before he continued. "But, you still haven't told me just why you want to be a teacher? Is it because you admire Rosemary so much?"

"Well, yes, partly," answered Margaret slowly, thinking it over in her own mind, "although I could never be as pretty as she, but it isn't only that. I hated the farm and my father's strictness and the only way that I could ever see of becoming independent of it and him, was to get an education so that I could leave when I became of age. I have always yearned to go places and see things and know all about books and music and be a lady!"

"Well," he said, pretending to laugh at her intensity to hide a deeper emotion, "that is quite a program all in all, but it isn't impossible to realize. In the first place, a lady is born, not made, and that part of your wish you already have. It is because you have a kind and tender heart that you are so good to a middle-aged cripple like myself!" He was watching her reaction to his words closely, but to his immense relief his excoriation of himself caused no change in the earnest expression with which she was regarding him. His heart leapt in his bosom and he thought within himself that had she thought of him in those terms she would have protested. The fact that she did not, he found tremendously reassuring and his voice quickened as he finished, "I see that you do not realize that fine feathers do not always make fine birds!"

"They would help a lot!" said Margaret wistfully, her eyes on her clumsy boots. He was touched, but he dared not show it too obviously. Rosemary Abbott had told him how her father had insisted upon appropriating all her earnings and he had been puzzling for some time over the problem of finding a way to give her some pretty clothes without hurting her feelings or wounding her fierce young pride, as he well knew his wife and Parker had already done. He longed to see her adorned in attractive clothes which his money had paid for and to witness her delight in them, but so far he had discovered no solution to the problem. It irritated him not to be able to outfit her as he chose, but he was well aware that his wife was watching his every move and he had no intention of giving her any just cause for further persecution of his little protege.

He thought fiercely that if he only had the use of his legs he could protect her adequately, but as long as he was helplessly bound to his chair, he could never be sure that she was not enduring petty persecutions at the hands of the two hostile members of the household. He must, therefore, proceed with caution and that very fact annoyed him. He frowned and returned to Margaret's description of a lady. "As far as knowing *all* about books and music, that is a pretty large order and I am afraid is a goal that very few reach. However, we are well on the way. We are going through my library and it is a singularly complete one, if I must say so myself, and we are learning some new music every day. As for the travel, I am afraid that that part of your program will have to wait a little while." He glanced down at his helpless legs bitterly. "That is, unless you want to leave me!"

Her soft answer set his heart to pounding. "I'd rather be here with you than any place I can think of. As long as I have you, I can get along very well without God!"

He took the matter up with Michael the next morning while he was having his massage. He hated to have Michael rub his useless, clumsy limbs but the doctor insisted, and Michael was meticulous in obeying the doctor's every command. Charles Stillwell lay on his back, his long arms folded under his head, his eyes on the frescoed ceiling. "Michael, she is lovely!" Michael did not need to inquire who she was.

"She certainly is that, sir!" he agreed heartily.

"But," continued the man on the bed, "her clothes are

awful. Something has got to be done about them. I can't bear to have her go on wearing those dull, drab, ill-fitting things, but I do not know what to do about it. I don't want to hurt her feelings. Can you think of something?"

Michael, who had a quick Irish wit, was ready with a suggestion, thankful to get his master's mind off the detested massage. "Well, sir, there is a way of yer payin' her more money without ye'd be hurtin' her feelin's. Last week Minnie burnt a hole in one of them tray clothes. She'd used it without Parker's permission an' she was beside herself fer fear she'd find it out and dock her wages. But the young miss, she mended it so neat ye'd niver have known it was hurt. Parker wouldn't of known it nither if she hadn't been aspyin' round the kitchen and seen Norah and Minnie admirin' the work. So what does the old battle-ax do, but arsk the young miss ter do some of the household mendin' fer her. She hates a needle like sin does that Parker. She's sure ter give her some more ter do, and then ye can pay her fer doin' it!"

The head of the house grinned at his faithful body servant. "Michael, you are priceless! I do not know what I should ever do without you. You keep your eyes open and let me know the moment Parker gives her some mending or sewing."

Michael agreed with alacrity. " 'Tis a pleasure ter be sure, sir. I'll be after watchin' that Parker like a hawk, and I'm thinkin'," he grinned back at the man on the bed, "that she won't be likin' it at all, at all!"

Chapter Seven

It was a rainy afternoon in early September and Margaret had been out for a walk at her employer's insistence that a little outdoor exercise would be good for her. The day had looked pleasant enough when she had left the house, but she had been caught in a heavy shower. She had taken refuge in the doorway of a building, but when it became obvious to her that the rain was not going to let up for some time, she had decided to risk a wetting rather than leave her employer alone too long.

When she arrived at the house and rang the bell, she looked terribly bedraggled. Her shoes and skirt were soaked and her hat was a limp mass. Parker opened the door. Margaret had never been offered a key and she hesitated to ask Mr. Stillwell for one. As she stepped into the hall she saw to her dismay that the green drawing room was full of chattering women. The lady of the house was giving a whist party. As Parker closed the heavy front door, she said with an ill concealed sneer, "You look like something the cat dragged in!"

Margaret flushed and bit her lip. She had on her oldest gown and she was fully aware without being told that the rain had not improved its appearance. Parker, a gleam of satisfaction in her small close-set eyes, indicated the room full of women with a wave of her hand. "Mrs. Stillwell wants you in the drawing room."

Margaret drew back and was on the point of refusing when the shrill voice of her employer's wife rose above the polite clatter. "Is that Miss McAskie, Parker? Send her in here please, at once," and Margaret knew that they had deliberately set a trap for her to fall into when she looked her very worst. There was nothing to do but to face the music. Margaret squared her slim shoulders and advanced a few steps into the room, uncomfortably conscious of her mended gloves, battered hat, and bedraggled garments amidst the lavish display of the latest fashions.

Mrs. Stillwell was playing at a table near the door. She raised her shrill voice to even a higher pitch to make herself heard above the hubbub. "Girls, this is my husband's new secretary." All eyes turned to survey Margaret standing helpless and alone near the door which Parker had firmly closed behind her. A dowager raised her lorgnette and surveyed the girl critically. Then she leaned down and addressed her hostess across the table. "The one you have been telling us about?" she asked, obviously amused.

Mrs. Stillwell laughed a sneering little laugh which cut across Margaret's sensibilities like a file. "The very same, my dear Maisie."

Maisie peered at Margaret through her lorgnette as if she were a freak in a side show. Then she turned to her hostess. "It must be nice for you, Ada, to have someone you do not need to worry about to keep that handsome husband of yours amused." The implication was obvious. Several of the ladies tittered.

Margaret gathered the tattered shreds of her dignity about her and addressed her employer's wife evenly. "Was there something you wanted of me?" Mrs. Stillwell waved her bejeweled hand vaguely. "Oh, no. Nothing special. I only wanted my friends to see you. You may go now if you wish."

Margaret, humiliated to the very core of her being, made good her escape. The women she left behind her made no attempt to lower their voices and their parting remarks were calculated to follow her retreating back. "My dearest Ada, you do not need to worry about that little country bumpkin. Why, she looks like a plucked chicken . . . " This, to the accompaniment of shrill laughter.

"Girls, did you ever see such clothes in your life? She looked like a scarecrow in a grain field . . . "

"You didn't tell us the half, Ada . . . "

"I scarcely believed Adele Miller when she described her, but I see she did not do her justice . . . "

Margaret fled up the stairs, her ears smarting and her cheeks burning. When she reached her room she flung herself across her neatly made bed and burst into a torrent of tears. Oh, she hated them; she hated them all! The mean, lazy, selfish things. If she had their money or their opportunities she could look as well as they and better! Inevitably, when she was upset, her thoughts reverted to her father. If he had not been so stingy and so pious, she would not have been laid open to this humiliation. She hated him as much as she hated them. So they thought her a crude little country bumpkin, did they? She writhed inwardly in shame and disgrace. Worn out by her emotions, she lay across the bed and let the minutes tick away, too exhausted by her storm of tears to rise and tidy herself. "I'll show them yet," she thought bitterly, "I'll show them! Someday I am going to have all the pretty clothes I want and jewels and a carriage and as beautiful a home as any of them and then nobody will ever guess that I have ever seen a farm or worn drab clothes or worked for a living! I swear I will. I'll show them!"

Parker fell right into the trap set for her by Michael. So pleased was she with the help she was getting from Margaret that she showed some of her handiwork to her mistress, who immediately saw a way of using the girl to her own advantage. She was extremely fond of hand-embroidered underwear, but she hated to pay the fancy prices that the shops charged for such garments. She would have some things made to order and stamped and Margaret could embroider them for her. She knew that her husband's young secretary would never dare to refuse her request, and she would be saved a neat sum of money. The housekeeper assured her that the girl had been mending the table linens while Mr. Stillwell read to her and that he had not even noticed what she was working on. But the two schemers had reckoned without Michael. He knew what was afoot and he cautioned his master to keep his eyes on Margaret's handiwork.

Margaret, the evening after Parker deposited a great pile of silken garments on her bed, took one downstairs with her. After an hour of music and a game of chess, she and her employer settled down to a book which he had been reading to her, and she brought out her sewing. Mr. Stillwell was all ready for her. "That chemise seems rather large for a little thing like you," he commented mildly.

The color came up under Margaret's clear skin. Cornered, she had to confess. "It isn't mine; it belongs to Mrs. Stillwell."

He raised his eyebrows questioningly. "Did she ask you to make it for her?" Margaret began to feel uneasy under his direct gaze.

"Well, no, not exactly. Only to embroider it for her. But, I don't mind," she hastened to assure him as she saw the gathering anger on his face, "I love to listen to you read and I am not used to sitting idly without some work in my hands. Besides, I love to work on material like this; it is so soft and smooth."

Her pleading did not eradicate the deepening scowl with which he was gazing at the soft piece of silk heaped in her lap. "Did she offer to pay you for the work?" he asked her bluntly.

"Oh, no!" Margaret replied quickly, "but, I did not expect it. You pay me a very generous salary as it is and I enjoy doing it, truly I do. I have never had anything so lovely to work on." She watched him anxiously. She did not mind making trouble for the woman who had been so hateful to her, but she trembled inwardly at the thought of the lengths to which her employer's wife might go in order to pay her back. Seeing no lessening of the sternness of his glance, she finished somewhat lamely, "It is a pleasure just to hold such beautiful stuff in my hands."

When he answered her, his tone was dry. "Well, I've no doubt that it will be a pleasure for her to wear it when you have finished it. You may finish that if you like, but we will see what can be done about rewarding you suitably."

'But, I don't want anything for doing it!" protested Margaret uneasy and embarrassed. "You do so much to give me happiness as it is . . . "

His stern expression softened at her distress, but he remained adamant. "The arrangement which I made with you has nothing to do with Mrs. Stillwell. Besides, any happiness you may have derived from our association, is as nothing to the happiness which your coming brought into my life. Let us continue where we left off."

Nothing more was said about the matter and Margaret concluded with relief that he was going to let it drop. But, a few evenings later he announced that they were dining in the big dining room with the lady of the house. As soon as the soup was served, he harked back to Margaret's handiwork. He fired his opening shot directly at the target. "That is very pretty embroidery that Margaret is doing for you, my dear."

His wife looked up from her plate uneasily, uncertain just how to answer him. When he called her 'my dear' or 'my love', he was usually trying to bait her, but tonight his tone lacked the heavy sarcasm with which it was usually weighted when he used such expressions.

He did not seem to be particularly upset so she ventured an enthusiastic, "Yes, it is rather nice. Vera was in today and she simply raved about the dressing sack she is doing for me." Maybe, she thought, the girl will get the work done a little faster if I show a little appreciation. Getting no audible response from either her husband or his secretary, she went on, "It is hard to get work like that done outside of a convent."

The master of the house looked down the table at his wife with satisfaction in his eyes. "And is convent embroidery so hard to get?" he asked solicitously.

She fell into his trap at once. "Oh, no! But it is terribly expensive."

"Well, is that so?" His eyes narrowed. "And you are getting it done for nothing."

Too late she perceived her mistake. She was on the defensive immediately. "Miss McAskie seems to enjoy doing it."

He considered the matter while he served himself to the croutons a servant was passing. "Yes, she seems to, but she is doing it on time which rightfully belongs to me. So, I feel that you should reimburse one of us."

Mrs. Stillwell flushed under her rouge. "Well, of course, if Miss McAskie insists upon being paid for the work. . . "

He did not let her finish, "She has no such idea, but I have. I want you to get Miss Brophy in and have her fit three new dresses for Miss McAskie. I will select the material myself. And for every garment she finishes for you she is to have enough material to make one just like it for herself."

Mrs. Stillwell's face became purple with indignation and her eyes snapped. "I'm sure that I do not see where she would go to wear such things as I have!"

Mr. Stillwell smiled down the table at the irate woman to whom he was married and there was deep satisfaction in his eyes as he replied blandly, "She can wear them for my pleasure, my love. Please ring for the roast."

The following day a small dapper man with a waxed mustache arrived from one of the exclusive shops in the city, accompanied by numerous boxes and bundles. He spread out his wares before the enraptured girl and her more critical companion. After they had selected enough material for a suit and three dresses, the clerk produced some new shirtwaists which he held up temptingly. "Very nice with skirts," he observed. Mr. Stillwell immediately ordered half a dozen in Margaret's size. This strategy was so successful that the young man produced a box of shoes and stockings and another containing hats. He departed with a substantial order in his pocket and a firm conviction that Mrs. Stillwell had better keep her eyes open. Margaret was the possessor of the makings of a wardrobe, the like of which she had never contemplated in her wildest dreams.

Miss Brophy, a tall, angular, flat-chested woman with a great passion for smart clothes, arrived the following Monday and set to work. She deplored the girl's flat bust, but she considered her slimness an asset and set to work with nimble fingers to give Margaret a fashionable silhouette. She fashioned several corset covers of nainsook and lace which were gathered into tiny ruffles and clusters to emulate the full bosom that fashion decreed and she concocted small pads which were to be tied about the waist with a string to give the rounded hip and slight back bustle which were the current mode. The shoulders of the dresses were padded out to such an extent that when she was at last ready to give Margaret a fitting, the girl stood transfixed, gazing enraptured at the fashionable figure which presented itself to her in the pier glass.

Miss Brophy took the pins out of her mouth and stood back eyeing her handiwork critically. "That's as good a job of deception as I ever accomplished!" she remarked crisply. "A man'd never know it wasn't all you till he got you home!"

As soon as her first dress was finished, Margaret wore it downstairs to show Michael and Mr. Stillwell. She walked into the room trying not to appear self-conscious and pivoted, her arms outstretched so that they might get a full view of her new finery.

After whirling about breathlessly, she came to a stop beside the invalid's chair. "Do you like it?" she asked eagerly.

He smiled indulgently at her. "It certainly is stylish, but the real question is, how do you like it?"

She pressed her small hands to her bosom, "Oh, it is beautiful! I feel just like a fashion plate in *Godey's Lady Book!*"

"And is that a satisfactory way to feel?" he asked, laughing. "I have always thought that Godey's Ladies were singularly stiff and unbending."

"Oh, that is merely their fashionable exterior," she assured him. "At heart they are really quite different. Like this." Bending gracefully she dropped him a deep courtesy, "It's simply wonderful to know that one is as stylishly dressed as everybody else and that one does not have to be ashamed of the way one looks. I love it and thank you very, very, much, kind sir!"

Chapter Eight

One evening toward the middle of September as Margaret and her employer sat lingering over their evening meal, he said to her, "I have a surprise for you." She looked up at him quickly with the swift upsweep of heavy black lashes that he loved to watch.

"For me?"

"For you, no less. I have made arrangements for you to go to normal school. You are to attend classes from nine 'til one, daily except Saturday."

The complete unexpectedness of his announcement left her breathless. "But — what about our work? How are we going to get that done?"

"Oh, we'll have plenty of time. We have all afternoon and besides, we have made such good headway this summer that now I think we can let up a little. For that matter, there is no real hurry about the book. I only undertook writing it to amuse myself before you came, but if you will let me help you with your assignments, I can get just as much pleasure out of that, I know. Now, don't look so dubious! I thought that you would be pleased."

"I am pleased, but I am also overwhelmed and I am afraid that you are not being fair to yourself."

"For a young lady whose greatest ambition is to become a teacher, you seem strangely reluctant all of a sudden. Don't you want an education any longer?"

"Oh, yes, more than anything in the world! It isn't that. I'm wondering what you will do without me all morning long."

To hide his real feelings, he made light of the matter. "So, you think that I have grown to be so dependent on you that I cannot get along for a few hours without you! Such conceit! What do you think I did before you came? I have my books and my music and I've been contemplating teaching Michael to play chess."

He turned away from her troubled look and abandoned his levity. "Besides, my dear, I want you to go. If you do, I shan't feel quite so selfish as I do now, absorbing all your time and attention. You can be home every day for lunch and we can go over your lessons together. I'm sure there is much that I can learn, even at the advanced age of thirty-six. So, you see you will really be benefiting me by keeping my mind alive and active."

Margaret rose from her low chair and went and knelt on the floor by his chair. "How can I refuse you when you put it like that? You are the most kind and thoughtful person I have ever known. Before I met you and Miss Abbott I never knew that anyone could be so unselfish and considerate. I do not know how to begin to thank you." Tears which she made no attempt to hide stood in her clear gray eyes.

"Don't try!" he said somewhat huskily. "Between you and me there should be no such thing as thanks."

It was a rainy evening late in October. A roaring fire was leaping up the chimney and Margaret and her employer had their chairs drawn up close to the dancing flames while they concentrated upon the chess board. Margaret was studying her next move and the cripple was studying the small heart-shaped face bent earnestly over the chess men, when Michael admitted the doctor. Margaret sprang up at once and made room for him by the fire. Charles Stillwell smiled up at his old friend. "It is a long time since we have been honored with your presence."

The doctor rubbed his big hands together. "I've people much sicker than you to give my attention to, my lad," he replied jovially.

"Are we to consider this visit a professional one, or is it purely social?" asked the invalid.

The doctor fished an old pipe out of his pocket. "From the looks of you, it might as well be social, but, inasmuch as it may be some time before I can return, we had better combine the two. Between babies and epidemics, I haven't had much time for two people who seem to flourish quite well without my ministrations." He turned to Margaret, "I am glad to see that you are putting on a little weight, Missie!"

Margaret, who had returned to her seat, arose. "I feel better than I can ever remember," she said quietly, "and if you want to examine Mr. Stillwell, perhaps you will excuse me. I've lots that I can do."

The doctor nodded his consent and Margaret departed. For a while the two men she had left by the fire said nothing. The doctor stood with his back to the cheery flames, fondling his cold pipe, seemingly intent upon his own thoughts, and the invalid sat staring abstractly into the heart of the fire. With a hiss and a flare the logs fell apart and the doctor looked up. "You are in love with her, Charles."

The invalid was instantly on the defensive, "Well, what if I am? I've come to the place where I've got to have some interest in life or cut my own throat! When she is with me I can forget that I have to sit here like a log all day."

The doctor took an ancient tobacco pouch out of his pocket and slowly filled his pipe, methodically tamping the tobacco into the pipe bowl. "But when you are alone, it makes it worse, doesn't it?"

Charles Stillwell admitted it reluctantly. "Yes, I suppose so, but she doesn't realize that I love her, so it can't do her any harm."

The doctor put a match to his pipe and puffed without speaking for a few moments. He was carefully considering his answer. When at last he spoke, his tone was gentle and kind. "No, I don't suppose it will, you being what you are."

The invalid was once more on the defensive and his anger was obvious. "What do you mean by that? Because I am a hopeless cripple?"

Again the doctor ignored the irritation and bitterness in his patient's deep voice. "You know perfectly well what I mean. You being the honorable man that you are!"

The bubble of his wrath deflated by the doctor's quiet tone, Charles Stillwell harked back to the first issue. "After all, it is my own business."

The doctor nodded his gray head in assent. "That is what I have been trying to tell myself for some time. I have hesitated to mention the matter because she has done you so much good. More, I am sorry to say, than I have been able to accomplish. But, I am beginning to wonder. I have grown to like and respect the child. She is very sweet and her side of this situation requires some consideration. Unless I completely misjudge human nature, that child is made for love. She has a vital, eager quality about her that is just asking for it, although at present she doesn't recognize it in the least. She is very intense and when her emotions are once aroused they are going to control her whole life. There is nothing promiscuous about her. With her it will be all or nothing. You would not want to arouse in her a feeling," he hesitated and continued even more slowly, choosing his words with care, "which you could not satisfy. You think that you are in a bad spot now, but if that happened, you would be in hell. . . " His word trailed off and he sat gazing into the fire, not daring to look at his friend's face. He was expecting a tirade, but to his great surprise, none came.

Instead, Charles Stillwell's deep tones answered evenly, "I fully realize that what you say is true, doctor, but there is one point that you have not taken into consideration. You said before that I was 'in love' with Margaret. That is where you made your first mistake. I am not 'in love' with her; I love her with every fiber of my being, a very different thing. When Ada came along I fell 'in love.' That was nothing but infatuation and I remember you tried to warn me that it wouldn't last, but I wouldn't listen. I've been thinking about the difference in the way I felt then and the way I feel now, and I have come to the conclusion that what you call being 'in love' is merely illusion colored with passion. When I was passing through that experience I thought of nothing but myself and that I must have what I wanted. I was young and headstrong but decent, and so marriage was the only answer. I know now that I could have had Ada without offering marriage, but my early training had been such that it never occurred to me to suggest such a thing. I was 'in love' which is the same thing as saying that I was so involved with my own passions that I couldn't rest until they were satisfied. All I thought of was Ada's body and of possessing it. With Margaret, it has been quite different. From the moment that she walked into this room dressed in those awful clothes, but with her head high, and I saw the fear and the courage struggling with one another in her eyes, I loved her. I loved her for holding up her head crowned with that terrible hat, in spite of the fact that she was nearly scared to death. Certainly there wasn't much of the physical in her to attract a man when she first came. She was pale as a ghost, and thin, but her indomitable spirit showed in her eyes and I loved her for what she herself was and not for the way she looked. Perhaps I was able to love her that way because, for me, there can be no more involvement physically, so that aspect of the situation did not enter my consciousness. I do not know. I only know that the feeling that I have for her is as different from the feeling that I had for Ada as day is from night. I do not know exactly how to explain it to you and make you understand.

"When I had once possessed Ada's body there was nothing else left, for her soul was as lean then as her body is now fat. When passion was satisfied the whole thing turned sour. Once when I was quite young I read a story in the Bible about a man, I think he was one of David's sons, who felt about a woman as I once felt about Ada. He could not rest until he had had her. He schemed and connived and lied until he finally got her and the account says that when he had succeeded in doing so he hated her as much as he had once desired her. His so-called love was lust and once it was satisfied there was nothing left. At the time, I did not understand that story, but," a shadow of pain passed across his face, "the day came when I did."

The doctor cleared his throat. He was more touched by his patient's revelation than he cared to admit. To change the subject he asked, "What about your book?"

"Oh, we will make a pretense of finishing it, but it does not really matter, as you perfectly well know. It was only something with which to pass the time, and in watching Margaret unfold and develop, I have something far more fascinating and interesting. When she leaves me," his face clouded again, "as I suppose she must some day, she will no longer be a simple little country girl, but an accomplished woman. Don't you think achieving that is a far more interesting project than writing a book?"

The doctor rose and kicked the dying fire together with the toe of his boot before he turned to his friend. "There isn't much you leave me to say, Charles, and if I have misjudged you, I am sorry. The only thing is, that playing at being God is rather dangerous business, and I do not want you wounded any more than you already have been. You have had enough hurts for one lifetime."

For the first time that evening, the invalid smiled confidently. "That is one thing that you do not need to worry about, my dear doctor. Now, shall we call Michael and get to work on my body? I think that my soul has had enough treatment for sometime to come. Ring the bell, will you, like a good man?"

Chapter Nine

It was a balmy day in the spring before Margaret's twenty-third birthday. The doctor and Charles Stillwell sat in the garden watching Margaret supervise the transplanting of some shrubs. She was at the other end of the grounds, but they could hear her clear laugh at some remark of Patrick's directed toward Jimmie, whom he considered incurably stupid. The doctor waved his pipe at Margaret and addressed the invalid. "You've done a good job there, Charles, much better than I expected."

The invalid could not forbear to chide his old friend a little. "You did not think that I could be trusted, did you?"

The good doctor looked at him over his glasses quizzically but fondly. "It was not a case of trust, but rather fearfulness for the weakness of the flesh. 'You are a better man than I am, Gungha Din!'"

The invalid flushed with pleasure. He found the doctor's congratulation very sweet. "What are you leading up to? Another lecture?"

The doctor took his pipe out of his mouth and frowned at it.

"No. This is by nature of being a mere suggestion, and I have been pondering over it a long time."

Charles Stillwell smiled at his friend. "Don't be so obscure, man. Out with it."

But the doctor was still reluctant. "The truth of the matter is, I don't want to get your hopes up, but. . . "

The man in the wheel chair turned the upper part of his big body toward the doctor and grasped his arm in a death grip. "You've heard of some new cure for my legs?" He could not keep the hope out of his voice.

The doctor nodded. "There is a man in New York who is doing some remarkable surgery on cases of your type. I would like to get him up here to see you. But," he cautioned, "it would be very painful and I cannot promise what the results might be."

Charles Stillwell ignored the last part of the doctor's sentence. "If there is any chance, *any* in this world that I might be cured, I want to take it. How long would it be?"

"That I cannot tell you, but several weeks, surely. After surgery and convalescing, you would have to go through the tedious process of learning to walk again, provided," he amended hastily, "that the operation was successful. If it was not, you would be no worse off than you are now, except for the strain on your heart during surgery and the pain that you would have to endure."

"Could it be done here?" He could not hide his eagerness.

"I do not think so. You would have to go to New York. Michael and I would go with you."

"I would not want her to know anything about it," Charles Stillwell said as his eyes strayed to the end of the garden, "at least until I was assured of the results, one way or the other."

The doctor's tone was sardonic. "And, just how do you propose to accomplish that?"

The invalid's quick mind had already tackled and solved that problem. "I will wait until the normal school closes. She will get her degree in a few weeks now. Then, I will send her to the Exposition in Chicago. I will give her the trip for a graduation present and then she will think nothing of it. She is mad to go. We have been following all the preparations in the papers. I have a cousin who lives there and with whom she can stay. If she takes the slow boat trip through the Great Lakes out and back, that will take up almost two weeks and she can spend at the least two weeks there. By the end of that time, I should be safely home again. We must find someone to chaperon her. You must know lots of people who are planning to go and could find some nice family for her to travel with."

The doctor grinned. "Perferably without any handsome young sons, I presume. You certainly work fast when once you make up your mind, Charles. But," he could not forbear another word of caution, "you must not count on success. Try to remember that I cannot promise anything as to the outcome of the operation."

Charles Stillwell's hands grasped the arms of his wheel chair feverishly. *"Anything,* any chance, is better to take than to sit like this, day in and day out, forever!"

Margaret, coming toward the two men with her hands full of spring flowers, was momentarily puzzled by the sudden look of animation on her employer's thin face, but he erased it quickly and she forgot about it as she dropped down on the porch steps and entered into a light conversation with the doctor.

Margaret McAskie stood between the white columns of the Peristyle of the Court of Honor at the World's Columbian Exposition and gazed eagerly about her. She had the whole day to herself to do exactly as she pleased. Her hostess, whom she privately thought a silly and empty-headed woman, had been kept at home by the sudden illness of her favorite child. Margaret had ignored her feeble protests that she should not go about the fairgrounds unchaperoned and had started out with a light heart. She much preferred her own company to that of her employer's talkative relative. Now she would be able to see what she wanted to see when and for as long as she wanted.

As she stood looking about her, with the whole day and the whole Exposition before her to enjoy as she chose, a smile of anticipation curved her lips. A young man who was lingering nearby gazed at her intently but she ignored his obvious interest and set off to enjoy herself. For once in her life she had plenty of money and she intended to spend as much as was necessary to do just as she pleased and see all that she wished. MacMonie's fountain was extremely beautiful and so was the Lake Front Mile, but what she really wanted to see was the Midway Plaisance Mile, at which her aristocratic hostess had turned up her nose. This was her one chance to see it and she intended to make the most of it. The great circle of the giant Ferris wheel had beckoned to her for days. She started off, her small feet as light as her heart.

It was almost noon when she emerged from the Transportation Building. As she stood on the walk trying to decide where to go for lunch, she heard a bell ringing wildly. Immediately, the crowd started running towards the Cold Storage Building. One man yelled, "Fire!" as he sped past her. Margaret had never witnessed a big fire and she decided that lunch could wait while she followed the crowd. As she neared the scene of the commotion she saw that the man had not been exaggerating. The Cold Storage Building, a rather squat building with a high tower rising out of it, was the center of attention. The fire had broken out near the top of the tower. A fresh breeze, blowing off the lake, had fanned the flames into a bright blaze. In a few moments some firemen appeared near the top of the tower, dragging their fire fighting apparatus with them through a window from the inside of the building. Fascinated, the crowd watched their red helmets bobbing in and out of the flames, but the wind worked faster than they could. Horrified, Margaret counted the tiny figures struggling valiantly against the superior forces of nature. There were eleven. The crowd at the edge of the building had increased to considerable proportions, but they stood as one person, transfixed with horror at the scene being enacted before them. Margaret suddenly wanted to tear her eyes away from the ghastly spectacle, but she could not do so. She stood with the rest, completely hypnotized while the fire grew in size and intensity.

Suddenly, someone in the crowd gave a loud cry of dismay. A great sheet of flame had suddenly and unexpectedly emerged from the base of the tower. In an instant's time it became apparent to the watching crowd that the firemen's only means of escape had been cut off. A moan went through the crowd. A woman screamed. For a breathless second the tower appeared to sway in the wind. The struggling men at the top ceased their unequal battle and for a split second stood gazing down into the inferno below them. Realizing their plight, they did not hesitate but a moment. Joining hands they jumped as one man into the leaping flames which were reaching out hungry hands to envelope them at the precise moment that the tower collapsed under their feet. The horrified people on the ground stood transfixed and silent. The crackling flames danced before Margaret's staring eyes and the awful wrenching sounds of the collapsing tower made her feel dizzy and ill. In front of her a woman dropped like a stone. Everything about her suddenly appeared out of focus and she felt herself falling, but at the same moment a pair of strong arms grabbed her and someone lifted her slight body and carried her through the crowd. In her fading consciousness, she heard a deep, rather husky, male voice, which reminded her vaguely of Mr. Stillwell's, demand a transport-chair and in a moment she felt herself lowered into one and realized that it was being set in motion.

As she felt the transport-chair move slowly under her, her mind pictured the horrible scene she had just witnessed and she fainted. Returning to consciousness, she felt something wet and cool being wiped over her face. Dimly she came to the realization that someone was wiping her face with a handkerchief rung out with cool water and that her head was supported by a blue-clad shoulder which felt very strong and comforting. For a long moment she did not stir and then the same low, husky voice which she vaguely remembered addressing the transport-chair boy, asked her a direct question: "There, doesn't that feel better?"

She roused herself to answer him, but she did not dare to raise her head for fear that the awful enveloping blackness would descend upon her once more. One word was all that she could manage. "Much," she answered him faintly.

Her rescuer went on gently passing the wet cloth over her face and forehead and in a few moments Margaret pulled herself together sufficiently to raise her head. She found herself gazing into a pair of dark brown eyes from whose direct and open gaze she felt no desire to turn away.

"I feel better now, thank you." Immediately he laid her back against the cushions and got out, motioning the transport-chair boy to pull away from the curious crowd which had gathered.

Margaret lay back, her eyes closed, thankful not to have to make any physical effort. Her companion walked beside her, but he had the delicacy not to try to engage her in conversation.

After some minutes, Margaret peeped at him from under her eye lashes. He was a tall young man with hair of deep rust red. His shoulders were broad and his hips slim and he walked lightly on the balls of his feet with a peculiar rolling swing that Margaret could not identify. His profile was clear-cut and classic with a straight nose and a good square chin. She decided inside herself that other than her employer, he was the handsomest man she had ever seen. He had an easy confidence, too, for he walked along beside her with his free, rolling gait, not at all embarrassed that he was carrying her hat and handbag. He was dressed like a gentlemen and he was certainly acting like one, Margaret thought to herself. Looking down, he caught her glance and smiled. His charm was undeniable and as pleasing as his boyish grin as he inquired, in an impish way, "I hope you like what you see. I'm really quite respectable. My name is Jonathan Wellfleet and I come from Boston."

Margaret blushed. He had caught her red-handed but he ignored her confusion and continued smiling as he said, "I do not blame you for examining a perfect strange man who makes off with your handbag." He held it out to her. "It is a wonder you did not call the police!"

She took it from him and held it shyly in her lap. "You have been most kind and I am grateful for your help. I am all alone and I wouldn't have liked reviving in some police station."

He nodded. "I know. I have been following you ever since I saw you standing looking around at the Peristyle, but I couldn't get up enough courage to speak to you until the fire gave me a chance. I hope you don't mind. I do want to get to know you most awfully, so please don't snub me, although I know I deserve it."

In spite of herself Margaret found that she wanted to respond to his evident sincerity. She answered him simply and without affectation. "I do not see how I can snub you when you have been so kind."

He grinned down at her, with a mischievous twinkle in his eyes. "My mother always told me that it paid to do good deeds, but I didn't believe her until now. If you really mean that, will you have lunch with me? I'm sure some hot food would make you feel better."

Margaret did not hesitate more than a moment. "Thank you, I would be glad to. That is, if you will give me my hat."

He handed it to her promptly, gave the boy pushing the transport-chair orders to stop, then stood watching her pin it on. "It's a crying shame to cover those magnificent ebony braids, but I suppose the proprieties must be observed. Won't you tell me your name so that I may know with whom I am to have the pleasure of dining?"

"My name is Margaret McAskie," said Margaret gravely and gave him her hand, so he could help her out of the transport-chair.

Dusk was deepening to darkness and the darkness being chased away by a myriad of twinkling lights as they approached the giant Ferris wheel. They had had lunch and dinner together. They had ridden on the toy railroad and floated leisurely over the canals in a gondola. They had entered every concession on the Plaisance Mile and watched the hoochee-coochee dancers — whom Margaret thought greatly overrated — as well as a fan dancer, and they felt that there was not much that they had missed as tired, but happy, they made their way toward the Ferris wheel. As they sauntered along, they passed a tent which was brilliantly lighted and to which crowds of people seemed to be hurrying.

"I wonder what that is?" Margaret inquired idly.

He answered her question at once. "The evangelist, Dwight Moody, is holding a meeting there. Want to go in?"

She drew back at once. "No, thank you. I have no use for religion. I had enough of it while I was growing up to last me the rest of my life."

He smiled at her vehemence. "Do you know, that is just the way I myself feel about the matter, so you see, we have something else in common."

Margaret had a sudden feeling that she should explain her attitude. More than anything in the world she did not want him to think ill of her. He might be agreeing with her just to be polite, although he sounded sincere enough. "My father is very religious, but his religion has not made him kind nor considerate of others. The very kindest and most thoughtful person I have ever known has no religion at all and I long ago made up my mind that if he can be what he is and get along without religion, so can I."

He caught her up instantly, "Did you say 'he'?"

"Yes, and what is more he is a cripple. He hasn't walked for years. If he can endure what he has had to endure and be as good as he is without the aid of religion, I don't see why anyone needs to bother with it."

The only word Margaret spoke that registered in Jonathan Wellfleet's mind was the word *cripple*. Suddenly he felt happy and very gay. Taking her arm, he steered her toward the twinkling arc of lights which outlined the huge Ferris wheel. "Let's have a ride shall we?"

Margaret agreed at once. "Oh, yes! But after that I must be getting back to where I am staying."

He did not argue with her and as soon as they had had their ride they left the grounds in search of a two-wheeler, which they soon found, and got in. As the horse clopped, clopped, over the cobblestones, he told her where he was staying and begged her to meet him the next day at the Exposition. Margaret hesitated, not being certain that she would be free of the unwelcome presence of her fluttering little hostess, and finally promised either to meet him at the same restaurant where they had lunched together or to send a note to his hotel.

As he helped her out of the carriage and up the steps of the house where she was staying, he said simply, "This has been the best day I ever spent. I hope that you enjoyed it half as much as I did."

She looked down shyly; he was standing below her on the steps. He had removed his hat and the light from a nearby lamp post gleamed on his copper-colored hair. He held out his hand and she placed her small one in it. The pressure of his hand-clasp sent an electric shock through her. Startled and confused, she murmured that she, too, had enjoyed it and fled into the house.

All was quiet in the lower hall. The housemaid who had admitted her whispered to her that the young master was awful sick and that the mistress wanted to see her the minute she came in. She was to go to the upstairs sitting room and wait. Margaret, her conscience troubling her about the lateness of the hour, steeled herself for the lecture she was sure awaited her, but when her hostess hastened into the room she was too full of her own troubles to take notice of the fact that it was way past the hour that a young, unescorted woman should be out. Her precious youngest son had had an attack of acute appendicitis and would need an operation and Margaret must leave at once. She was terribly sorry, but she could no longer have her stay. She must arrange to leave the first thing in the morning. There was nothing to do but to pack her things. Her hostess had made a return reservation for her and it never occurred to her to change it. When she had completed her packing she sat at the little writing table and tried to compose a note to Jonathan Wellfleet. Completely inexperienced in such matters, she did not know how to convey her regret and at the same time not appear forward. After a dozen attempts, she merely explained the reason for her sudden departure and signed her name without telling him where she was going nor giving him an address where he might reach her. "After all, what is the use?" she thought forlornly. Boston was a long way from the city where Mr. Stillwell lived and she would probably never see Jonathan Wellfleet again. Suddenly, she felt utterly weary and deeply depressed. She undressed and climbed into bed, but she could not sleep. It was early morning before she fell into a light slumber. Then, she dreamed that an auburn-haired young man was holding her against his blue-clad shoulder and awoke with a start to find her pillow wet with tears.

The trip home by train was by no means as interesting to her as the trip out by boat had been. Her hostess had insisted that, inasmuch as it was necessary for her to travel alone, it would be best for her to go that way and she had listlessly assented. Inexpressively weary all of a sudden, she failed to enjoy a trip that would ordinarily have fascinated her. Within herself she wondered if her lassitude meant that she was succumbing to illness. Worn out in mind and body, and oddly depressed, she arrived at the big station which had overwhelmed her less than five years before. She had sent a telegram to Mr. Stillwell and she hoped to be met, but Patrick's ruddy countenance was nowhere in evidence so she took a cab to the house.

Parker admitted her with a cold, "So, you're back again; I can't say we were expecting you."

Margaret dropped her bags on the floor with a thud. "I sent a telegram. Didn't Mr. Stillwell receive it?"

Miss Parker drew in her lower lip, a look of satisfaction which she made no effort to conceal on her dark face. "Mr. Stillwell isn't here."

Margaret could not believe her ears. She thought that she

surely was going to be ill and that her hearing was failing her. "But where is he?" she stammered, confused and taken off her guard.

The housekeeper drew herself up. "I cannot see that that is any business of yours, Miss," she stated emphatically and finally. "Your room is ready when you decide to go up."

Realizing that she would get no further information out of the hostile woman, Margaret picked up her heavy bags and ascended to her room, her tired mind in a state of utter confusion. If Mr. Stillwell was gone, Michael must be with him. Unless — her heart leapt at the thought and missed a beat — he was dead! But no, that was not possible. There would have been black crepe on the front door if it were true. She wished that she dared to go downstairs to the kitchen and get some information from the servants, but she was afraid of encountering the housekeeper and she felt too weary and dispirited to cope with her. She undressed and lay down on the comfortable bed. In spite of her distress of mind, her weary body overruled, and she fell into a light doze, from which she awakened at dusk to find Minnie standing over her with a match in her hand on the point of lighting her bedside lamp.

She came to herself with a shudder and sprang up at once. "Oh, Minnie! Where is Mr. Stillwell?" Minnie blew out the match and tossed it into the fireplace.

"Did I frighten ye, Miss? I'm that sorry. The marster's gone ter New York wid Michael and the doctor ter git his legs fixed. We don't spect 'im back for a week or more. It's that surprised he'll be ter be seein' yer. He told Michael he was plannin' ter git home hisself first. That Parker read yer telegram and give it ter herself but Norah saw it lyin' on her dressin' table and she figured as she could read it if Parker could, so when she was reddin' the rooms she done so and that's how we knew yer was here. We tried ter watch fer ye, but Parker tole us ter stay below stairs so we couldn't warn ye. It's that sorry we was that there wasn't no one ter meet ye, Miss, but they (there was no mistaking whom Minnie meant) kept both Patrick and Jimmie busy on purpose all afternoon. Patrick was fit ter be tied, he was fer sure."

Margaret relaxed on the bed with a long, drawn-out sigh. "You don't know what a relief it is to talk to you, Minnie. I've been imagining all kinds of horrible things."

Minnie sputtered angrily, "That Parker might've tole ye if she'd a mind ter, but she's just plain too hateful. Now, Miss, ye look all tuckered out. I'll run ye a nice hot bath and then ye can have yer dinner in bed. Parker didn't give no orders about yer meals but we won't let ye starve. Cook's got a tasty chicken all cooked with the kind of noodles ye like."

True to her promise, Minnie produced a tempting dinner on a tray. The warm bath and the hot food were very comforting to the girl, worn out with the emotional strain through which she had just passed. Minnie tidied her room while she ate and told her all she knew. No word as to the success or failure of the operation had been received and the mistress of the house was as much in the dark as to how matters stood as were the servants. There was nothing for Margaret to do but to settle down and wait as patiently as she could for the master of the house to return. She kept out of the way of Miss Parker and Mrs. Stillwell as much as she could and the servants gave her her meals in Mr. Stillwell's rooms.

She amused herself in the garden and with her books and music as best she could, but somehow they did not seem to have the same flavor for her they once had had. She wondered vaguely what was the matter with her. She felt so listless all of the time. Had the doctor been at home, she would have gone to visit him.

The evening following her return from Chicago she was at her employer's big grand piano softly playing over, "My Heart At Thy Sweet Voice," when all of a sudden her head went down on her arms on the keyboard and she burst into violent weeping. Appalled and ashamed of herself, she was glad that there was no one about to observe her lapse into maudlin sentiment and closing the lid of the piano, she went slowly up to bed. She must need sleep, she concluded wearily, as she dragged herself up the stairs. All the sightseeing she had done and the endless miles she had tramped at the Exposition had taken more out of her than she had realized. She must see to it that she got some rest and felt better when Mr. Stillwell returned. He would need all the cheer and comfort she could give him, especially if the operation was not successful. She wished with all her heart that he might be cured and all of a sudden some nameless impulse within her made her think of asking God to help him, but as quickly as it had been born, she discarded it. If God would not help her keep her lamb safe, He certainly would do nothing about Mr. Stillwell's legs. It was useless to even ask Him. Scowling at herself in the mirror of her dressing table as she combed her heavy hair, she spoke to her image in the glass. "You must pull yourself together. You can do more for him when he comes home than God can, and no matter how it comes out, he will be sure to need you more than he does God."

Although she wanted for nothing and was surrounded with every comfort and had had two good nights sleep, she was still vaguely unhappy and depressed the next day. Her thoughts wandered to the young man who had been so kind to her at the time of the fire and she wished that she had thanked him more adequately. Perhaps he had come to the conclusion from the stiffness of her note that she did not want to see him again. This thought she found most disturbing and she castigated herself mentally for a fool to entertain it. Nevertheless, she thought of a dozen different and better ways of expressing herself now that the opportunity for doing so was past and gone. Resolutely, she shut the matter out of her mind, only to have it return insidiously again and again. Suddenly, she was bitterly ashamed of herself. Here was her employer who had been so good to her lying ill and alone in a distant city, and all she could think of was a young man with dark brown eyes and auburn hair whom she scarcely knew.

Resolved to forget all about him, she picked up her violin, determined to practice until her mind was entirely clear of any thought of Jonathan Wellfleet. She had been practicing only a few moments when Nora came into the room all a-flutter. "There's someone ter see ye in the drawing room, Miss," she exclaimed, her eyes round with the unexpected excitement of the occasion. "A man!"

Margaret looked up in surprise. The doctor was away and the music professor had classes at this hour in the morning. Besides, he did not know that she was back. She quickly put down her violin, straightened her dress, patted her hair, and ventured out into the hall.

Miss Parker stood on the landing at the head of the hall, peering over the stairs, curiosity and disapproval written in every line of her sparse figure. Margaret crossed the hall without hurrying and closed the drawing room door behind her with a finality that brooked no interference.

A tall, blue-clad figure rose at once from one of the loveseats and strode over to her, taking her cold hands in his. "Did you think," said the deep voice that had haunted her dreams, "that

I could let you go out of my life like that, once you had come into it?"

Her caller was Jonathan Wellfleet!

Chapter Ten

The patient livery stable nag plodded slowly over the dusty road, the reins slack upon his back. Occasionally a fly lit upon his black coat and his tail switched in momentary irritation, making a thumping sound against the dash board of the surrey. Margaret sat relaxed and content against the padded seat, her eyes absorbing the peace and beauty of the quiet countryside through which they were passing. The fringe on the top of the surrey swayed with the motion of the carriage, casting dancing patterns of light and shade across her lap and lent an illusion of coolness to the hot afternoon. Her companion held the reins loosely, allowing the horse to take its own pace so that he might keep his eyes on the slight figure of the girl beside him.

At the arrival of Jonathan Wellfleet, life, which for days had seemed insipid and stupid and inexplicably dull, suddenly took on new color and charm. Margaret's listlessness fell away like a discarded garment, and time, which had hung heavily upon her hands since her return from Chicago, took on the speed of light. From the moment that she had walked into the green drawing room and he had taken her cold hands into his big warm ones, until the present buggy ride, they had been on the go. Ignoring Miss Parker's and Mrs. Stillwell's inquisitive glances, Margaret had come and gone with him whenever and wherever he asked her. He seemed to have endless plans for their amusement and entertainment. Today they were on their way to a traveling carnival which had been widely advertised in the city for a week.

The carnival had established itself in a large meadow just outside of a small town situated about seven miles outside of the city. They had spent the day in the woods having a picnic lunch, and now in the late afternoon, they were on the way to the carnival which was in full swing.

There were various concessions and booths and a Ferris wheel about which many children and several adults were crowded. It looked like a pigmy to Margaret and Jonathan, compared to the immense one at the Exposition, but it was painted a bright red and was gay with gilt. A wheezy tune emerged from the shack at its base and the crowd was entranced by the wheel's rotation. There were more applicants for seats than there were seats to hold them. Jonathan and Margaret made the rounds of the booths and concessions and by the time they had returned to the Ferris wheel the crowd had thinned and the evening shadows had lengthened across the grass. Jonathan asked if she cared to have a ride and she nodded her assent. The cars were so small that they only held four people, facing each other in pairs, their knees crowded together in the narrow center space. Margaret was glad that no one else wanted to ride in their car, for Jonathan had to fold his long legs sidewise as it was and even then his knees touched the opposite seat. Although the barker held up the progress of the wheel fully three minutes trying to drum up trade, only half of the cars were filled. Either from fear or from lack of funds, the rest of the crowd standing about did not succumb to his blandishments so he finally nodded to the mechanic and with a great creaking and groaning of machinery, the wheel got under way. The small cars swung out and back as the wheel revolved and the little breeze they stirred up was very pleasant. They rose above the fields toward the darkening sky and looking up, Margaret thought how much cooler the stars looked than the lights of the town beneath them. They had made a full revolution only a half dozen times when the mechanic brought the machine to a stop and the barker began to unload the passengers.

There was considerable protest from several boys who felt that they had not received their money's worth, but the barker told them hardheartedly to come back the next day. They went away grumbling, only to turn slyly when they were some distance down the road and pitch stones at the two men who were operating the wheel. Most of them missed, but one small stone, aimed more truly than the rest, whizzed past the mechanic's head as he ducked and clattered into the machinery. With a shriek and a whine the wheel, which was turning slowly to allow the rest of the passengers to dismount, came to an abrupt halt. The mechanic swore loudly and the barker started to chase the boys, but they were too quick for him and were out of sight behind some trees before he got into motion. With a discouraged grunt he returned to the wheel and watched the disgruntled mechanic tinker with the machinery. After a few moments he cupped his mouth with his dirty hands and bellowed up at the remaining passengers to keep their seats.

Jonathan and Margaret were at the very top of the Ferris wheel. Below them, two cars were filled with giggling girls and their swains. With much cursing and swearing, the mechanic continued to bang around with the machinery. It was so dark by then that the barker had to hold a lantern for him so that he could see what he was doing. The barker peered anxiously over his shoulder and watched his futile efforts to start the machinery. By this time a few loiterers had assembled and one of them suggested that if they had a ladder they might be able to get the people down. He was at once dispatched to fetch one. When he returned the ladder was placed upon the flimsy platform and by propping it against the side of the wheel and pressing every available man into service to steady it, the two cars below the one in which Margaret and Jonathan found themselves, were emptied to the accompaniment of grunts from the boys and shrieks of dismay from the girls. When the passengers were safely on the ground, they abused the barker so roundly that he could only appease them by returning their ticket money. This did not improve his disposition and when it became evident that the ladder would not reach within six feet of the topmost car he swore loudly and at length. Finally, in disgust, the mechanic threw down his tools and they held a consultation *sotto voce*. The sweating mechanic wiped his grimy hands upon a piece of waste and the barker, his voice harsh from a long day's work, croaked up at Jonathan and Margaret that he could see nothing for it now but that they must spend the night there for it was too dark to see what they were doing and they could not locate the trouble in the machinery.

The two men then started down the road after lighting all the lanterns that were available and placing them on the platform at the base of the wheel. The two young people crowded into the tiny car could barely see them turn now and again to peer up through the gathering dark at the victims of this unforeseen accident. The small group of loiterers gradually dispersed, talking and laughing. Jonathan Wellfleet had said nothing through all the commotion, but from the tightness of his big mouth, Margaret knew that he recognized as fully as she, the seriousness of the situation in which they found themselves.

Here and there a lantern blinked amongst the tents, an animal howled, a dog barked, and then all was dark and still. Margaret kept her eyes on the stars and resolutely tried to push into the back of her mind what her employer's wife would have to say when she returned to the house in the morning, having spent the whole night somewhere with a man. But, in spite of herself, these troubling thoughts kept intruding themselves into her consciousness. It had been unconventional enough to have gone out during the day unescorted, but to stay out all night would produce a situation of which Mrs. Stillwell could take full advantage. Margaret wished with all her heart that Mr. Stillwell was at home to protect her. He at least would believe her. Thinking of what awaited her when she returned to the Stillwell house in the morning, she sighed.

Her companion said simply, his deep voice full of regret. "I'm awfully sorry. I wouldn't have had this happen for the world."

She answered him just as simply, "You couldn't help it." In spite of her concern for the unfortunate situation in which they found themselves, she somehow had a curious desire to comfort him.

"I was a fool to let you get into this wheel," he continued bitterly. "I should have known better, and now that it is too late I remember that there was an auxiliary engine for the wheel at the Exposition and an expert mechanic on hand in case of trouble. They would not have taken such elaborate precautions if there had not been good reason for them. That simple fact should have occurred to me before this. And now you are paying for my heedlessness and folly.''

Eager to distract him, Margaret said hastily, "Let's talk about something else. Tell me about yourself. You know a good deal about me, but so far you haven't told me anything about you. Won't you please?" Her shyness was forgotten in a quick surge of desire to turn his attention away from the regret he so obviously felt. For some reason she could not bear to have him castigating himself on her account.

She leaned back against the hard seat and unpinned her hat. Her companion twisted about in the narrow space trying to find room for his long legs. They could scarcely see one another. The moon had risen, but it was so young that it shed little light. The small car creaked and swayed gently in the slight breeze which had sprung up with the gathering darkness. The mingled smell of the sawdust which had been spread about on the ground near the animals' tents and the sweet grass with which the meadow below them abounded, ascended to their nostrils. The village lay quiet and at rest at their feet. The occasional cry of a child or the bark of a dog were the only sounds which disturbed the stillness. The distant, but persistent croaking of many frogs near the river's edge seemed merely to accentuate the quietness which wrapped them about like a mantle. Gradually the lights in the houses of the villages went out one by one and the new moon climbed higher and higher into the heavens. Finally, in answer to her question, the man broke the companionable silence which had fallen between them.

"What do you want to know?"

Now that she found him willing to talk Margaret hardly knew how to continue. Her heart cried out that there was nothing about him that wouldn't interest her, but her better judgment made her reply to his question with a sedate, "What you do and where you live." She suddenly abandoned her stiff attitude by saying, "Oh, everything!"

He laughed as he twisted about in the seat to give her more room. "Those are the very questions I wanted to ask you the first day I saw you."

"But, now you know most of the answers about me, but I really know nothing about you except that you come from Boston."

"That doesn't seem fair, does it? Well, here goes! I suppose

102

that to make my life's story really interesting, I should be able to start with: 'I come of poor, but honest parents,' but, I'm afraid that I can't. For generations both my father's and my mother's people were in the coastal trade. They made a very good thing of it, too, what with tea, spices, Jamaica rum, and one thing and another, but my mother hated the sea as much as my father loved it. When she was a little girl she had stood on the deck of her father's five-masted schooner and watched them consign her mother's body to the waves. She loved her mother dearly and I do not think that she has ever recovered from the shock. She is convinced that had her mother taken ill on land where competent doctors could be had that she need not have died.

"When she married my father, he already had his captain's papers and had been twice around the Horn, but she was sure she could woo him away from the sea. They did not need the money that the business brought, and she had a very strong will. But my father's will was even stronger. She never succeeded in getting him away from the sea although she made his days ashore miserable by nagging him about it. I was the youngest of seven children. I have a sister seventeen years older than I and in between us there were five other boys. I scarcely remember them, for they all died in an epidemic of black diptheria before I was five. My father was at sea at the time and my mother would come home from burying one to find another dead. How I happened to be spared, I am sure I do not know, but from that time on, the struggle between my mother and my father became more and more intense. My mother blamed my father for not being there when my brothers died, although what he could have done to have prevented their deaths, I do not know. My father became very bitter and blamed my mother's God for allowing such a catastrophe to come to pass. He owned a small fleet of vessels by this time and it was his dream to see one of his sons commanding each of them. I was torn between my mother's determination that I should never go to sea and my father's equally strong determination that being the last of our line I should follow in the footsteps of my ancestors."

"What did your mother want you to do?"

"She wanted me to become a minister. In her sorrow she had turned to religion for consolation, and to her the ministry was the only ideal occupation for a man. My father, of course, snorted at the very idea and told my mother that no son of his would be brought up to be a milk sop."

"It must have been hard on you!" said Margaret softly.

"It was. My earliest recollections are of the acrimonious and heated quarrels between them. In the beginning I was torn between my loyalty to them both. I felt sorry for my mother, but I loved my father and as I grew older the romance of the sea gripped me as it had my ancestors before me. I determined in my secret soul to follow in their footsteps as soon as I was old enough. I never told my mother, but my father understood. When he was home we spent every minute I could spare at the wharves, but the minute he left, my mother would start in on me with tales of tragedies at sea. I remember her taking me to South Boston, showing me the small cupolas with which many of the roof tops were furnished, and telling me that they were called 'widow's weeps' because women went up into them to watch for men who never returned from the sea and to weep for them! She left no stone unturned to discourage me from doing what my father wanted me to do and I learned not to express any interest whatsoever in anything connected with a seaman's life when I was near her."

Margaret moved a little closer to her companion. She did not know how to express her sympathy, but she wanted him to feel it.

"I entered Harvard when I was sixteen because my mother wanted me to, but my father insisted that I spend my summers with him, afloat. I lived for those summer vacations. My father promised me that when I graduated I could be with him permanently and I pinned my hopes on that promise and resolutely pushed from my mind how my mother would feel about it. I did not dislike Harvard, but to me it seemed rather a waste of time when men were out doing real men's work."

He stopped speaking for a moment, but Margaret's eager, "And, did you go?" spurred him to further speech.

"No. My father's vessel went down off Cape Hatteras with all hands aboard only a week after I graduated from Harvard!" A deep sadness filled his quiet tones.

"Oh!" exclaimed Margaret on an indrawn breath. "How sad! I suppose that your mother said 'I told you so!'"

"She did more than that." He tried unsuccessfully to keep the bitterness the memory brought to him, out of his voice as he continued. "She got rid of everything in the house which reminded her of her husband or of the sea. Down came his portrait and those of both of their male ancestors because they were painted in their captain's uniforms and they were relegated to the attic. She could not quite bring herself to destroy them, but she did destroy all of his oil paintings of the sea, a really superb collection, and she smashed his numerous models of clipper ships and my most choice possession, a model of my father's schooner set up inside of a green glass bottle. It had taken my father's first mate a year to make it."

For a few moments, he sat staring into the darkness in front of him as if his eyes once more beheld the frantic woman holding the broken bits of green glass and shattered wood in her hands and a wild look upon her set face. Margaret yearned to slip her small hand into his to express her sympathy, but she was too shy so she just sat quietly beside him and waited for him to go on with his tragic story.

He stretched his long arm along the back of the seat before he continued wryly, "The ironical part of the whole thing was that the house was full of things that had been brought over the sea in his ships; rugs from the Orient, brocade and scenic wallpaper from France, teakwood from India, porcelain from Japan and knicknacks from all over the world. She sold the business for a mere song because my father had been foolish enough not to make a will, thus keeping me from getting it. Naturally, that about broke my heart, for I had been planning to carry on with it. She was quite wild and nobody could do a thing with her. There was only one course for me to take and I determined to take it. I would run away to sea and ship on whatever vessel I could find that would take me, but before I could make any arrangements mother was taken ill, quite violently ill. I simply didn't have the heart to run off and leave her until she improved in health, for I was afraid that the shock would kill her. When she was able to see me she told me that the doctors had told her that she might never be able to walk again. She said that it was some form of creeping paralysis. She begged me for her sake to start in with my theological course and stay near her, at least until she improved a little in health. I hated the very idea, but all that summer I stayed home and when fall came I started in with my studies again. My mother did not leave her bed, but my sister told me that my being at home was making all the difference in the world to the state of her health and was aiding immeasurably in her slow recovery."

He took his arm from the back of the seat and straightened himself. He evidently felt the closeness of the small space in which they were confined. Margaret wished that he would finish his story, but she did not want to hurry him. Finally he said slowly, "There is only one more chapter and it is a hard one to tell. I had only been attending classes at the theological school for a few weeks and was at home for the weekend, when the weather turned suddenly cold. One night I got up and went in search of more covers for my bed and found my mother walking in the hall as normally as you or I. She pretended to fall in a faint, but after I got her back in bed and had called the servants, I put my sister on the carpet and she finally admitted to me that mother had been able to walk all the time, but that she had used her illness as an excuse for keeping me with her and making me to what she wanted. I left the house that night and the next day I shipped out with an old friend of my father."

Before she thought, Margaret said, "So, that is why you walk the way you do!"

He laughed, "You flatter me. I did not realize that I had acquired a seaman's roll, although I have had the deck of a ship under my feet for the better part of nine years."

"Have you liked it as well as you thought you would?"

"Aye, aye, sir, and better. The sea has been all and more than I ever dreamed she would be. My father once told me that she was a capricious mistress, but a charming one and that she never bored a man. I found out that he had spoken the truth. I am now first mate on the vessel on which I first shipped and I will have my captain's papers when I return. The only reason I went to the Exposition was that I was waiting for them to come through and had nothing else to do for a few weeks."

The way he expressed himself about the sea sent a chill to Margaret's heart. Unwilling to analyze the cause of the sudden dread which enveloped her, she asked him another question.

"Did you ever go back home again?"

"Yes. At the end of two years I went home. My mother was an old woman and I realized that she might want to see me. I was willing to forgive her for what she had tried to do to me and I thought that she would be glad to see me."

"Wasn't she?"

"If she was, she did not show it outwardly. She had aged terribly, but she had not changed. She asked me point blank if I was ready to give up my life on the sea and when I told her that I was not, she said that if I did not abandon the godless life I was living she would cut me off without a cent. I tried to tell her that a seaman's life was not necessarily godless, but she would have none of it. She insisted that sailors were an immoral, licentious lot and nothing that I said to her could make her change her mind. I tried to tell her that I was leading a decent life and had done nothing of which either she nor my father need be ashamed. She insisted that I choose between her and the sea. When I clung to the sea she told me that she never wished to see me again. She was beside herself and she left me no choice. I kissed my sister, left the house and have not returned since, but, wherever my father is tonight," he lifted his dark head to gaze into the heavens, "I hope he knows and is glad."

Margaret followed his gaze with her eyes. "Do you believe in heaven?"

He shrugged his broad shoulders. "That depends upon what you mean by heaven. The heaven that my mother had all fixed for the godly always seemed too pat to me, just as the hell she imagined for the godless or anyone else who failed to agree with her seemed a little too convenient! Who knows?"

For a few minutes they sat in silence. Then Margaret said softly, "My father believes the same way your mother does, but his beliefs have never made him kind nor considerate of others, but only condemnatory and bigoted. It is a queer thing what religion can do to people, isn't it?"

When he did not answer immediately, she continued, "The very kindest and most considerate person I know hasn't any religion whatsoever. Religion has not improved any person whom I have ever known. It is for that reason that I have decided to leave it out of my life."

She paused a moment wondering if he was shocked at her brashness, but when he turned to her and said simply, "That is just about the way I feel myself," her heart leapt within her breast. To quiet its wild beating she twisted about in her seat.

He moved along to try and give her a little more room. She wished that she could put her feet up on the opposite seat and stretch out a little. As if he divined her thoughts, he said, "If you would lean against my shoulder, instead of that hard seat, and put your feet up on the opposite seat, you would be much more comfortable."

Without words, she did as he suggested. He put his arm around her and settled himself more comfortably into the corner. His hold was quite impersonal and it was inexpressively sweet to her to rest her tired head against him and to feel the roughness of his coat under her cheek. The night wind gently rocked the little car and she was able to lie back relaxed and content, forgetful of the dark void beneath her and the trouble she knew lay ahead.

At last he broke the silence which enfolded them. "Life is a queer thing. Do you know that I feel more at home sitting up here in this silly little car telling you the story of my checkered career than I ever did in the home I was born in?"

Margaret murmured somewhat breathlessly over the wild beating of her heart, "I'm glad!"

"Perhaps," he continued, "there is more truth in the old saying that 'home is where the heart is' than I knew." When the girl beside him did not answer, he went on gently. "From the first moment when I saw you standing between the columns of the Peristyle gazing out over the lake, I knew that my heart had found its home and I had to follow you. I owe a special debt to those poor men who lost their lives in the fire because it enabled me to scrape up an acquaintance with you. I had about despaired of making an opportunity of speaking to you, although I had followed you about all morning."

He waited for her to say something, but the sudden jump her heart had taken at his words had deprived her of speech. She was so unused to love-making that she did not know how to act nor what to say. She was glad that he could not see the telltale blush which had spread over her face and neck. When he realized that she was not going to say anything he asked softly, "You are not asleep, are you?"

She shook her head against his shoulder and his arm tightened about her. "Perhaps you could catch a nap if I stopped talking." She wanted him to go on and on forever, but she did not know how to tell him so without appearing forward. He slipped his other hand into an inside pocket and taking out a watch, snapped open the case. Somewhere inside the mechanism, a tiny bell rang eight times. "Midnight," he observed as he closed the case and returned it to his pocket. "Are you warm enough?"

Again, she nodded her head against him without words. He reached over and took her two small hands into his big one. In spite of her assurance, he found them cold. Immediately, he shrugged out of his coat and insisted upon her donning it. He silenced her feeble protests with, "Nonsense, I am used to being out in all weathers and I've a great deal more flesh on my bones than you have to keep me warm. There, doesn't that feel better?"

She had to admit that it did. The wind had freshened and she had become more chilled than she realized. When he had her comfortably settled, he once more gathered her hands to him and held them against his breast. She could feel the pounding of his heart beneath them as the warmth of his big body slowly penetrated through them. Gradually, his body warmth began to steal through her also. She lay against him snug and content and in a short while she had drifted into slumber.

A man's shout awakened her rudely. She came to with a start to discover that while she had slept, her companion had lifted her bodily in his arms and that she lay against his breast, cradled in his arms like an infant. He smiled into her startled eyes, but he did not relax his hold. "Don't sit up too rapidly or you may become dizzy. They have started tinkering with the machinery again and if the amount of good they are doing can be gauged by the noise they are making, we should soon be on *terra firma*. I wouldn't look down if I were you. I haven't looked at my watch for the last hour, but it must be somewhere near five o'clock."

Margaret sat up slowly and he lifted her onto the seat. Her hands flew to her hair. It felt warm to her touch where his cheek had rested against it. Quick color flooded her face as she tried to tidy it. He shook his head at her, amusement in his eyes. "Don't bother. It looks pretty all fluffed up like that. Keep that coat around you until we get down to the ground. I don't want you taking cold."

She obeyed him without comment and he sat up and stretched his long arms and legs to get the stiffness out of them and to start the blood circulating. The racket below them had increased and by dint of much hammering, pounding, and cursing, the wheel was set in motion and bit by bit jerked around until the car in which they sat reached the platform. The mechanic opened the little door, Jonathan stepped out, and assisted Margaret to alight. For a moment she could hardly stand and he put his arm around her to steady her.

Embarrassed by the stares of the small group of carnival employees who had gathered to watch the mechanic work, Margaret shrugged out of Jonathan's coat and handed it to him. The barker approached them rubbing his dirty hands together and trying to appear nonchalant. He did not like the look in the young man's eyes nor the set of his square jaw and he concluded somewhat hastily that he had better try to compensate them for the inconvenience they had been caused. "How'd it be if I give you fifty dollars?" he inquired hoarsely, his small shrewd eyes on Margaret. "That ought to pay you for the predicament you were in." He ended with a coarse laugh whose meaning was obvious. Margaret flushed and Jonathan paused in getting into his coat to give him a long level look.

Alarmed, the barker hastened to settle the matter as soon as possible. He pulled a fat roll of bills out of his pocket and peeling off several, shoved them toward Margaret.

One of the bystanders snickered and said in an audible whisper, "Wish I'd git paid for pawing a pretty woman all night."

Jonathan swung about, his eyes flashing angrily. "Who said that?" he demanded and his voice was as cold and hard as his eyes.

The man who had made the unfortunate remark tried to justify himself by blustering to the barker. "Well, he was. I saw him a'strokin' her hair and holdin' her when I went ter the well ter git water fer the animals. He was . . . ."

His words degenerated into a gurgle as Jonathan stepped forward and with lightning speed, punched him on the chin. The man crumpled to the ground. Jonathan eyed the little group belligerently. "If any of you has anything more to say, he had better say it now!"

They shifted around in awkward silence, cowed by the young man's anger and made no effort to help their fallen companion. Jonathan turned from them with contempt, took the money which the barker was still holding, counted it, and courteously handed it to Margaret. She had not been willing to take it from the barker, but she took it from him. Some of the fury died out of him at the sight of her standing there, small and embarrassed. Without a backward glance he offered her his arm and led her down the road to the place where they had tied the horse and surrey. He made no apologies for having lost his temper, but assisted her into the carriage and took up the reins. They were out of sight of the carnival before he spoke. "I think we had better try to find some breakfast in the village before we go back to the city."

Margaret nodded, knowing that she would need all the

strength she could muster before she faced Mrs. Stillwell.

It was only a little after seven when they drove under the porte-cochere of the Stillwell mansion. Mixed up with Margaret's troubled thoughts she had been wondering if Jonathan Wellfleet planned to stick by her through the coming ordeal or not. It was now perfectly obvious to her that he was not going to desert her and her heart lifted somewhat. Nevertheless, the fingers with which she pressed the bell trembled. Although Mrs. Stillwell never rose early, Parker was sure to be on hand. Nor had her fears proved false, for it was the horse-faced housekeeper who personally answered the bell. Her thin-lipped mouth pursed itself into a tight line of disapproval as she opened the door a few inches and peered out. "Well, Miss, it's about time you got back!" She entirely ignored the young man's presence. She opened the door sufficiently to admit Margaret's slight body and would have closed it sharply behind her, but Jonathan was too quick for her. He put one foot in the crack and when she tried to slam it in his face, she could not. Icily she stared at him and he returned her look without flinching. "I am coming in with Miss McAskie," he said firmly and, somewhat to her own surprise, the hostile housekeeper found herself allowing him entrance.

Not for a minute was she willing to relinquish her advantage, however, and turning to Margaret with ill-concealed triumph in her voice, she announced, "Mrs. Stillwell wishes to see you in her upstairs sitting-room the minute you arrive."

Margaret could not hide her surprise at this unusual departure from custom. "Is she up already?"

Miss Parker unbuttoned her tight mouth sufficiently to admit that her mistress had left orders that she was to be informed as soon as Margaret returned, no matter what the hour. The inference was plain that she personally would not have been sorry had Margaret never returned! "The young man," Miss Parker would not dignify him by saying gentleman, "can wait for you here."

Margaret paused, defeated, with her slender foot on the first step of the stairs and turned apologetically to Jonathan, but he was not in the least intimidated by the hostility of the housekeeper. He looked that personage directly in the eye and announced in firm tones, "I am coming with Miss McAskie." Miss Parker glared at him for a moment unable to frame a suitable reply, but she could not stare him down. He gave her look for look and she finally succumbed wordlessly to his superior strength of will and turned to lead the way upstairs, her expression more dour than ever.

Mrs. Stillwell's sitting room was silent in the early morning light, but in considerable disorder. Jonathan had to remove a copy of *The Ladies Home Journal* and a bit of needlework from a small love seat before he and Margaret could sit down. He wanted to stay as near as possible so that she might sense his support. Miss Parker watched this maneuver out of the corner of her eyes before she deigned to depart and announce their arrival to her mistress.

Jonathan took Margaret's trembling hands in his. "Please, don't look so upset. I got you into this and I will get you out."

Vaguely comforted, she loosened her hands and rose to straighten her hat, hair, and clothing in front of the mirror over the fireplace. When she again took her seat beside him, she gave him a feeble smile. Somehow she did not feel quite so forlorn.

They waited in silence for some time. Miss Parker had evidently informed her mistress that the young man had insisted upon coming in with her husband's protege and Margaret suspected that she was going through her usually complicated toilet for his benefit. Nor was she mistaken, for when Mrs. Stillwell sailed into the room at last, she was arrayed in a beribboned peignoir and her hair was as elegantly and fussily dressed as if she were going to a ball. Jonathan arose at once and waited courteously for her to trail her draperies to a chair. She looked him over curiously. It was the first time she had had a good look at him and the look of surprise that crossed her florid countenance at his good looks and good manners was an open insult.

Somewhat disgruntled, she flounced to a seat, wondering within herself how such a plain piece as Margaret had been able to attract such a handsome young man. She had counted upon dealing with the girl alone and the young man's presence was a setback.

Jonathan gave her no opportunity to fire an opening shot. He introduced himself at once. "My name is Jonathan Wellfleet, Mrs. Stillwell, and I am here to apologize for the mishap which kept Miss McAskie out all night."

Mrs. Stillwell was somewhat taken aback by the promptness and openness of his explanation. She crossed one plump leg over the other revealing several inches of silk stocking and satin slippers into which her plump feet had been forced. She raised her eyebrows. "I cannot imagine what you can possibly have to say for yourself, and her." There was overt contempt in the glance she directed at Margaret.

Jonathan's even tones did not change as he answered her. "We drove to Wellsville to attend a carnival and went up in the Ferris wheel. Some youngsters threw a stone into the machinery and it stuck, so that we had to stay there all night."

His story was evidently quite different from the one she had expected to hear. She could think of nothing to say but, "Were you the only ones to get stuck?"

"No, there were others, but they succeeded in getting them down with the aid of a ladder. The car in which we were riding was higher than the rest and the ladder did not reach us."

Mrs. Stillwell found this controlled young man's manner most disconcerting. She found herself almost believing his fantastic story. This would never do, she thought. She must carry the battle into the enemies' country! She would never be given a better chance to get rid of the girl and she must make the most of the opportunity. She had waited too long, to be foiled now. Margaret had insinuated herself into her husband's good graces for too many years as it was and she must not let a handsome and engaging young man rob her of her revenge. She, therefore, threw back her head and sneered, "Indeed! A likely story, young man! You must think I was born yesterday!"

Margaret gazing in nervous terror from one face to the other, saw Jonathan's generous mouth tighten at the woman's words and the same burning look came into his eyes as had filled them when he had knocked down the workman at the carnival, but he managed to control his temper and say quietly, "Miss McAskie has fifty dollars in her bag to prove my story." He picked up Margaret's bag where she had placed it on the love seat beside her and opening it, took out the roll of dirty bills. "Here it is. Would you like to count it?"

Mrs. Stillwell made no effort to take the money, but she refused to relinquish her advantage. "Do you imagine that it is worth fifty dollars to ruin a girl's reputation? I certainly hope that nobody saw you and that this doesn't get into the papers. I wouldn't want such a scandal attached to this house."

Jonathan's big hands clenched themselves into fists, but he

113

answered her evenly enough. "Inasmuch as nobody got our names, and the horse and carriage came from a livery stable, I do not see how that could happen."

Mrs. Stillwell did not like to have the wind taken out of her sails in this high-handed manner, so she returned to her first point of attack with a sharp, "Well, it certainly has not improved Miss McAskie's reputation for you to keep her out all night!"

Jonathan's eyes narrowed, "Inasmuch as nobody knows anything about the matter but the occupants of this house, no one would be any the wiser if you kept quiet about it."

This was too much for Mrs. Stillwell, for that was not exactly what she intended to do. She had waited too long for this advantage not to seize it when it presented itself and she had every intention of making the most of it. His coolness angered her and she answered him sullenly, "It's impossible to keep the servants from talking."

He looked directly at her. "I'm not talking about the servants. I am talking about you."

Knowing herself to be in the wrong, her quick temper flared, "There is only one decent way of settling the matter right and to quiet the gossip and that is for you to marry her!"

Margaret sitting between them, her face flushed and her heart sick with embarrassment, felt like a helpless pawn being moved any which way by the whim of cruel fate. This spiteful woman was not only determined to discredit her in the eyes of the household but was going to leave no stone unturned to get rid of her before Mr. Stillwell returned. She wished dully that the earth would open up its mouth and swallow her. But, she had reckoned without Jonathan. He was not only undismayed by the proposition which Mrs. Stillwell presented, but he was saying evenly and clearly, "That is exactly what I intended to do from the first minute I saw Margaret. That is," he amended turning to the girl beside him, sitting huddled in the corner of the love seat, "if she will have me!"

Mrs. Stillwell gasped, overcome with the success of her ruse, "Well, I never!" Then she collected herself and continued sneeringly, "I suppose, under the circumstances there is nothing else for her to do. She'll probably jump at the chance, although I don't suppose she knows much about you!"

Jonathan's eyes were still on Margaret's downcast countenance and there was a deep softness in them as he regarded her.

"The only thing she needs to know is that I love her and have done so ever since the first moment I saw her and I can only hope that she can learn to love me. As for my background, my family is in the Social Register and she can easily look me up if she wishes."

Mrs. Stillwell's mouth fell open, disclosing several gold fillings of considerable size. Too late she saw that she might have been too hasty. She had a great and overweening respect for anyone whose name was listed in the Social Register and she began to think that she might have done better had she let this matter take its course. But the two on the loveseat were not paying any attention to her. Jonathan had lifted one of Margaret's small, cold hands and had kissed it tenderly and she was looking up at him with her gray eyes full of the tears she could no longer restrain. He took out of his pocket a large handerchief and wiped them gently. As he did so he read the confusion in her eyes, for he rose and lifting her to her feet, faced the irate woman across the room. "And now, madame, if you will excuse us, we will go somewhere and conclude the matter which you have so crudely precipitated upon us in this unseemly manner. I wish you good morning."

He led Margaret to the door without a backward glance. Miss Parker was hovering about in the hall outside, so very near to the door that they knew that she had her eyes and eares glued to the panel and the keyhole. Jonathan looked through her coolly and still holding Margaret's hand led her down the wide stairs and through the hall to the front door. As he assisted her into the surrey he once more kissed the little hand he held.

Nothing more was said until he found a quiet spot beneath some trees. At that early hour of the morning they were quite safe from prying eyes. He stopped the patient nag and hooking the reins over the dashboard of the surrey, he took both her hands in his big ones. He sat holding them quietly until her agitation subsided somewhat and she could bear to look up at him. His eyes held hers as he said gently, "I have wanted to say what that miserable woman forced me into saying ever since I first saw you, my darling. I do not want to be so bold that I frighten you, but I want you to know that I love you with all my heart and I hope that in spite of what has happened you will marry me before I return to my ship. Not beçause you must, but because I do want you to so very much. Will you?"

115

Almost before she knew what was happening, Margaret heard herself promising to become Jonathan Wellfleet's wife.

Chapter Eleven

Jonathan and Margaret Wellfleet were sitting in the doctor's waiting room awaiting his return from the Stillwell mansion. Not knowing how to reach Mr. Stillwell, they had sent a note to the doctor's house announcing their marriage and asking him to break the news to his patient. They had received a telegram from him the day before announcing his return and expressing a desire to see them as soon as possible. They were early and the doctor's pretty young nurse eyed them curiously. She thought the young woman was obviously pale and nervous and the young man very concerned. When the consulting room door opened to disclose the doctor's haggard countenance, Margaret started. He brushed aside his nurse and motioned for her to enter. Jonathan rose to accompany her, but she shook her head at him. The doctor was her friend and she preferred to see him alone.

The doctor had preceded her into the office and was standing by his desk in a characteristic pose, his hands under his coattails. As he turned to face her and the bright sunshine illuminated his face, she was shocked at his appearance. All the heartiness with which she always associated him was gone and he looked gray and old and extremely tired. A deep sense of guilt flooded her soul as she realized that she had seized her own happiness in both hands and had hardly had time for days to give a thought to the man who had been so kind to her. She crossed the room swiftly and took hold of the doctor's arm. "Oh, doctor, how is he? Was the operation successful?" she asked eagerly.

The doctor freed himself from her grasp and put her gently into a chair before he answered her, but when he did he came directly to the point. "There wasn't a thing they could do. He was eager to take the chance on the operation so we took it — but it didn't work!" The muscles of his tired face twitched as he turned away from her and seated himself at his desk. "And now that he needs you more than ever, you have run off and gotten married." There was no censure or condemnation in his voice, only a great weariness.

Stung to the quick, Margaret's eyes filled with tears. "There wasn't much else I could do. I went to a carnival with a young man whom I met at the Exposition, and we got stuck in the Ferris wheel all night. When we got back in the morning, Mrs. Stillwell told him he had to marry me. She was ready to throw me out of the house. You know she has never liked me . . . "

Her voice trailed off and she opened her bag to procure her handkerchief so that she might wipe her eyes.

The doctor's keen eyes had never left her face. "So, that is how it happened!" Reaching over he took hold of the small gloved hand lying on the edge of his desk. "Don't cry, child. No problem was ever solved by shedding tears. And are you happy, my dear?"

The rich blush which spread over her face and neck at his question, was all the answer he needed. He sat back in his swivel chair and fitted the tips of his fingers together in a gesture which was characteristic of him when he was pondering a weighty problem. "Well, that is something to be gained. What does your husband do for a living?"

"He is a sailor. He has just obtained his captain's papers and before we met he had signed on for a six-month voyage. The company who owns his vessel will not allow women on their boats, so I thought that perhaps I might stay on with Mr. Stillwell until he returns."

The doctor cleared his throat, "Well, that is the first piece of good news I have had in weeks, I must say! Mr. Stillwell's condition has been too precarious for me to risk informing him of your sudden marriage." He peered at her over the tops of his glasses. "He is very fond of you, you know, and this is bound to be a shock to him. He was no sooner settled in bed than he demanded to see you, but I put him off for I hadn't the heart to tell him that you had left him, so soon after having to tell him that his case was hopeless. I insisted that he must have some rest before he saw anyone. When does your husband have to leave?"

"The day after tomorrow."

The doctor leaned forward in his chair. "My child, I am going to ask a great favor of you. I want you to go back to the Stillwell's with your husband and stay there till he leaves. I know it is a lot to ask of you to cut into your honeymoon like this, but if you really want to help Mr. Stillwell, you will persuade your husband to do this for you. Oh, don't worry," as he saw a protest rise to Margaret's lips, "I will go with you and I'll make it as easy for you as I can. I know that it will mean a great deal to Mr. Stillwell to see the young man. Where is he, by the way? In the reception room? Well, get him in here. Mr. Stillwell is not the only one who is anxious to make his acquaintance!"

The invalid was lying in the big bed in his darkened bedroom when the doctor arrived. The effect of the opiates he had been given had worn off, but he was still somewhat drowsy. The doctor drew up a chair and sat down by the bed. The invalid moved his head restlessly on the pillow. "What brought you back so soon?"

"I just thought that I would like to have a look at you. How do you feel?"

"About the same. It was actually a relief to get back into this bed, although I would never have believed it once."

"I'm glad to hear it, for I want you to stay in it for at least a week."

The protest the doctor expected came at once. "Oh, doctor! Have a heart. I want to see Margaret and I can't let her see me in bed."

But the doctor was unrelenting. "If you want to see her in the next week, that will be the way you will have to see her. Of course, if you don't, I'll tell her to keep away!"

The invalid groaned. "You are a hard taskmaster. You know perfectly well that the only thing that has kept me going is the desire to see her."

The doctor fitted his long fingers together and regarded the tips fixedly. "You're sure you want her to see you in bed? Wouldn't you prefer to wait until we can get you into your wheelchair again?"

The invalid moved his head so that he could get a better look at the doctor's face. "What is this anyway? First you say I have to see her in bed, if at all, and then you try to talk me out of seeing her. What is the matter? Nothing has happened to her, has it?" And then, when the doctor's answer was not immediately forthcoming, "For God's sake man, have pity on me! I have had about all I can take for awhile!"

The doctor leaned over the bed and his eyes were troubled. "I'm an old fool, Charles. There is nothing the matter with Margaret. Indeed, she looks better than I have ever seen her."

The invalid relaxed. "You shouldn't frighten me like that. How did she take it when you told her about me?"

"She cried."

The invalid sighed on an indrawn breath. "Life can be very cruel."

The doctor seized his opportunity. "It has been for you, but you don't want it to be that way for her, do you?"

Charles Stillwell's tones were crisp as he answered, "That is an extremely foolish question coming from you. What exactly do you mean by it?"

"I mean that I am going to give you an opportunity to put her happiness before your own."

"I always have."

"But this is different. I guess I'm just a blundering old fool, Charles, but what I am trying to tell you is, that while you were away, Margaret got married."

The drowsiness fell away from Charles Stillwell like a hastily discarded garment. He uttered one word, "Married!" and it sounded like a pistol shot in the quiet room.

The doctor went on talking evenly, his intent eyes on his patient's face. "She met a young man at the Exposition. He followed her here. She had to come back early because of illness in your cousin's house. He took her to a carnival in Wellsville and they got stuck all night in the Ferris wheel. When they got back in the morning, Parker was waiting for them and so was Ada. Please lie quietly, Charles. It will do you no good to thrash the upper part of your body about like that. You'll only feel it later. You remember I warned you about Ada some time ago. She is a woman and human and she took her revenge when she could. She told the young man that the only way he could make it right was to marry Margaret. Don't groan. He was more than willing. In fact, it seems that he followed her here for that very purpose. He is a nice lad, Charles. I've talked with him and I like him. I think you would, too, if you would let yourself."

The invalid turned his head aside on the pillow so that the doctor could not see his face. Quietly, the doctor reached over and felt his pulse. He ignored the tear he saw creeping down the pallid cheek turned away from him. It was not the first time he had seen a strong man weep in his extremity. He sat slumped forward in his chair waiting with the resigned patience he had acquired in the hard school of having to watch the sufferings of others. The clock on the mantle chimed the quarter hour and still the man on the bed did not speak.

The doctor continued quietly, "She is very happy, Charles, and very much in love. If you want the best for her, I think she has found it."

A moan came from the man on the bed. "That ought to make me happy, but it doesn't. Perhaps when I get used to the idea it will. I never meant to be a dog in the manger, but, oh, doctor, it is hard to take."

The doctor leaned forward and put his hand on his friend's shoulder in silent sympathy. After a few moments the invalid said, "Where is she?"

"Right here. There is one good thing about all this, Charles. Her husband is a sailor and he has signed on for a six-month voyage, on which he cannot take her. Margaret is more than willing to spend that time with you, if you want her to. They have been staying in a downtown hotel, but he has to leave the day after tomorrow and I persuaded them to come here, just in case you might want to see them."

The invalid turned his head and the despair in his sunken eyes tore at the doctor's kindly heart, but when he spoke, his voice was controlled enough. "Thanks, doctor. You are good to me. I'm glad that you told me before I saw her. This is what I wanted for her, of course, but I did not imagine that it would be so hard to take when it came. When I realized that nothing could be done about my legs, I thought that I had resigned myself to giving her up completely, but I didn't think that I would have to face the issue so soon. Coming so quickly after the other it rather hit me below the belt. Perhaps it is just as well to get all my disappointments over at once. Please tell her that I want to see her and her husband and that I will see them in the morning. I-I need a little time to get used to the idea of — of her being married."

The bedroom was bright with sunshine the next morning when Michael admitted Margaret. At the doctor's request, she had come alone. She crossed the room swiftly and knelt beside the bed hiding, as best she could, her shock at the wasted, gray look on Charles Stillwell's face. The operation must have been far more painful than she had realized. He searched for face eagerly for a long moment of silence. Satisfied at what he saw there, he put out his hand and she clasped it in both of hers. He could think of nothig better to say than, "Have they taken good care of you?" and when Margaret nodded, "Get up off the floor, child, and get Michael to bring you that chair by the dresser. It is the most comfortable one in the room. I've a thousand things to ask you. What do you mean by going off and getting married as soon as my back was turned?"

His tone was light and bantering and Margaret smiled as she accepted the proffered chair. "I couldn't help myself. Didn't the doctor tell you?"

"Yes, he told me, but not half enough. I'm most anxious to meet that husband of yours." The jesting left his tone as he inquired, "Is he half good enough for you?"

Margaret's eyes lighted. "Oh, yes, sir! He is much too good for me and so kind. He is all I ever dreamed about in a man!"

To cover his hurt, he teased her. "Have I lived with you all these years and not known what was going on under those black braids of yours? I did not think that I had given you time to dream about any other man!"

Margaret blushed. "It was really your fault that I ever started to dream at all. I never had much use for men until I came to you. My father was a tyrant and the only man I knew, except our minister who was a hypocrite of the deepest dye, whom I loathed. When I came here I had about made up my mind that I had seen all of the male sex that I ever cared to see and do you know?" she laughed softly at the memory, "I had fully determined never to marry. But you were so kind and considerate and thoughtful in a thousand ways that I began to change my mind. We had so much fun with our music and books that I began to think that a husband like you might be very nice to have." She was twisting her wedding ring about on her slender finger and regarding it lovingly as she talked so she did not see the pain in his eyes at her words.

Charles Stillwell cleared his throat and said somewhat huskily, "Tell me something about this young upstart who has stolen you from me."

Margaret looked up and her eyes were like stars. "He is tall like you and big, but he has the same long slender bones. I have always liked your hands." The hands under discussion clenched themselves under the covers. "And his are like yours. His hair is auburn and his eyes are brown and he is the most charming man I have ever met — except you," she said shyly. "He knows how to do things and he does everything so well. He . . . "

But the invalid interrupted her gently. He could not bear to have her go on eulogizing the man who had succeeded where he failed. "Where is this paragon of perfection?"

Margaret scarcely noticed the interruption, so pleased was she to be talking about her beloved. "Out on the porch. I will go and get him if you like."

But he was not yet ready to see the man who had taken his place in her affections. "Tell me first, everything just as it happened."

As Margaret launched into the story of her adventures, he watched her intently, taking in every change of tone and inflection. When she reached the part of the story where she had returned to find him gone, she said naively, "I was so unhappy and I didn't know why. You were gone and I was worried about you, but it was more than that." A shadow crossed the invalid's face, but she did not notice it, so intent was she on finishing her story. "When he came, I knew that it was because I was afraid that I might never see him again."

To save himself, he could not keep a twinge of irony out of his voice. "And when you did, he was forced into marrying you!"

But the irony was entirely lost on Margaret. "Yes, but he claims that that was what he came for in the first place."

"And, how about you?"

Margaret dimpled. "I hadn't thought much about it until he kissed me, but then I did."

Charles Stillwell turned away from the flushed and radiant face so near his own. This was even more difficult than he had anticipated. The unconscious manner in which she revealed to him how close he might have come to winning her for himself, had he been whole, did nothing to decrease his mental anguish. He found it almost impossible to control his voice and that angered him, for he held weakness in high contempt, but Margaret did not even notice his agitation. She was too engrossed with herself and her own happiness to see an inch before the end of her straight little nose. As he lay there watching her, afraid to speak lest his voice betray him, that incontestible fact began to insinuate itself into his consciousness and it enabled him to pull himself together as nothing else could have done. When at last he yanked the bell pull which hung by the side of his bed, there was no one to notice that he nearly pulled it off the wall, but when Michael answered the summons, he was able to make his tone light. "Go find the young man, Michael, and ask him to come here. I want to see this young Lochinvar!"

It was not until she was almost asleep that night that Margaret recollected that nothing whatsoever had been said about the invalid's operation and suffering. She felt ashamed of herself that she had been so concerned with herself and her affairs that she had failed to express her sympathy!

Chapter Twelve

Michael moved softly about the room trying to find things to do to keep him near his master. The young lady had left for Boston as soon as her husband had gone to sea, leaving the crippled man despondent and lonely. Michael wished that he would talk to him, but Mr. Stillwell's only interest in life seemed to be centered in the letters he received from Margaret and the hope that the next mail would bring him another. He kept her letters in a teakwood box close at hand and read and re-read them until they were limp. Michael glanced up at him. He was as absorbed in them again as if it were the first time he had read them. Michael sighed. As long as the invalid had started in on them again, it would be safe for him to go down to the kitchen for a few moments. He had timed the reading and knew that it would take at the very least twenty minutes.

Charles Stillwell had the letters arranged by dates and he was careful to keep them in order. With Margaret gone, they were his greatest comfort in life. The salutation of the first one always made his heart leap, no matter how many times he read it.

Dear Charles,

I cannot get used to calling you that, let alone writing it. It still seems odd to me that just because I have entered the married state you should feel it necessary for me to start using your given name. However, I shall get used to it in time and I am glad that it pleases you. I wish that there were more things that I could do to please you. You have always been very good to me and I feel that I have done very little in return.

I hadn't been gone from you an hour before I was wondering why on earth I consented to make this trip alone to Boston. For all I knew Jonathan's mother's supposedly dangerous illness might only be a hoax to get me where she could look me over. I told you how she played that trick on Jonathan in order to keep him near her, and I wished that I had thought of that before I left. If Jonathan had been there, or you had cautioned me, I don't think I would have come. I can only hope that my coming will be able to accomplish something worthwhile. I know that Jonathan feels the alienation from his mother keenly even though it was entirely her fault. I would love to be able to achieve a reconciliation between them and that is the real reason that I came. Just now that does not seem possible, but I must get back to the beginning.

The train trip was very tedious and, of course, I was dreading what lay ahead of me which did not help. I had thought that perhaps Phoebe, Jonathan's sister, would meet me at the station, but she did not. Instead, I was met by a couple of colored servants in the house named Sarah and Zach. However, I must admit that the warmth of their greetings somewhat compensated for not being met by my sister-in-law. they very evidently adore Jonathan and they simply beamed at me. while I am on the subject, I will tell you a little about their history. when they were young lovers they were put up for sale on a southern slave market. It so happened that Jonathan's grandfather was in port unloading his vessel and he attended the auction out of curiosity. When he witnessed their deep distress at the thought of being separated he bought them both and took them north with him, and they have been in the Wellfleet family ever since. Jonathan's father eventually gave them their freedom, but I am sure that nothing would persuade them to leave the Wellfleets. They must be quite old, but they are spry and they do not show their age. Zach is the coachman and Sarah the cook. All the way home,

Sarah entertained me with a running discourse on Jonathan when he was young and I, of course, loved it and began to feel much better about the whole situation.

But when we arrived at the house, my heart sank. It is a high narrow brownstone set in a block of similar houses and as I stood on the sidewalk looking up at it, it seemed most forbidding. As Sarah led me up the steps she whispered to me, "Don't you pay no mind ter the Missus, Missie. She's as ornery as a mule." So you can imagine how I felt, as I entered!

Again, there was no one to welcome me, but I was taken at once to my mother-in-law's room. I cannot make you understand what it was like unless I describe her to you. She is a tartar for sure and rules the whole household with a rod of iron! Before she said a word to me she rebuked Sarah for coming upstairs without being summoned when she had ordered one of the other maids to bring me to her room. Sarah had done it to lend me moral support, I know. I think I'm going to like Sarah. When she had bobbed a curtsey and retired, I received a very cold and frigid welcome: "So, you are the young woman my son married!" I admitted that I was and stood my ground. She looked me over as if I were a piece of meat in the market which had begun to spoil and I gave her look for look. Phoebe was puttering nervously about the room and her mother finally introduced us and commanded her to show me to my room. I can assure you I was glad to go. When I am more rested and am allowed some time to myself, I will write you a complete description of the household, but just now I am too tired and sleepy to keep my eyes open for another moment.

Good night, dear Charles, I wish that I had stayed with you!

Your somewhat weary and dispirited secretary,

Margaret.

Dear Charles,

After several days of living in this household, I am now ready to reveal all. To be quite truthful, it is a tremendous help to have someone to tell everything to and every night before I go to sleep I write both you and Jonathan a few lines and when the *number of lines achieve the respectability of a letter, I send them off. I do not write to Jonathan, as I do to you, however, for I do not want to hurt him and you have no idea what a comfort it is to me to unburden my soul to you.*

To begin at the heart of the matter, let me tell you about this mother-in-law of mine. I told you she was a tartar and I never said a truer thing. Everyone in the household, except Sarah, is scared to death of her. She has Phoebe completely cowed and under her thumb. Poor Phoebe! I'll tell you about her later, but I want to describe my mother-in-law first. She is a tall woman (even seeing her in bed, I can tell that) and very lean. Her hands are long-fingered and bony and she keeps them folded in her lap with the air of a martyr. Even in bed she sits up as straight as a ramrod and every word she enunciates is uttered in a cold, hard, irritated tone. It does not matter whether she is nagging Phoebe or ordering her meals, she speaks and looks as if she could chew nails and enjoy them.

Now I come to Phoebe. She is pathetic and I alternate between pitying her and despising her for letting her mother dominate and absorb her. She must be nearing fifty, but she jumps at her mother's every word. She is as plump as her mother is lean and the reason is that her one joy in life is nibbling. Her mother knows this and is continually heckling her about her appetite. She hardly eats a mouthful in her mother's presence (we have many of our meals in her room) and her one joy in life is to sneak down to the kitchen and devour the dainties that Sarah hides for her in a place known only to them.

She jerks her shoulders and shuffles her feet and her hands are never still. She has a nervous habit of laying her thumb along the side of her nose which is anything but attractive, and to which her mother alludes frequently in a most scathing manner. Her eyes are weak and she has to wear glasses. They are always sliding down on her plump little nose and she peers near-sightedly over them in the most pathetic or annoying manner, depending on how one feels about her at the moment.

The rest of the household is comprised of Sarah's twin granddaughters who are respectively the upstairs maid and the waitress. They are quite light in color and are very pretty, but in disfavor right now because they have had the kink taken out of their hair. According to Sarah, their mother, who was her only child, ran off and married a "no-count northern white nigger" who abandoned her long before the twins were born. She died at their birth and Sarah has raised them. They are petrified in the presence of the mistress of the house who keeps a sharp eye on everything they do, but they are fond of Phoebe and frequently smuggle little tidbits into her room.

Life has settled down into a routine now, but I cannot say that I am enjoying it. We, that is Phoebe and I, do nothing but attend prayer meetings, church, and temperance meetings when not giving attendance to Jonathan's mother when we are at home. You will never know how I long for our cozy times about the fire with our music and games and books.

The only books which are read in this house are religious ones and they are dry as dust. There is a large library on the second floor, but it is full of such things as Bunyan's "Pilgrim's Progress," Milton's "Paradise Lost," and numerous theological works and commentaries. Sarah tells me that Mrs. Wellfleet relegated all her husband's books to the attic. Someday she is going to sneak me up there and show me the family portraits.

So far, my mother-in-law has not left her bed, but I am sure that she could if she wished. The longer I stay, the less possible it appears that I shall accomplish much by staying, but somehow, for Jonathan's sake, I cannot bring myself to leave just yet.

I miss you more than you will ever know and my resolves are weakening. Your letters are such a joy. It is good to know that you are reading and thinking. I particularly enjoyed the newspaper article you sent. It is ages since I have heard from Jonathan although I write him regularly. I hope that that means that he is nearing the last lap of his journey.

Your affectionate secretary,
Margaret.

Dear Charles,

I am very, very cross. In fact I am what Sarah would call "fit to be tied." What do you think happened? My mother-in-law set her minister after me! Evidently they had decided between them that I had heard enough sermons on hell and damnation to persuade me of the error of my ways. The minister came to call one afternoon (personally, I think he was sent for) and

Mrs. Wellfleet sent down word that she was resting and would I please give him tea. At first, I did not see why Phoebe could not have done so, but after a few minutes conversation with him, I saw the reason. It was undoubtedly because her mother told her not to. He is a pompous ass and smooth as butter; that is, he looks as if it wouldn't melt in his mouth. I am sure that he thought he was extremely tactful, but I found him merely oily and ingratiating. The gist of his lecture, (I cannot give it any other title) was that I had a great responsibility, not only for my own salvation, but also for Jonathan's and that I should repent of my sins and see to it that he did the same. As he was talking and I was glaring at him (I am afraid) the reason for my mother-in-law getting me to give him tea became apparent to me. She is determined to get at Jonathan through me. I let the minister run on without comment, but when he suggested that he pray with me, I am afraid that I gave vent to my thoughts. I told him that neither my husband nor I had any use whatsoever for religion and the reason that we did not was that we had both been made to suffer so severely by people who called themselves religious that it had soured us completely on the subject. He seemed somewhat taken aback, but he finally murmured that religion should not be judged by the failure of its exponents. I replied, somewhat icily I fear, that if one's religion was not powerful enough to make one decent to live with, it was not, in my opinion, worth much. He was obviously shocked and asked me if I was not worried about going to hell. I told him that neither Jonathan nor I believed in hell. At this brashness he was so taken aback he almost stuttered as he informed me that such talk was blasphemy. I then informed him that the only reason I could see for hell was to make people who called themselves religious and acted like the devil, suffer as they made others suffer, but that personally I thought there was enough suffering on earth without adding a hell hereafter. He then gasped like a floundering fish and finally managed to enunciate, "But, what about heaven?" Having had quite enough of him and his platitudes, I rose and announced very curtly that heaven would not be heaven to me if some of the people I knew who called themselves Christians were in it (meaning, of course, my father and Jonathan's mother) and I sailed out, leaving him open-mouthed and as convinced as my mother-in-law that I am on the way to perdition.

I do not know how much more of this I can take. I did want to stay until Jonathan's boat docked, for it would then be perfectly natural for him to come here and get me, but I do not know whether I can hold out that long.

Your extremely riled and disgusted secretary,
Margaret.

Dear Charles,

This is to announce that I am coming back to you as soon as I am able to pack. The reason is as follows: Phoebe and I went out this morning to do the marketing. Zach took us to a place called Faneuil Hall. We go there every Friday. There are booths and stalls and you walk through and choose what you want. It is very colorful and interesting; much more than any of the meetings I have been forced to attend since I have been here! But the important thing is what happened when we returned to the house. We had been instructed to pick up some packages which were not ready, so we got back much earlier than we expected. I went at once to my room and what do you think? There was my mother-in-law sitting in my rocker calmly reading my letters from you and Jonathan! She had the box open on her lap and the letters properly separated into two little piles with the pink and blue ribbons with which I hold them together lying on the table. As you know, I am light on my feet and she did not hear my approach until I had opened the door and was almost upon her. She rose at once and dropped everything on the floor, but she made no apologies or excuses. I was so angry I was speechless for a moment, but when I recovered my voice I said plenty, some of it not very nice, I am afraid. Her only reply was that Jonathan was her son before he was my husband and she had every right to read his mail. When I then accused her of reading your letters also, she turned upon me with a most vitriolic look and told me that her suspicions about me had been fully realized: I was not only godless, but I was immoral, carrying on correspondence with a man who was not my husband! With this parting shot she sailed past me and I had all I could do not to strike her. The situation is hopeless, simply hopeless! I see that now and I wish that I had never come.

*Perhaps, it is just as well that I am leaving for I have been
feeling very unwell for some time, but I did not want to worry you
by telling you about it. Today at the market I fainted dead away,
much to poor Phoebe's horror, and came to on the floor with my
head in Sarah's lap. A kindly farmer's wife from one of the stalls
gave me a cup of fresh milk and after a bit I was able to get up
and return to the carriage. I made Sarah and Zach and Phoebe
promise not to tell Mrs. Wellfleet. It was bad enough to feel as I
did without having her acid inquiries as to the state of my health
added to my difficulties. If I do not feel better, I shall have to
ask our kindly doctor to look at me. I am sure of one thing and
that is that I will never let my mother-in-law's doctor touch me.
Either he is a fool whom she has completely taken in with her pretended illnesses or else he has connived with her to deceive and
in neither case would he be trustworthy. I want Zach to mail this
so I will close. I will be seeing you very soon, I am very glad
to say.*

  Delightedly yours,
  Margaret.

When Charles Stillwell had finished reading Margaret's letters he sat in deep thought for a few minutes, then with a deep
frown he picked up the other letters in the box and commenced
to read them. The first was from Jonathan.

Dear Mr. Stillwell;
  *I deeply appreciate your concern for Margaret's welfare.
When she did not return to you at the time set, you must have
been as frantic as I would have been in a like circumstance. I
am so sorry that my mother did not answer your letters. I cannot make any excuses for her conduct and I can simply say that I
am deeply regretful that you should have been caused such distress of mind. Sending Patrick to find out what had happened
was the only thing you could do and I wish he might have been
able to have obtained more reliable information for you. Margaret was in bed and out of her head with fever, and Sarah, who
would have been glad to have given him any information he*

132

wanted, was spending every waking moment with her. Sarah was the only person who could quiet her or whom she was willing to have near her.

But to get back to the beginning of the trouble. Margaret was pregnant when she came to my mother's house but she did not seem to realize why she felt as she did. Then she had the extreme misfortune to contract diphtheria. After she got her letter off to you telling you that she was returning, she collapsed and Sarah put her to bed. She has been there ever since and she has been a very sick girl. She almost choked to death and if the doctor had not quickly inserted a tube in her throat to facilitate her breathing, she would have died. She came very near it as it was, and the fever seemed to cling to her. Her recovery has been very slow not only due to that, but to her pregnancy. By the time I got here she was merely a shadow of her former self and she was never very well filled out as you know. I could have wept when I saw her. The doctor had forbidden my mother to go near her for every time she did, the fever shot up. Margaret tells me that she has written you what happened between them. I regret the whole thing deeply. The only excuse that I can make for my mother is that since she lost five sons with diphtheria she is not quite normal and she is extremely bitter because her children died while Margaret lived. There is no reasoning with her and I no longer try. I spend my entire time with Margaret and she is very slowly but, I hope, surely, improving. When I hold her in my arms she is still as light as a feather, but she had no fever yesterday for the first time and she tries to eat to please me. You may be sure that I stay with her every possible moment and when I am not with her, Sarah is. She is receiving every attention, but the doctor tells me that she has so little stamina, her recovery will be lengthy.

I shall take her away from here as soon as she is able to travel. I am afraid that she had been most unhappy in my mother's house and I know that the fault is not hers. When she told me why she came I wanted to curse or weep! I am afraid there just is no possibility of a woman of my mother's age changing. It saddens me that there is no middle ground on which we can meet.

She informed me of what she calls Margaret's carrying on with you and although I tried to explain the situation to her and even told her that I knew you and had stayed in your home, she would not listen to reason. She insists that I must give up Margaret but that I will never do. I wanted to remind her that her own Bible says that a man should leave his father and his mother and cleave unto his wife, but it is only a waste of breath to try to argue with her. Once she gave me my choice between her and the sea. I chose the sea that time, which should have taught her a lesson, but I am afraid that it didn't, for now she insists that I choose between her and Margaret and naturally there isn't any choice. The situation is impossible and as soon as I am able to leave Margaret for any length of time during the day, I shall see what I can do about getting something to do on land. From what the doctor tells me, she will need me for some time to come and I do not feel that I can go off and leave her when she has been so ill and she is still pregnant. I have already notified the company to find another captain for the "Matilda Lee' when she sails. I will write you further developments.

   Sincerely yours,
   Jonathan Wellfleet

   The morning mail was delivered at the Stillwell mansion at eleven o'clock, and Michael was at the door waiting for the postman. It took all the courage he had to go back to his master whenever there was nothing in the mail from the young lady. It gave him actual physical pain to see the eager look on the invalid's face change to one of disappointment and discouragement. But today there was an envelope addressed in the handwriting of the young lady herself. Michael almost broke his neck getting up the stairs to the master. He was panting and red in the face when he handed the letter to the invalid, but the look on his master's face more than repaid him for his effort. Michael placed the letter opener on the table and departed with a light heart. Now his charge would be cheerful for the rest of the day.

   Alone in his room, Charles Stillwell ripped the letter open and hastily scanned its pages. Then with an audible sigh of relief he settled down to re-read its contents more carefully.

Dear Charles,

It is a very long time since I have been able to write you and I am afraid this will have to be brief. Jonathan has written you about all that happened to me in Boston. I do not let myself think about it when I am awake, but sometimes I have nightmares and I dream that my mother-in-law is trying to choke me to death. When that happens, it is such a comfort to find Jonathan here beside me when I awaken.

We are all settled and waiting for the baby to put in its appearance. Jonathan has taken a job managing a sail loft. It belongs to a sea captain who was a great friend of his father's. He is a widower and we are living in his house. It is really only a cottage and very quaintly furnished, but it is comfortable and has a lovely garden. It is quite near the harbour and the salt air is supposed to do something or other for me, I have not yet been able to discover just what.

I spend most of my time in bed and am not allowed to lift a finger. Perhaps it is just as well as I really don't seem to have much energy. Sarah and Zach are taking care of us. They walked out on Jonathan's mother. I wonder how she likes it, having them desert her in such a high-handed manner, but I really don't care. I hope that I never have to see her again as long as I live. Everytime I think about her, I get all trembly inside, so I try not to.

I must close now, but I did want you to know, from my own hands, that I am pretty well and most awfully happy. We are near the sail loft and Jonathan comes home everyday for lunch. I see no one, but I do not care as long as I have him.

Your recuperating and utterly contented friend,
Margaret.

Chapter Thirteen

Dr. Nicholas Shelby Thorpe sat on the floor playing with Margaret Wellfleet's twins. He was still in his uniform, but he had not wanted to take time to change before he saw her. In his eagerness to reach the house he had forgotten that it was by his express command that she napped every afternoon and when Sarah had told him that she was asleep, he had had to content himself with the twins. They had grown tremendously since he had been off to war and they were certainly a cute pair of four-year-olds.

The boy was a sturdy, handsome replica of his father, but the little girl with her dark coloring and delicate frame made him think of Margaret. She was so much smaller than her brother and so unlike him in coloring that it was hard to remember that they were twins. The children were fascinated with the toys that he had purchased for them as soon as his boat landed in New York from Cuba, and after their first ecstatic greeting, they became absorbed in their play.

He sat and watched them. He was very tired. He had enlisted as soon as war had been declared on Spain and he had certainly been kept busy. Typhoid, dysentary, and malaria had taken more toll of men than the enemy's bullets and the conditions under which he had been expected to labor had been deplorable. He was glad when it was over and he could return at last.

He frowned as he watched the children playing at his feet. He was a fool and a knave, but he was madly in love with the mother of these children and, instead of helping matters, his being away from her had only intensified his feeling for her. He had reminded himself a thousand times that it was absolutely insane to be in love with a woman whom he had attended in childbirth, but no castigation of himself by himself could alter the fact that he still loved her madly. That he liked and admired her husband more than any man he had ever known did nothing to alter that unpalatable fact. That she quite openly adored that same husband did not seem to affect his feeling for her either. He knew that it should, and he told himself so again and again, but it did no good.

His soul was as weary as his body from flagellating himself for his folly. He had determined a hundred times over not to come back, het yere he was in spite of himself, hardly able to contain himself for a sight of her. He passed his hand over his forehead and closed his eyes for a moment. As always when his mind was not engrossed in directing his body, his thoughts reverted to her. The birth of her twins had been a very difficult case. Not only had the delivery been long and hard and her strength too slight to meet her body's needs, but after he had succeeded in pulling her through by the skin of her teeth, she had developed childbed fever and been ill for months. He had fought for her life and he had saved her, but she would never be strong as long as she lived and she would never be able to have any more children.

His sweetest memory in life and one that had sustained him during the past years in many a difficult spot was of a day when she had been ablaze with fever and had started to call wildly for her husband. He had sent Zach running for him, but Jonathan had left the sail loft to do an errand and they could not find him. To satisfy her he had bent over the bed and lifting her bodily in his arms, the way he had seen Jonathan do a dozen times, settled with her in the low rocker that stood by the bed. In her delirium she had not known that it was not her husband who held her and she had calmed down at once and clung to him through the blankets in which he had wrapped her, until at last she had fallen into a fitful sleep.

He held her gently as long as he dared, her dark head on his wildly beating heart and she never knew the difference, but for him, life changed completely that day and he swore within himself that as long as she needed him, he would be where she could reach him, even though she would never know that for him she was the only woman in the world. He sighed. His father had been like that, a one-woman man, and he supposed that he was like him. Rather a disadvantage to a man when there was no chance of getting the one woman!

He had not realized what a difficult role he was setting for himself that day, and as time went on, his guilty secret weighed on him to such an extent that when war was declared, he was glad of an excuse to get away. He had persuaded her husband that he should not leave her for any reason whatsoever and he had departed, if not with joy, at least with a lighter heart than he had carried for some time, for he had not only saved her life, but he had seen to it that she did not need to worry about her husband's going off to war.

He had decided then, that for his own sake, he had better not return, but when the time came for him to be mustered out of the army, he had turned down several tempting offers to establish a practice in other cities and come directly to her. This Sunday afternoon, Sarah had told him that Jonathan had gone for a walk and he hoped fervently that he would not return until he saw her. He wanted no other eyes on their meeting.

A clock chimed five and his quick ear caught a light step on the stair. He arose and in a minute she was in the room, her cheek's flushed with sleep and her eyes bright. "Why, Nick!" her exlamation of surprise and delight made his heart leap in his breast, "Why ever didn't you have Sarah wake me for such an occasion as this? How long have you been waiting?"

"Not too long," he managed to mutter, her two small hands in his big ones. "You should not expect me to break my own rules."

"But it has been such a long time," she said, looking up at him with smiling eyes. "Come and sit down and I'll have Sarah bring us some tea."

He settled down in a chair opposite her, preferring to be where he could watch her. She sent one of the children to ask Sarah for tea, and in a few moments Zach brought in a well-laden tray and Sarah took the children away for their early supper. She poured his tea, remembering that he liked three lumps of sugar and handed him the cup, but before she took her own cup, she looked across at him and her eyes sobered.

"Oh, Nick, I *am* so glad that you are back. I have so much to tell you and I need your help and advice. Will you help me, if I confide in you?"

"Did I ever refuse to help you?" he asked, trying to keep his tone light.

"No, you have been one of the best friends we have ever had." He wished that she had made the pronoun a singular one. There was an obscure hurt in the word *we*. For a moment she kept her eyes on the folded hands in her lap, evidently considering how she should commence her revelation.

He reached over and poured her tea for her. "Before you start, you must have your tea. You cannot expect to keep up your strength if you eat like a bird."

She took the cup from him, but the abstraction did not leave her eyes. He handed her some sandwiches and she took one absently.

He decided to distract her attention until tea was over. He did not want her confidences interrupted by Zach or Sarah.

"Aren't you going to ask me about Mr. Stillwell?"

Her abstraction left her in a moment, "Oh, yes, did you see him?"

"Yes, both coming and going. I wrote you about the first time. Now I would like to tell you about the second."

"Oh, yes," she said eagerly, forgetting her own troubles. "Do."

"He was about the same this time, as before. He gets no better and no worse."

She shook her head, crowned with its heavy dark braids. "If only somebody could do something. Do you think there is any chance?"

He, too, shook his head. "I'm afraid not. He sent you his love." As he said the words, Nick thought within himself that the poor devil was in the same fix he himself was in, as far as she was concerned, but did not have the diversions to distract him that he, Nick, had. At least his profession kept his mind off of her for long periods of time while poor Charles Stillwell had no such outlet.

"Thank you for telling me," she said simply. "I do what I can by writing him daily, even if it is only a line."

The doctor nodded, "I know. He told me." He thought it best not to tell her, but he knew that it was only those letters which kept the cripple from committing suicide. A strange effect this small woman had upon the men who loved her. Two of them could never have her, but they couldn't seem to get along without her!

He had eaten a substantial tea, but she had not even finished her sandwich. He made her do so and take another before he would let her have the tea things removed.

She pouted at him prettily. "Here you are, scarcely home and you start bossing me about. If I weren't so glad to see you, it would make me cross."

He hid his deep concern for her physical welfare under banter. "Somebody has got to make you toe the mark. I cannot see that you have gained an ounce since I left."

She looked up at him. "But, I did, really I did, only I've been so worried of late, that I am afraid I have lost it all."

He leaned toward her, "What is worrying you?"

Her eyes were once more on her hands and she was twisting her wedding ring about on her finger as she had a habit of doing when she was upset. "You won't laugh if I tell you?"

"Have I ever laughed at you?"

"No, but this is enough to make a horse laugh and you may not think that it is worth worrying about, but it is to me."

He reached over and took one small hand in his. "Anything that is important to you is important to me. If it does not make you laugh, I am sure that I will not find it in the least amusing."

What, he was wondering to himself frantically, can be the matter? Has Jonathan run off with another woman or has she stopped loving him? As that thought crossed his mind, he reminded himself crossly not to be an idiot. Jonathan was as much in love with her as he was; his letters testified to that. Nick's weariness made him irritated at her uncertainty. He was on the point of demanding point blank that she tell him her trouble when she looked up at him and all the irritation went out of him like a snuffed candle.

She withdrew her hand from his and leaning back in her low chair told him her difficulty. "It may not seem tragic to you, Nick, but it does to me. Jonathan, of all people, has been *converted!*" She gave the distasteful word a disgusted emphasis.

His relief made him let out a long sigh.

She looked at him reproachfully. "You see, you do not think that it is very important."

Lest he divulge to her his real feelings, he replied somewhat crisply. "Anything which concerns you interests me. After all you are my patient. Tell me exactly what happened."

Margaret commenced her story. "A lot has happened, one way or another, since you have gone. The business was not very good, for steam has made such advances the last few years that there is nowhere near the demand for sails that there was. So I persuaded Jonathan to go into a sideline, the making of awnings. Cloth awnings are much more fashionable than the old wooden ones and he had done quite well with it." She was still twisting her wedding ring and her agitation was obvious to the doctor's trained eye, but he felt it best not to interrupt her. After a moment's hesitation, she continued.

"From that, he branched into making tents. I was delighted because I am anxious to get out of this house and buy a house on the hill. This place is too crowded since the twins were born and besides, the neighborhood is running down fast. It is no place to bring them up. When they go to school, I do not want them associating with the children from River Street and that is what will happen if we go on living here. Besides, this house is too old fashioned and quaint for me. Jonathan has been trying to buy the business from Captain Marvin and so there has been no money for houses. That was one reason I was so pleased about the awnings and tents."

She paused for breath and the doctor thought within himself, "Poor Jonathan! That means that he plans never to go back to sea, which he loves. How this woman sitting opposite me has changed and affected the lives of the men who love her!"

But he had no time to ponder on this line of thought, for Margaret was continuing her account of what had happened.

"The Methodists in town were having a revival meeting and they wanted a tremendous tent in which to hold the meetings. They gave the order to Jonathan. Naturally, we were pleased about it, so when the man who was the head of the committee invited us to attend the meetings the first Sunday afternoon, we felt that we could not refuse." She bit her lip as the painful memories of that fateful afternoon returned to her.

"It was pretty awful. Hard wooden benches and sawdust on the floor. There were all kinds of people and all kinds of smells. It was very hot. Jonathan and I looked at one another and decided we would just have to endure it. We sat near the back so that we could get out as soon as it was over, but it dragged on and on. First we listened to a singer who really had a magnificent voice, if he had been singing something besides hymns. Then an evangelist, a man named Moody, started to preach." The distasteful memory made her hesitate a second time.

"He was pretty crude, but he certainly held the people's attention. He was so eloquent that he swayed that huge crowd of people as a fresh wind ripples through ripe grain. I did not pay too much attention to what he said, for I was busy watching the facial expressions of those about me. It was not long before he had many of them in tears. I despise a public display of emotion and I have always had particular contempt for this form of mass emotionalism, but I had to admit that this man was a past master of the art. One minute he had the crowd weeping and the next, laughing. He was certainly an artist in his own field.'"

Margaret paused but when the doctor made no comment, she continued slowly, "I turned to look at Jonathan. To my surprise, I found him listening intently. He merely glanced at me when I touched his arm. I wanted to leave, but I did not feel that we should make ourselves conspicuous. When the evangelist had finished, a sigh that was almost a groan went through the vast crowd. I started to rise so that we could depart, but Jonathan whispered to me that we should wait, nobody else was leaving. Evidently, there was more to come." Her lips tightened. "There certainly was. What my father would have called an *altar call*, for the evangelist commenced to plead with people to come forward and accept Jesus Christ as their Saviour. Dozens of people went. The evangelist and his helpers herded them into a smaller tent in back of the big one, but still he did not dismiss the crowd." She frowned down at the ring she was twisting on her finger.

"I began to be very restless and most indignant at being held there against my will, when all of a sudden, Jonathan turned to me and said, 'I want to go forward. Will you go with me?' Nick, I couldn't believe my ears." Tears she could no longer hide sprang into her eyes and crept down her cheeks. "Jonathan, who had always felt as I have, that he had enough religion in his youth to last him for the rest of his life! At first, I thought he was joking, but one look at his face soon disillusioned me on that point. He meant what he said and, Nick, I am afraid that I lost my temper, for I told him tartly that I wouldn't dream of such a thing and that he must be crazy. He answered me very quietly that in that case he would have to go alone and he got up and went. I felt as if he had suddenly and unexpectedly slapped my face." Again Margaret stopped, overcome by her own emotions. The doctor said nothing, feeling that the best thing to do to relieve Margaret was for her to be able to talk about it to someone she could trust. In a moment, over the lump in her throat, Margaret went on with her recital.

"I was so angry that I got up and left, whether I was dismissed or not. I came straight home and waited and waited, but he didn't come. I was just about frantic and on the point of sending Zach out to find him, when he walked in."

Again she paused for breath and the doctor asked quietly, "And what did he have to say for himself?"

She gave a sharp sigh before she answered him. "Very little. He did not try to excuse himself nor give me a sensible explanation of why he had done what he had. He merely stated that he had been talking with the evangelist all that time and where once he was blind, now he saw. When I asked him what he saw, he replied, 'If Jesus said to come to Him and I refuse to come, that makes me a sinner, who is essentially a person who wants to go his own way instead of God's.' He told me that he personally had accepted his responsibility in the matter and made his peace with God and had been born again." She bit out the despised words, her eyes still on her hands. "I could have cried and I almost did. I guess he saw how I felt, for he was sweet, as only Jonathan can be. He put his arms around me and told me that this did not need to make any difference between us."

Margaret was so engrossed in her own problem that she did not notice the shadow that passed across her listener's face at her words, nor the tightening of his mouth. She went on with her story. "But, oh, Nick, it has! It has in a thousand ways, and I am just sick about it."

She was very near to tears once again, and he asked her quietly, "How do you mean?"

"Well, Jonathan now spends time reading the Bible that he once spent reading secular matter to me and he insists upon having prayers at the table and in reading the Bible to the children and the servants. I had enough of the Bible in my youth to last me the rest of my life and now I am having it stuffed down

143

my throat all over again and I *hate* it!" She stopped and gulped back her tears.

Dr. Thorpe's nails bit into his palms. He longed to help her, but she had brought him a problem which was out of his province, although he realized that it in a way affected it very closely, because if she kept on in this highly emotional state, she would be ill and he must spare her that at all costs. She took a handkerchief out of the pocket of her gown and blew her nose before she continued. "And, that isn't all. He insisted upon going to church. I wouldn't go with him, so he went alone and insisted upon taking the children. He hasn't been nasty about it, but he is as adamant as the Rock of Gibraltar and I have just about as much chance of changing him as if I tried to move it. The whole thing is ruining my happiness." Once again tears came to the surface and she had to stop to wipe her eyes and blow her nose.

"I tried to go his way. I even went so far as to investigate a church in a better part of town than the one that he insists upon attending and I found a very nice one, Grace Church. Perhaps you know it. All the best people go there and there are a great many social events scheduled. I went to a service and I found the minister never mentioned sin or hell or damnation. I began to think that I wouldn't mind being a member of that particular church and, after attending quite faithfully for three months and taking part in many of their activities, I broached the subject of joining to Jonathan, but he wouldn't even listen to it. He stated flatly that that church did not preach the truth, that the minister did not believe the Bible, and that it was nothing but a social club and not a place in which to worship God. I was flabbergasted at his reaction; I am sure I do not know where he got his information, but he was very sure of himself.

"Then, I tried to point out that if we went there the children would meet other children of their own class and that it might do his business good because a lot of wealthy people attended it, but he told me gently, but firmly, that he did not go to church to improve his business or his children's social standing; he went to worship God. He wasn't cross and he didn't lose his temper. I wish he had. At least that would have given me something legitimate to complain about in his conduct since he got converted, but he doesn't even give me that handle to grasp. He is as dear and loving and considerate as ever, but oh! Nick, he isn't all mine anymore! His religion is separating us and I hate it! Oh, how I hate it!"

She could no longer control her emotions and was now frankly weeping. The man, who was watching her with a distress equal to her own, felt something hot and sticky on his fingers. Looking down at his hand, he saw that the paper cutter he had picked up from the table next to him to distract himself from her unhappiness had bitten into the palm of his hand and drawn blood. He took out his handkerchief and wiped it automatically without glancing at the damage he had done.

A deep sense of inadequacy and discouragement swept through his weary body. He had come back to be of use to her where he could, and he felt that he was making a very poor start. If he could not be happy himself, at least he wanted to do everything in his power to secure her happiness. That he could see no immediate solution for the very first problem she had brought him irritated and at the same time depressed him. But he could not bear to see her cry. To him, it was worse than being under fire. He got up, and going to her, knelt beside her chair. Taking her handkerchief out of her hand, he wiped her eyes. Some of the tenseness went out of her at his kindly touch. As for him, being so close to her made him feel slightly dizzy.

Hastily, he rose to his feet, but when he spoke, his tone was gentle. He was thankful that she would never know the effort it cost him. "You musn't cry. Tears never yet solved a problem. They will only exhaust you. If you will promise me not to worry about this, I will tackle Jonathan and we will see what can be done. Where is he, by the way?"

The gray eyes looking up at him were full of gratitude. "He went for a walk around the harbour and out on the point. He does that more and more lately. Oh, Nick, you are an angel! Perhaps he will listen to you. It is wonderful to have you home again!"

It was not more than a week later that an opportunity presented itself to broach the subject to Jonathan. Margaret was helping with a bazaar at Grace Church and she planned to spend the evening there. Jonathan was not interested in bazaars, so the doctor suggested that they have a game of chess together. Jonathan, who admired and respected Nick and thoroughly enjoyed his society, invited him for dinner. The doctor accepted the invitation with alacrity. He was anxious to witness the prayers which Margaret hated so much.

When the meal was finished, Jonathan rang for the servants and the children who had been fed earlier and now were ready for bed. When they came in, Sarah and Zach sat down against the wall. Jonathan would never permit the old couple to stand through prayers the way his mother had insisted upon their doing. One child climbed up onto Nick's lap and the other onto Jonathan's. When they were comfortably settled and the children were quiet, he commenced to read from the Psalm Forty.

"I waited patiently for the Lord; and he inclined unto me and heard my cry. He brought me up also out of an horrible pit, out of the miry clay, and set my feet upon a rock, and established my goings."

The doctor listened intently. He hated to admit it to himself, but he enjoyed it. Jonathan's deep voice and the perfection of his enunciation, combined with the magnificence of the language, appealed to him strongly, and he thought to himself that it must be the personal antagonism within Margaret's soul that made her hate prayers so. Not having the motive within himself, he rather enjoyed them and was almost sorry when his host had concluded the short passage.

The children at once closed their eyes and folded their small hands and the servants did likewise. Then, Jonathan Wellfleet began to pray, and his friend watching him covertly beneath lowered eyelashes, knew that whatever Jonathan had come to believe and feel, it meant a great deal to him. When he had finished, the children said good night and Sarah bore them away. The two men retreated to the living room fire and for a while they sat by its warmth without talking. Finally, Jonathan roused himself, "Shall I get the board?"

Nick shook his head. "If you don't mind, I'd rather just talk. I am more weary than I realized since I have been able to let down and relax a little."

"Of course." Jonathan unfolded his long legs and drew his chair closer to the fire. "I don't suppose that you want to talk about your war experiences?"

"Not particularly, but there is something I do want to talk to you about — your conversion."

"So, Margaret has told you about that?"

"Yes, she unburdened her soul the first day I was here. She seemed very much upset."

Jonathan sighed, "I know and I am truly sorry, but I don't know what to do except pray that she too may come to know Jesus in person."

Nick took his pipe out of his pocket and Jonathan lighted it from a taper ignited in the glowing coals. The doctor drew on it a few moments in silence. He must consider carefully his next words. He had the feeling that he did not want to hurt Jonathan's feelings any more than he wanted to fail Margaret.

At last he said slowly, "What worries me is that she will make herself ill over this. Adverse emotions can make people sick. Margaret hasn't much physical stamina, as you know, Jonathan, and she has been through a lot."

Jonathan's eyes darkened. "I know, Nick. It bothers me as much as it does you."

Nick took his pipe out of his mouth and regarded it quizzically. "I don't suppose you could give it up?"

In spite of his concern, Jonathan smiled. "I see that you do not understand what has happened to me any better than Margaret does. Of course she doesn't try." The smile left his face and a shadow passed across it.

The doctor said, "I'd like to try."

Jonathan looked into the fire. "It is a hard thing to explain to someone who has never experienced it. To say simply that one has been born again isn't enough. There is, at first, no tangible evidence of new life to prove the hypothesis. That I have been born physically is perfectly obvious because I have a body to prove it, but to be born spiritually, to be converted, is another matter altogether. I have nothing but my own inner feelings and outer actions to demonstrate the existence of this new life. There is nothing tangible about it and that is why people who have no personal knowledge of it find it impossible to understand the significance of conversion."

The doctor asked, "Just what *do* you mean by conversion?"

"It's rather hard to define. I suppose the best way to describe it is to say it is a right-about-face. All my life I have followed my own dictates, I have gone the way that seemed best to me and have done what I wanted. When I was converted, I recognized that God, being my creator and my saviour, has claims on my life and I have put His claims before my own. I no longer want to serve only my own ends and live to fulfill my own selfish pride. I find myself wanting to be an expression of God's love through my life and actions." Jonathan sighed, his glance begging for the doctor's understanding. "I am afraid that I am expressing myself badly." Not knowing what else to say, the doctor replied, somewhat tersely, "All this is a little hard on Margaret."

"I know, and it gives me just as much concern as it does you, but I cannot see what can be done, for birth on either the physical or spiritual plane is something which we cannot ignore, as you know. There is a difference between life on the spiritual and the physical planes, however, and that difference is that physical life can be destroyed. Life on the spiritual plane is quite different from life on the physical in that once it is generated within a person it never dies but goes on and on forever."

Jonathan stooped over to mend the fire before he continued. "Physical life is finite, meaning that it has definable limits: the day of our birth and the day of our death. Spiritual life is infinite and has no definable limits. Nothing can destroy it and nothing can kill it. No matter how hard I might try to smother it, now that I have been born by the Spirit of God, I cannot lose the new life He has given me. If I did smother it or turn my back on it, I would get to heaven but I do not want to sneak in by the back door, so to speak. If my Saviour loved me enough to die for me, I should be able to live fully for Him."

For a long moment the doctor gazed into the glowing coals. It was hard to say what had to be said. It meant either hurting his friend or failing his love. To him, there was no valid choice, for Margaret always came first. He squared his tired shoulders and asked, "No matter what the effect may be on her?"

Jonathan groaned and clasping his big hands about his knees, leaned toward his companion. "I see that I have failed to make you understand. I love Margaret with all my heart. She is as my very soul, a part of me, but if I do as you want me to do and abandon the call I hear from God, for her sake, I would again make myself the mainspring of my existence by choosing her instead of God."

The doctor's patience was wearing thin. The evening was nearly gone and he had accomplished nothing for Margaret's cause and in spite of himself he had to admit that what Jonathan said made sense, but he could hardly tell Margaret that. The conflict within him put an edge on his voice when he spoke. "There is a perfectly sensible explanation back of Margaret's hatred of religion and one that you should consider."

"I know. She is utterly against it because she believes that God failed her in not preserving her lamb, but I think that she was premature in forming an opinion of God. She *did* get away from the farm even without the money the lamb would have brought. I tried to show her that God might have sent the teacher in order to help her, but she would have none of it."

Nick frowned. "I cannot see that Margaret is too much to blame for the way she feels. After all, if I remember the Bible at all, it does say that Jesus promised to answer prayer."

"It certainly does, but you cannot expect to lift that verse out of its context and understand its true meaning." Picking up a Bible which lay on the table beside him, Jonathan turned quickly to the Sermon on the Mount. "Here it is in Matthew 7:7, but if you read the whole passage, which starts at Matthew 5:1, you will see that Jesus was preaching a sermon to His own disciples, who *already believed* in Him. Nowhere did He promise to hear the prayers of an unbeliever unless that unbeliever is asking Jesus to be his saviour. In fact, in another part of the Bible it says that the prayer of an unbeliever is an abomination to God. By her own admission, Margaret was not a true believer at that time."

"What do you mean by a *true* believer?"

"I mean a person who believes *all* that God has to say, not only parts of His Word that he happens to like personally. The Bible is full of the sin of man and the means that God took to forgive it, the blood His Son Jesus shed on the Cross."

Somewhat sullenly, the doctor said, "I do not see what blood has to do with it!" For a moment Nick sat in silence, irritated with himself that he had not been able to corner Jonathan successfully. Jonathan, not wishing to lose the doctor's interest, turned from gazing into the fire and decided to put the matter on a basis the physician could understand.

"Well, speaking of the shedding of blood, I remember your fear that Margaret might bleed to death when the twins were born and your remarking at the time that unfortunately there could be no birth without the shedding of blood. If this is true on a physical level, why should you question the same rule on a spiritual level?''

The doctor's quick mind instantly perceived that he was being put in a corner. He would have interrupted his friend, but Jonathan would not allow it. "God has a law that there could be no forgiveness of sin on His part without the shedding of blood. Therefore, in order for us to become reconciled to God, someone had to shed blood. Ordinary human blood was useless for it was contaminated by sin. The only person who lived life entirely without blemish or sin was Jesus Christ. Therefore, His blood was the only blood which would meet God's requirements.''

Nick thought that at last he had a point from which to argue, and he seized it eagerly. "Why should God make such a law?''

"Because God has every right to set up whatever standard He chooses in the spiritual realm. You have no right to question Him, because you do not know about spiritual life, not having been born again.'' His voice was gentle but firm; there was no inferred criticism in his tones. "Oh, Nick, it is so simple, if you would only see. The twins have Margaret's life principle within them because she is a human being and could, therefore, transfer to them that human life principle at birth. But only God can transfer the spiritual life principle. As a doctor you know that certain requirements have to be met before human birth can take place, which is also true of spiritual birth. God's requirements have to be met. You do not quibble at the requirements which generate human life. Why should you quibble at God's requirements for generating spiritual life? His requirements are very simple: that we recognize our true state as sinners wanting our own way, instead of His, and that we accept by faith the sacrifice His Son has made for us on the Cross as being the means of changing our hearts. The very minute we do those two things we become children of God and have within our spirits His life principle. But people frequently reject these requirements. That is what Margaret is doing.''

Failing in one direction, Nick took another. "You'll have to admit that part of Margaret's hatred of religion is due to the way in which she was treated by those who say they believe the Bible, her father and your mother.'' For a moment he wondered if he would draw blood with that remark, but Jonathan did not seem to be offended. Instead he nodded his head. It was evident that he accepted his mother's responsibility in influencing Margaret against religion.

"I know, and to be quite truthful I felt much the same way about mother."

"Whatever changed you?" The doctor's tone was sarcastic, but Jonathan refused to be baited.

"When God got hold of me, He showed me how unreasonable it was to ignore His claims just because a few people who had professed to have accepted them acted in an unchristian manner. What I was doing was pinning their failure on God and that is unjust because God would have changed them, had they allowed Him to."

"If He is so all powerful, then why didn't He?" asked the doctor.

"Because salvation and living to please God are matters of *choice*. People must make their own choice because God will not force anyone to believe in Him or to love Him. Margaret is choosing to reject God, and that is why she is so bitter and upset."

At that moment the two men heard Margaret's step on the porch. There was no time to argue further, but the doctor flung out one more tart question. "And, what do you propose to do about this unfortunate situation?"

Jonathan bent his head. "There is nothing I can do but pray," he replied softly.

Chapter Fourteen

It was Sunday afternoon and Margaret was putting the finishing touches on her daily letter to Charles Stillwell. She had a picture of the twins in front of her which she intended to enclose and she could not help smiling at the two little pictured faces. As she nibbled her pen and wondered what else she could add that might entertain and amuse the crippled man, she thought of the struggle she and Jonathan were having about this matter of religion and the smile left her face. That would give her plenty to write about, but somehow she could not quite bring herself to write her old employer about it. She still hoped that between her and Nick they would be able to show Jonathan the error of his ways. Nick was a good ally because Jonathan was fond of him.

He had not had much to say about his first encounter with her husband touching the matter, and she suspected that he had not come off as well as she had hoped, but probably that was because he had not had time to marshal his arguments. As she sat pondering the matter, Jonathan entered the room. He had had the children out for a walk and now he sent them to the kitchen to get their supper. Their parents could hear them chattering with the two servants as they ate their meal.

Jonathan sat down in a chair that was close to the small desk and crossing his long legs, addressed his wife. "When you are through with the pen and ink I would like to use them."

Margaret nodded but continued finishing her letter. When she had done so, she enclosed the pictures, sealed and stamped the letter and put it aside to be mailed. She did not attempt to hide her surprise at her husband's request, for Jonathan almost never wrote letters at home. She inquired curiously, "To whom are you writing?"

Jonathan looked up from arranging the writing equipment. "Mother," he said briefly.

The swift anger, which any mention of his mother brought forth in Margaret, welled up within her and she inquired with an edge on her voice, "In heaven's name, why?" To the best of her knowledge, Jonathan had not spoken of or written to his mother since they had walked out of her house with Sarah and Zach behind them.

Her husband ignored the sharpness of her tone and answered quietly, "To tell her about my conversion. I have thought for some time that I should do so. It would make her happy."

This was too much for Margaret and she flared, "Why should she be given that satisfaction and be made happy? What happiness has she ever been the means of giving you and me, I would like to know?"

Jonathan put down his pen and looked across at his wife with understanding in his eyes. "I know. That was how I felt about it at first, but I don't any longer."

His look of affection and the mildness of his manner completely won her and pushing aside the writing material she perched herself on his lap with the question, "Then why bother at this late date?"

His long arms went about her as he settled her more comfortably on his knees. She nestled her head on his shoulder and he stroked her soft hair with one hand. "Because I have been thinking the matter over and I have decided the resentment isn't very becoming in a Christian."

She jerked her head away from his touch and leaning it back against his shoulder looked up at him, rebellion in her stubborn look. "She doesn't deserve it!"

He nodded. "No, but neither do we deserve the grace of God."

She stirred against him restlessly. She hated to hear him talk like that. He looked deep into her eyes, his own pleading for understanding. "Don't you see, my darling, that it is wrong of me to remain silent out of spite?'

But Margaret wouldn't give an inch and she still insisted petulantly, "She doesn't deserve it!"

He nodded, "I know, but neither did I deserve my Lord's dying for me!"

Margaret said stubbornly, "I can't see what that has to do with it."

He sighed and she pushed her advantage. "I don't see that she deserves any consideration whatsoever after the way she acted. A fine Christian she is!"

"That is just it. Do you want me to be the kind of a Christian my mother is, small and spiteful and vindictive?"

Somewhat taken aback that he should admit to these traits in his mother so readily, Margaret had to confess rather ruefully, "Well, no, I suppose not, but then," she added bitterly, "I still do not see why you should bother with religion anyway. We have enough between us without that. You don't need it and neither do I."

He ignored her bitter words and tightened his arms about her. "Don't you see, my darling, that my mother and your father *believe* the right things? They just have not let their beliefs make any difference in their dispositions and they should have. It is because I want to be the kind of Christian Jesus wants me to be that I want to do this! He said that when we were slapped on one cheek we should turn the other. That is what I am trying to do to my mother, and I am not doing it for *her* sake, but for Christ's. When He was reviled He reviled not again, and that is the pattern I want to follow."

His beautiful deep voice ceased speaking. For a moment, Margaret was almost persuaded to accept his ideas by the very grandeur of his words, but then she remembered what she had been through at her mother-in-law's hands, and fury and resentment overcame her. She drew away from him to cry, "It isn't fair! It isn't fair! She doesn't deserve it. Oh, please, for my sake, don't tell her."

His troubled eyes sought hers. "You really mean that?"

Margaret nodded her head. "I do! Yes, I do!"

"But, Margaret, she is old and ill, and supposing she should die? Then I would feel very bad at not having told her, just for spite."

But Margaret would have none of it. "Nonsense, she isn't half as sick as she makes out to be! She just does that to get her own way. She pretended to be sick to make you go to theological school, and she did the same thing to get me there so she could insult me. You know she did." Tears of anger and resentment welled up in her eyes. "Don't you think that it is hard enough for for me to have you take the children and go downtown to that insignificant little church while I go all by myself uptown to Grace Church, without doing this to me, too?"

"But, darling, you are being as vindictive as mother by acting like this, don't you see that?"

"Well, I'm not a Christian, and I don't pretend to be one, and if I'm vindictive it is because I've been so badly treated that I've a right to feel as I do. If you really love me you will do as I wish about this."

Jonathan sighed. "Even though I am persuaded that it is the wrong thing to do?"

Tears of self-pity filled Margaret's eyes. "Your mother treated me very badly and said awful things about me and yet you want to act as if nothing had happened. Don't you think that it is hard enough having you persist in this matter of religion without adding that humiliation to it?"

Suddenly, it seemed terribly important to Margaret to get her own way about this letter. There was no reason why her hateful mother-in-law should not be made to pay for her sins. Margaret knew that one of the first questions the old woman would ask Jonathan, if relations were re-established, would be whether his wife had been converted. When he, in all honesty, would have to answer no, she would undoubtedly enjoy saying, "I told you so!" In her secret heart Margaret determined that, if she could help it, her hated mother-in-law wouldn't be given that opportunity, so she let her tears flow unimpeded.

Poor Jonathan was as agitated by the discussion as Margaret was.

Surely, it would not do any great harm to give in to his beloved wife. Perhaps later her heart would soften and she would relent. The sense of her wrongs was still fresh in her mind. His mother had been very cutting when she had tried to force him to give up the girl he had married. He, too, had been full of bitter resentment because of the things she had said, but when he had submitted the matter to God, some of the bitterness had gone out of him. His viewpoint had changed because he was now trying to let God motivate his reactions but Margaret's had not, and she could not be blamed for that. If this thing meant so much to her, perhaps he should yield.

He took his handkerchief out of his pocket and dried her eyes with it gently, as he conceded the point. "All right, darling, I'll promise not to write until you tell me I may, if you will only stop crying. You wrench my heart with your tears. I know that mother doesn't deserve to know about my conversion, but paying people back in their own coin sometimes turns into a boomerang and hits the person who intended to hurt. It seems to me that the only safe way is to obey God and turn the other cheek, but that command applies only to me as a believer and not to you, so we will let the matter rest for awhile."

Margaret, blowing her small nose vigorously on his big handkerchief, hardly listened to his words, so pleased was she to get her own way. He had not entirely escaped her if he would give in on this. Maybe after a while he would give up his other crazy religious notions, too, if she did not make too much of them. As she leaned back against his shoulder she thought to herself triumphantly, "There, that will fix her! She needn't think that she can malign me and get away with it! I'll make her pay for every mean thing she said! Even if Jonathan does want to forgive her, I won't, and if it's the last thing I do, somehow I'll keep him from doing so!"

Dr. Nicholas Shelby Thorpe stepped out the back door of his office and started on foot for the Wellfleet's. No one but his office nurse and his coachman knew how often he slipped through several back alleys to the back garden gate of the little house on River Street. Both of these old and trusted servants occasionally shook their heads at one another when it became necessary to fetch him for an emergency, but they spoke about the matter to no one.

Today, the doctor's long legs covered the ground between his office and her house in even a shorter time than usual. If he could manage it, he tried to see Margaret every day, if only for a moment, just to assure himself that all was well with her. He had been tied up for several days by a patient with a bad case of pneumonia and then a difficult and prolonged confinement, and now he could hardly wait for a sight of her.

When he arrived, Margaret was in the dining room hanging some new curtains she had just finished sewing. She was up on a ladder standing on her tiptoes to reach the rod above her head. He crossed the room with three strides and lifted her down bodily. Staring down at her angrily as he held her in his arms he tried to ignore the quickening of his heart and pulse. "You little idiot! What are you trying to do? Kill yourself or maybe cripple yourself for life? Haven't you given me enough trouble without adding a broken back or some cracked ribs to it?"

Margaret put up a small hand and stroked his cheek, laughing at his fury. "Don't be cross, Nick. It makes Zach dizzy to get up on a ladder and I wanted to see how the curtains would look. I just finished them."

He set her hastily on her feet. "Here, give them to me. I'll hang them for you, but I don't want you trying a trick like that again."

She stood off and watched him and when he had finished, she regarded her handiwork critically. "They are not as elegant as Mrs. Curtis's new curtains, but they suit the room."

He was not looking at the curtains, but at her. "What is so wonderful about Mrs. Curtis's curtains?"

"They are brocaded velvet and very elegant, and when my ship comes in I shall have some just like them. Of course, they would not be very suitable for this little cottage, so I would have to have a house to hang them in, a big lovely house on the hill."

His anger vanished as it always did under her light touch and he teased, "And when will that be?"

She pulled a fold of the curtain more to her liking and said absently, "That tie back could be a little shorter," and then in answer to his question, "Some sweet and happy day. Oh, Nick, do you know what I shall do when I am rich? I shall go to New York and stay at the Waldorf Astoria and buy every single thing that I see in the shops that appeals to me and walk down Fifth Avenue every evening in a new dress and buy curtains for the whole house all at once! The house on the hill, of course!" She laughed at him over her shoulder as she put away her sewing equipment and he smiled back, wishing with all his heart that he could give her her heart's desire.

He had the means, but he could not help but wonder if she would get the pleasure she anticipated out of them were any man but Jonathan to supply them. She wanted a house on the hill in the fashionable part of town and all that went with it, but she wanted Jonathan to provide it for her. Despair filled his soul because he could do nothing.

They went into the small living room and Margaret picked up the needlepoint she was working on. As she commenced to sew she said without looking up, "I want you to do something for me. Will you?"

He sat down opposite her. "Do you have to ask?"

She glanced across at him and smiled. "You really are such a dear, Nick. You ought to find some nice girl and marry her. You are much too nice to be running around loose." He made no comment so she continued gaily, "But, then what would I do?"

Somewhat grimly he asked, "Let's get down to cases. What is it you want?"

She snipped off a length of thread, threaded her needle, and commenced to sew again, before she answered him. "It's about Jonathan!"

It would be, thought the doctor, and groaned inwardly. In spite of his dereliction, Jonathan was still the center and circumference of her life.

"He is determined to join that awful little church and I've got to stop him somehow. They have had him on probation for six months. Imagine! They are so bigoted and old-fashioned that they do not allow their members to dance or go to the theater or play cards and they won't admit anyone to membership if they do those things. The six months is nearly up and he has passed muster so far, but I've got to do something that will make them think he has disobeyed their precepts!"

Nick crossed his long legs and regarded the toe of one well-shined boot. "And what do you propose to do? You can't blindfold Jonathan and lead him to McQuinty's tavern and let them see him there."

She looked up eagerly, forgetful for the moment of her sewing. "No, but I think I can persuade him to go to the Worden's with me next week. We have been invited. Mrs. Wordon is a member of Grace Church and she has been very nice to me."

"But they are giving a ball!"

"I know, but Jonathan doesn't, and if you keep your mouth shut, he won't. He never reads the society news in the paper, and I won't let him see the invitation. It isn't likely that the people he comes in contact with at the sail loft would enlighten him, for they will not have been invited."

"But when you get him there, what will you accomplish? You can't force him into dancing with you."

Her eyes sparkled. "I'll accomplish plenty! An account of the affair and a list of the guests will be published in the morning paper and when those narrow-minded church people read about it, they will refuse to accept him! It won't really matter then whether he dances or not!"

"Why do you call them narrow-minded? You really know nothing about them. They may be quite the opposite."

"I don't care what they are!" cried Margaret in exasperation. "I don't like them."

But Nick would not quarrel with her. "It doesn't matter. Don't be cross. I wasn't planning to attend the Worden's ball anyway."

"Oh, but you must! I'll need your moral support. Please, Nick, don't be difficult. I don't know what else to do. He won't listen to reason, but perhaps if they turn him down simply because he went to a ball without even trying to discover whether he was actually dancing or not, it will open his eyes to what they really are! Then he may be willing to give it all up. It is bad enough for him to insist upon attending there himself, but to drag the children along with him is more than I can stand. I don't want them brought up in such an atmosphere. They are getting such queer ideas as it is. The other day Timmie lost his temper with Zach over some trifle and do you know what he did? He went to him and apologized and told him that he had acted just like the devil and he was sorry. Imagine a child his age even thinking such a thing. When I asked him why he said what he did, he told me that his Sunday school teacher told him that he was born a child of the devil and that everytime he lost his temper he was serving the devil."

Nick considered the tip of the letter opener he had picked up intently for a moment before he spoke. He did not want Margaret upset and excited in this way, but on the other hand he felt that in all fairness to Jonathan he should try to make her see that she was making a mountain out of a molehill. Putting down the letter opener he leaned toward her. "I cannot say that I think it is so dreadful for the child to apologize to a servant. In fact it is a good thing. In the future he may come to have some consideration for the feelings of others just because of this experience. It certainly cannot hurt him any."

But Margaret would have none of it. "Oh, Nick, why are you so perverse today? That is only beggaring the issue. The point is that I do not want him to think of himself as a child of the devil. Why should he? He is an utter darling."

"Don't you think that you put undue stress on that phase 'a child of the devil'? Perhaps he has no real idea of its meaning."

"Oh, but he has! I talked to Jonathan about it and do you know what he said? He said that the child was right and that that was exactly how every child was born according to the Scriptures and that was why it was necessary for them to be born anew in order to become children of God! He is always talking about the new birth and I hate it! Didn't I have enough trouble with the twins first birth, without having to be concerned about a second? Such talk drives me frantic!"

Nick tried to present the best side of the picture. "Well, good manners will help, and personally I think apologizing for one's inconsideration is one of the foundations of good manners."

She looked across at him reproachfully. "It isn't that idea I object to so violently, and you know it. It's this 'children of the devil' business. When I rebuked Tim for using such an expression as 'acting like the devil,' he said he was sorry, but for a child of God to act as he had was certainly acting the way the devil wanted him to act, and not the way God did. I was so exasperated. You see, he has already picked up Jonathan's expressions and he considers himself a child of God."

"I cannot see that it can do him any harm."

"It will do him plenty of harm if he goes about talking in such an insane manner. People will think he is crazy. It was perfectly natural for him to have lost his temper. He has the same quick temper his father used to have. It goes with red hair. What I want is to get him away from that church before he picks up any more odd expressions. I want him to be normal and young and irresponsible like other children and not have his head filled with such silly ideas."

"And you think you can accomplish this by tricking Jonathan into going to the ball? I can't say I like the idea very much."

Margaret rolled up her work with her face set. "Very well. If you won't help me, I'll have to chance it on my own. I won't go on the way things are. We are a house divided against itself, and it can't continue. One of us will have to give in." Tears filled her gray eyes. "I am fighting for the children as well as myself. I was hoping that you would understand, but if you don't, I'll just have to get along without your help."

Her tears accomplished what no amount of argument could, and in a moment's time. He capitulated at once. "I'll do what you want. You know I will, even though I do not approve of the method. Don't cry, Margaret. I beg of you, don't cry, my dear. Here, take my handkerchief. Now, tell me just what you want me to do."

Margaret Wellfleet stood in front of the pier glass in the corner of her bedroom and, lifting herself on her tiptoes, turned herself about so that she could get the full effect of her new gown. She had made it herself, but there was nothing homemade-looking about it, she decided triumphantly. The material was a rich wine-colored moire taffeta and it was fashioned with an off-the-shoulder effect and a bouffant skirt which were very becoming. The unwonted excitement of going out to an evening festivity accompanied by two handsome men had brought high color into her usually pale cheeks and her gray eyes sparkled with anticipation. Jonathan might not be looking forward to the evening, but *she* was going to have the time of her life!

She had been practicing dance steps with Nick and she was not worried about acquitting herself acceptably on that score. She went to her dressing table and opened the velvet boxes lying beside her gloves. At Christmas, Charles Stillwell had sent her a complete set of garnet jewelry and she had chosen the color of her dress to go with them. She snapped the cases open and gazed admiringly down at the necklace, earrings, brooch, ring, bracelets, and combs which they contained. They were extremely handsome and she felt with a lift of her heart that when she had adorned herself with them she would be as charmingly and appropriately dressed as any other woman at the ball.

This was the first big party she had attended in the city and she was anxious to make a good impression. The Worden home was the kind of house she wanted to be received in and to have her children received in later on, and it was to that end that she was so anxious to leave their run-down neighborhood and move up on the hill where people like the Wordens lived. If only Jonathan wasn't so unreasonable he would see that all the best people, like the Wordens, attended Grace Church. But she wouldn't spoil the evening by thinking about that now. She picked up the combs and fastened them to her gleaming black braids. As she sat admiring the effect, the door was pushed stealthily open and two small heads appeared in the aperture. She nodded and her two children burst into the room.

They rushed over to the dressing-table, entranced with what they saw. Tim stood respectfully by her side, his eyes full of admiration, but small Peggy commenced to pat the lustrous material of her mother's gown. Margaret pulled away in irritation. Why did the child always have to touch everything? She would make her feel untidy. Margaret did not like to admit how excessively this small daughter of hers annoyed her. The child had a fluttering way of using her little hands which reminded her mother of Phoebe and she was beginning to display a nervous giggle similar to the one she had found so annoying in her husband's sister. At times, Margaret wondered in despair if the child was going to grow into the same type of silly female as her aunt. The little girl did not have the manual dexterity which Tim had, and she was always dropping things or breaking them. Her mother had to repress an impulse to box her ears a dozen times a day for her clumsiness. Peggy was a lighthearted little thing and flitted from one thing to another in rapid succession without paying proper attention to anything she did.

Margaret was vaguely aware that Jonathan had a special place in his heart for his daughter, but she felt that he was far too tolerant of her clumsiness and that she would never grow out of it if he coddled her so. As she impatiently removed the small, not-too-clean hands from her gown, she glanced at her sturdy young son and thought what a joy and comfort he was to her. He had not touched anything. He seemed to realize without being told that when she was all dressed up she did not want to be mussed and disarrayed at the last minute. His eyes, so like his father's, were full of admiration. "You look very beautiful, mother. You have a shining look. Are you happy?"

Swiftly she reached out and putting her arm about him drew him to her. She had no thought mussing her gown. It was a pleasure to her just to feel his touch. She answered him gaily, "Very, darling. We are going to a party and I love parties."

She released him and picking up the necklace, unfastened the clasp. Peggy, who had been standing in crestfallen silence, immediately begged to be allowed to put it on for her. Trying to keep the irritation out of her voice, Margaret protested, "No, Peggy. Your hands are sticky."

Seeing the disappointment in his sister's eyes, Tim intervened, "I'll take her to the bathroom and wash them for her, mother."

"Oh, very well," said his mother resignedly, thinking to herself that it was a good thing she had allowed plenty of time.

While the children were gone, Margaret fastened the dangling earrings into her ears and noted the effect with satisfaction. She had been afraid that she was too small to wear them, but her neck was long and slender and they looked very well. She pinned the brooch to the front of her gown, clipped the bracelets about her slender arms, put the ring on the fourth finger of her right hand and sat admiring the total effect while she waited for the children to return.

Once more the children burst into the room and Jonathan was right behind them. He was very handsome in his formal attire. The deep black and spotless white were a perfect foil for his thick auburn hair. Her heart lifted and swelled as she looked at him, and for the thousandth time she thought rebelliously that they would be the happiest couple in the city if only it were not for the religious bug that he had allowed to bite him. Peggy rushed up to the dressing table and picking up the garnet necklace let it slip through her fingers. Margaret uttered an exclamation of annoyance and it was all she could do to refrain from slapping the child. Peggy's face fell and she appeared about to burst into tears, but her father was across the room in a flash and had the necklace in his hands. He consoled Margaret and comforted the child at the same time. "It's not hurt, mother.

Now, Peg-top, let me help you fasten it. We must be sure that it is secure so that it won't get lost. Here, you hold it about mother's neck, while I fasten it. There, doesn't that look lovely?"

Margaret repressed a little shudder which involuntarily came over her at the touch of the child's small damp fingers against her flesh. She had evidently been in such a hurry that she had used cold water to wash them. Peggy's lips had stopped trembling at her father's kindly tone and touch, and she now stood back and gazed at her mother with eyes so full of worship that Margaret had the grace to feel ashamed. She bent toward the child.

"You may kiss me, just once, but don't muss my hair."

When Peggy had timidly complied, Jonathan said, "Now, we are all agreed that mother will be the belle of the ball." Margaret look up at him sharply. As far as he knew this was to be a reception. What had he found out? But, now, he was laughing with the children. He had only used a familiar expression and meant nothing by it. Margaret drew a sigh of relief.

Jonathan took each child by the hand, "Let's go downstairs and I will tell you a Bible story there. I think I just heard Uncle Nick come in. He is going with us so you may say good night to him when we leave."

The children accompanied him down the stairs and Margaret picked up her gloves and cloak and followed them. Jonathan never asked her to listen to his nightly Bible story but she was all ready and had nothing else to do. Besides, she would like to get Nick's reaction.

When she entered the small living room, Jonathan was already settled in the Boston rocker with one child on his lap and the other close beside him. It was Peggy, of course, who was in his lap. She was always climbing all over him. He did not seem to realize that she might muss his shirt front. Nick rose at once and taking Margaret's things made room for her beside him on the love seat. Jonathan looked up and tried to hide his surprise with a smile. This was the first time Margaret had ever come to listen to what he taught the children. Tim leaned against his father and he put his long arm about him holding him close. Peggy put up a small hand and stroked her father's cheek lovingly. Instead of brushing it away impatiently, as her mother would have done, he took a second to kiss it before he commenced his story.

"Tonight, I thought that I would tell you about the greatest love story ever written."

Peggy interrupted with, "Is it a Bible story, Daddy?" Margaret frowned at her. Interrupting was one of the child's most vexing habits.

Jonathan nodded, displaying no annoyance. "Yes, darling, and it is about a man who loved a woman more than he did God. The man's name was Adam and the woman he loved so much was Eve."

Tim spoke up, his eyes glowing, "I remember them, Daddy. They were the first people God made."

Again Jonathan nodded. "That is right, and they lived in a very beautiful place called the Garden of Eden. They were very, very happy because they loved one another and God came to the garden and paid them a visit every day."

Peggy interrupted a second time. "Did He talk to them the way you do to us, Daddy?"

Jonathan looked lovingly at his small daughter. "Yes, He did and He was very good to them. He had put all kinds of beautiful trees in the garden and He told them they could eat of the fruit of any of the trees they wanted except for one particular tree. Of that tree they must not eat. The name of that tree was the Tree of the Knowledge of Good and Evil and the reason God did not want them to eat of it was that up until that time they had known only good, and if they disobeyed God and ate what He said not to, they would know evil, too. God wanted to spare them that knowledge and if they had obeyed Him, they would never have known what *evil* is."

"What's evil, Daddy?" asked Peggy.

"*Evil* is the inner drive which makes strong people take advantage of the weak; which causes a person to think of his own needs above those of others; which gives energy to lie and cheat to get one's own way; which blinds the heart to God's truth. It is disease, and fear, and death."

Nick looked at Margaret, but she refused to meet his glance. He thought grimly within himself, "That rather puts us in our place for the job we are going to do tonight."

As for Margaret, she lifted her chin and ignoring the implication of the words, thought irritably that it was too much to expect children to understand that kind of talk.

Jonathan continued, "God had told Adam and Eve that if they ate of the forbidden tree they would die. You remember when your canary died? He couldn't eat or sing or fly any more and we had to bury him in the garden because he could no longer respond to us as he once had. Well, God was trying to tell Adam and Eve that if they disobeyed Him they would not be able to respond to Him any more, that He could not walk with them or talk with them or be close to them any more. For a while they did just as God told them and left that certain tree alone. But then the devil decided to get Adam and Eve to disobey God because if they did, then he could step in and take over. As long as Adam and Eve refused to disobey God, the devil was helpless, but the minute they disobeyed, he could use them for his own evil purposes.

"So what do you suppose the devil did? He got into the garden and one day, finding Eve alone, he started to talk to her. He asked her what God had told her about the forbidden tree and she told him that God had said that if she ate of it she would die. But the devil said that God was a liar and that she would *not* die. Now, she had a choice to make. She could believe either God or the devil, but she could not believe both of them. The opportunity to choose between God and His truth, and the devil who is the author of all lies, has been given to every person who has lived since then."

Peggy was impatient to get on with the story. "What happened next, Daddy?" she asked eagerly.

"I wish that I could tell you that Eve chose to believe God, but she didn't. She believed the devil and picked some of the fruit of the forbidden tree and ate it. Then she told her husband what she had done and offered him some. Now Adam was not fooled by the devil's lie. He knew that if God said they would die, they would die. But he loved Eve very much and he knew that unless he ate of the fruit, too, Eve would have to die and leave him. He did not want this to happen. On the other hand, if he ate the fruit he would have to leave God. His choice was not between God and the devil, it was between God and the woman. What did he want most? To walk and talk with God everyday, or to be with Eve? He could disobey God to be with the woman he loved, or he could obey God and be left alone with Him in the garden."

Jonathan ceased speaking and for a moment there was silence in the small room. The children were interested only in the story but each one of the adults was making the application to his own heart. Margaret thought bitterly, "Adam chose what Eve wanted, but Jonathan won't choose what I want." Jonathan looked down at Peggy's dark hair, so like in color and texture to that of her mother's, and thought, "If I give in to Margaret, I will lose contact with God, like Adam. No, Jesus paid too big a price for my salvation for me to deny Him." And Nick, his eyes on Margaret's rebellious face, thought, "That is the essential difference between Jonathan and me. Jonathan is willing to choose God, but I would have chosen Margaret — if only God had given me the chance!"

Peggy was bouncing with excitement by this time. "Which did he choose, Daddy? Which did he choose?"

Jonathan came back to his story. "He chose Eve. The woman meant more to him than God."

Peggy let out a small sound. Her mother thought, with rancor in her soul, that unlike Adam, Jonathan thought more of God than he did of her, and felt for a minute as if her husband had struck her a sudden blow.

Tim said softly, "Maybe he was sorry later."

Jonathan nodded. "I am afraid he was, son, but it was too late to do anything about it, for he never saw God face to face again as long as he lived upon this earth. It was a big price to pay."

His deep voice fell silent. The child in his arms lay quiet against his shoulder. He bent and kissed the silky tresses to hide the tightening in his throat. The child standing beside him slipped his arm up about his father's neck and laid his burnished head on his shoulder. There was something inexpressively comforting in the little lad's clasp and the man's heart lifted. All was not yet lost. God was still in His heaven and if he personally could do nothing with Margaret to make her see the truth, God was not limited. He would be faithful to draw her to Himself, and then they could be together once again.

Nick, his troubled eyes going from Jonathan's bent head to Margaret's erect sullenness as she sat beside him, thought he had better put an end to this painful scene. "Aren't you children going to kiss Uncle Nick good night?" he asked with what lightness he could muster and hoped within himself that this would make Margaret abandon her plans for the evening. But he had reckoned without her fierce pride. Now, more than ever, she felt that she must show Jonathan how wrong he was.

Rising to her feet, she said coldly, "It is time that the children were in bed and that we were going. Please call Sarah, Nick, and tell her to have Zach bring the carriage around."

Chapter Fifteen

Dr. Thorpe sat in front of a roaring fire in his big living room, a frown upon his face. He lived alone in one of the largest and handsomest houses on the hill, a house which he had inherited from his father. Being the most eligible bachelor in the city, he could have had the house full of guests anytime he chose, but he seldom entertained and he refused more invitations than he accepted. His housekeeper, a dour woman but an efficient manager, had bade him good night a few minutes before and had departed to some affair of her own and the other servants were attending a funeral. There was no one to bother him and he could spend a quiet and relaxed evening by himself, but he was neither quiet or relaxed. Instead, the usual struggle was going on inside him. It was Wednesday evening, Jonathan's prayer meeting night, and Margaret was sure to be home alone. He wanted desperately to spend the evening with her and was thoroughly ashamed of himself because he knew that no matter how much he might argue with himself, he would eventually give in and depart for the little house on River Street. Tired as he was, he almost wished that a call would come in which would prevent him from fulfilling his desire. As he sat gazing at the leaping flames, his thoughts went back over the last few years. Margaret's nefarious little scheme about the ball had worked only too well, and Jonathan's application for membership in the church he had wished to join had been refused because of it.

Margaret had been delighted with her success, but the doctor had been sick with shame at the part he had played in the affair. He knew perfectly well that Margaret would never have been able to carry out her plan without his help. Had he refused to teach her to dance, she would have been forced into abandoning the whole thing, but he had not refused. The very thought of having his arms about her, even in a dance, had been too much for him and he had allowed her to persuade him into aiding her. His trouble, he reflected bitterly, was that while he loved Jonathan as he loved no other man of his acquaintance, he was *in love* with Margaret. That left him utterly at her mercy when he was near her. When he had learned of the results of their chicanery, he had been bitterly ashamed. He knew that if he did not act while his shame was still strong he never would, so going to a patient of his, an elder in the church Jonathan wanted to join, he informed him that he had been at the ball and that while Jonathan Wellfleet had attended the affair, he had spent the entire time discussing politics and religion with his host.

Shortly afterwards, Nick had closed his office, packed his bag, and departed for Europe to study for three years. During that period he had heard frequently from both Jonathan and Mar-Margaret. He should never have left a forwarding address, but he had not had the moral courage to cut himself off entirely from her. As time progressed, Jonathan's letters revealed his deepening desire to become a missionary and Margaret's letters, her utter rebellion and fury at such an idea. The struggle had gone on for some months, but finally Margaret had won. She had taken to her bed and been, according to Jonathan, quite ill, and he had capitulated. The doctor could not help wondering if she had become so desperate that she had descended to using her despised mother-in-law's method of getting her own way. He excused her in his own thinking by acknowledging that she was so small and weak physically that she had to use whatever method she could.

A thousand times during those years the doctor had determined to establish his practice in some other city when his studies were completed, but when the time came to return, he found himself buying a ticket for the city where he had been born and brought up. After his return, he had tried to keep away from the little house on River Street, except when both Jonathan and Margaret were there, but he soon found that they were leading two separate lives. Jonathan had a regular schedule of events at his church which did not coincide with the multitudinous social activities in which Margaret involved herself. This made things both easier and harder for Nick: easier because he might see more of Margaret by accepting the numerous invitations to parties to which she was also invited, and harder because he would not allow himself to do so. He had to admit to himself that seeing her in large groups did not interest him anyway. It was seeing her alone and listening to her and watching the quick change of expressions on the small heart-shaped face he loved so dearly that appealed to him. Besides, he loved her too much to compromise her and he had been very careful to see that their names were not linked in any way.

"I've kept away from her for weeks," he told himself in justification for the action he knew he was going to take as he arose, banked the fire and went in search of his overcoat.

When Margaret heard the doctor's step on the porch, she ran to open the door and welcome him. She had been wanting to see him, for she had wonderful news to tell him. As she stood in the doorway with the light from the hallway streaming over her, he saw that she shone with happiness. His heart lifted as it always did at the sight of her, but tonight it leapt in his breast and he had to resist an overwhelming impulse to take her in his arms and smother the small glowing face with kisses.

Instead, he bent to remove his rubbers so that she would not see the expression on his face. As she drew him in by the fire, he managed to remark gaily, "Well, shiny-eyes, what has come over you? You look as if a candle had been lighted inside you."

"Oh, Nick, the most wonderful thing has happened!" Her heart-shaped face was wreathed in smiles as she looked up at him. "I could hardly wait to see you to tell you about it. If you hadn't come soon, I would have sent Zach with a note to ask you to come."

He drew forward her low rocker and held it until she seated herself. If he were to give her his complete attention he must not be too near her. He then took his accustomed place on the love seat opposite, where he could watch her undisturbed. She was too excited to pick up her work. She sat in the low chair, looking like a little girl at her first party, her hands folded demurely in her lap and her small feet planted squarely on the floor. The sight of her filled the empty places in his aching heart, but he covered his feelings with their time-honored jest. "Don't tell me that your ship has come in?"

She laughed gaily, "It hasn't docked yet, but I see it coming!"

"Well, well, has somebody died and left you a fortune?" Then, thinking of Charles Stillwell, he could have bitten his tongue for the crudeness of his remark, but, surely, he reasoned, she would not be so happy over a thing like that even if it did bring her what she wanted so badly, a house on the hill and all that went with it, but she was too excited to notice.

"No, but Jonathan has invented something which may get us the money we need to buy the things I want. And what is more he has sold it already and the thousand dollars he got for it is in the bank."

Nick laughed across at her, "Whoa there, Maggie! You're going too fast for me! What did Jonathan invent and to whom did he sell it?" Sometimes, when his heart was particularly sore because all her attention was centered on her husband, he called her Maggie because he knew she hated it. Invariably she would give him some attention by frowning at him or scolding him for using that hated nickname, but tonight she was so happy that she did not.

She went blithely on, her thoughts entirely centered upon her good fortune. "I don't understand much about the invention except that it has something to do with splicing steel cable. When he got it done he sold it to Mr. Cuyler, a member of his church. Mr. Cuyler is going to start manufacturing it right away and they are to share the profits. Jonathan supplied the invention and Mr. Cuyler, the money. Jonathan thinks there will be a gold mine in it, for no one has so far succeeded in perfecting anything that nearly approximates it in efficiency. I am so excited that I can hardly sit still. Just think what this means, Nick. At last, at long last, I can have the things I have wanted for so long!"

Nick frowned. He wished that Jonathan had come to him with his invention. He had more money than he knew what to do with and he would have been glad to have provided the necessary backing.

"What does Jonathan know about this Cuyler?"

"Nothing, except that he professes to be a Christian and you know Jonathan! That is enough for him!"

"When are they to start manufacturing?"

"Right away. They had already located an old factory building down at the south end and they will start as soon as it is equipped. I'm so happy that I could almost burst!"

He teased, "I suppose you have already picked out the new house?"

"Well, I have been looking around on the hill," she admitted, dimpling.

He laughed aloud. "And I suppose you have it nearly furnished, in your mind's eye."

"It's an inexpensive way of having fun," she defended herself.

Nick said gently, "It certainly is. You're very happy about this, aren't you?"

"Oh, yes," her gray eyes glowed, "and a little ashamed!"

He scowled, "Why, ashamed?"

She hesitated a moment, as if undecided whether or not to tell him, then she said, "Ashamed because I was beginning to wonder whether Jonathan really loved me the way he used to. He has been so stubborn and persistent about this religion of his and nothing would make him give it up. While you were away, I had such a terrible struggle to keep him from going to the mission field. It has seemed to me, sometimes, that God is all he thinks about. But now I know that he sometimes thinks of me or he wouldn't have spent the time he did perfecting this."

She sat looking down at her hands, gathering courage to go on with her revelation and a great pity welled up within the doctor's heart, not for the woman sitting opposite him, much as he loved her, but for the man whose heart was set on preaching the Gospel while his hands were kept busy splicing cable, in order to provide for the woman he loved things for which he personally cared not one whit.

A log fell apart in the grate sending up a burst of flame as Margaret continued slowly, "You do not know how hard it has been, Nick. I do love him very much and ever since he was bitten by this religious bug I have been so worried that he was growing to care more for that part of his life than for me. You remember the night he told the children the story about Adam and Eve?

173

That night I felt as if he had stuck a knife in my heart." She blinked her lashes rapidly to force back her tears, but two crystal drops crept down her cheeks and fell on her folded hands.

But Nick could not bear the sight of her tears. "Here, here, what is all this? When I came in, you were so full of happiness you were nearly bubbling over and now you are in tears! What a little chameleon you are! If this is the effect I have on you perhaps I had better leave."

Margaret shook her head. "No, please don't go. It is such a relief to talk this out with someone. Ever since Jonathan got converted," she made a little grimace with her mouth as she used the word, "I've had a feeling that I loved him a lot more than he loved me and it hurts to feel that way."

Poor Nick knew only too well what she was talking about, but he did not enlighten her as to that fact. Instead he said gently, "No two people ever seem to care for one another with the same degree of intensity. It seems that there is always one who cares more than the other."

"But, it wasn't like that when we were first married," she protested. "It is this religious thing that has come between us. I can't help but feel that if he really loved me and cared about how I felt, he would give it up."

"Isn't that a little unreasonable of you?" the doctor asked out of his inner hurt. "If you love him more than he loves you, why don't you try to get his viewpoint on the matter?"

She glanced across at him reproachfully. "You know perfectly well that it is as much for his sake and the children's as my own that I want this. I want security for them and a place in the community for him. Is that too much to ask?" Nick was silent and she continued, "I have seen what religion can do to people. It made my father small and mean and hard and it made Jonathan's mother cold and underhanded and revengeful. One of the reasons I hate it is because I am afraid of what it will do to him."

"Have you noticed any of these things since he became interested in religion?"

"Well, no," she admitted reluctantly, "but it has changed him toward me and that is all that matters. I must admit that he doesn't lose his temper as he used to and he is much quieter."

The doctor could not help smiling. These were not the ordinary reasons given to him by a complaining wife. Usually they were the other way around. "Did it ever occur to you," he asked her, "that the traits you dislike so in your father and his mother may have been in them and a part of their personality, irrespective of any religious experience they may have had?"

His question made her defiant. "Well, if they were, I think that their much vaunted religion should have eradicated them."

"But, Maggie, you aren't very consistent. That is exactly what you were objecting to about religion a minute ago! Most people would say that controlling one's temper was a decided improvement."

Margaret's fine black brows drew together in a scowl. She did not quite know how to answer that, so she took refuge in a rebuke. "How many times do I have to tell you not to call me Maggie?"

He ignored it and continued, "Besides I have had quite good evidence just lately that Jonathan is no plaster saint."

"You have?" she asked eagerly. "How?"

"You probably won't like it if I tell you. Are you sure that you want to know?"

Margaret was aggravated. "Nicholas Thorpe, you are the most annoying man! First you infuriate me by calling me Maggie and then you tease me by not telling me something I really want to know."

Nick grinned. He could take anything from her but tears and if by provoking her he could raise her ire sufficiently to make her forget her reasons for shedding them it was perfectly all right with him. "Do you know anything about this class that Jonathan holds so much store by?"

"No. We don't talk about religion when it can be avoided."

"Do you know what this class does?"

Margaret frowned. What on earth was Nick getting at? "No, and I don't particularly care."

"I'm afraid you will when I tell you." Nick began to wish that he had not gotten himself into this. "They have been conducting street meetings."

She uttered one word, "Where?"

"In the slums."

Her relief was evident. At least her husband was not making a fool of himself in the part of town which her friends frequented. "Who does the speaking?"

"Jonathan, and let me tell you he is good at it. He has a real gift for it."

"You've heard him?"

He looked rather sheepish. "Yes, several times."

"What kind of people listen to him?"

"Oh, the usual riffraff. There are a lot of saloons down that way. The saloon keepers are beginning to complain."

"Why?"

"Because when he starts to speak, men and women listen to him and they don't patronize the saloons."

Her small mouth was set. "When you started all this you were going to tell me something. What was it?"

"It was about Jonathan's temper. The saloon keepers sent out a man to heckle him the other night and he knocked him down."

The sombre expression left Margaret's face. "He did?" she asked eagerly. "What happened then?"

The doctor wished that she had not asked that question. "He commandeered my buggy to take the man to my office. He was quite drunk."

"And?"

"We sobered him up and Jonathan started to talk to him. When he found out that the man was hungry he sent out and got a meal and watched him eat it. He acted as if he hadn't seen food in days. He was a big Irishman by the name of O'Reilly and he certainly could eat! When he had had all he could hold he became tractable as a lamb and magnanimously offered to listen to anything Jonathan had to say."

"Don't tell me Jonathan wanted to preach to him after all that?"

"He not only wanted to, but he did."

"And what effect did it have on the man?" asked Margaret, her lip curling.

"A good deal. He was converted!"

Margaret drew in her breath. This was terrible. It would only whet Jonathan's appetite for more. How on earth was she to explain such eccentricities to her friends, were they to find out? It was bad enough for him to get converted himself, but to go out and preach was unendurable.

Watching her facial expressions anxiously, Nick went on. "Jonathan let him stay down at the loft and O'Reilly hasn't touched any liquor since." His words cut through Margaret's bitter thoughts like a hot knife through butter. Suddenly she felt

176

very tired. All the joy and pleasure she had felt earlier in the evening left her. What was the use of trying to get ahead when Jonathan undid everything she tried to do? People couldn't be expected to accept a man socially who went around preaching to drunkards. She felt as if the bottom had dropped out of everything.

Nick reached over and put one of his big hands over hers. "You mustn't take it so hard, my dear. No great harm has been done. The people you know will probably never contact O'Reilly or any of the other people Jonathan preaches to on the other side of the tracks." And then, as her face did not brighten he continued, "I thought that I had better tell you before somebody else did."

"There, you see," she said triumphantly, "you say none of my friends will find out about it, but yet you think you should tell me about it just in case they might! Oh, Nick, Nick! How can he do it? A Harvard graduate, with good looks and education and background? Whatever possesses him? How can he so demean himself?"

Nick withdrew his hand. As always her concern was only for her husband. "He doesn't consider what he calls preaching the Gospel demeaning," he said stiffly. "That is the only explanation I can give you."

In her heart Margaret was thinking how all this would please his mother were she ever to learn of it and she resolved that never, never as long as she was able to keep Jonathan from writing her, would she give her nasty, hateful, mother-in-law such a chance to gloat. Aloud, she said wearily, "I guess there is nothing to be done about it, so I might as well get to bed and get some sleep."

She rose, but the doctor would not leave her in such a mood. He was beside her in a moment, "You mustn't take it so hard. Perhaps it is only a passing phase."

"Liar," he told his own heart.

She looked up at him in despair. "You know Jonathan better than that," she said reproachfully.

His dark face was full of concern. As much as he longed to comfort her, he did not know how to go about it. They walked to the door. Spent with her emotions and utterly weary from the strife within herself, Margaret leaned against the door jamb with a sigh. "You are good to me, Nick, and I would rather hear it from you than an outsider. At least now I can armor myself against it."

This was too much for poor Nick. In an instant he had her in his arms and was carrying her upstairs like a baby. He put her down on her bed and, going to the head of the stairs, called Sarah. When she came on the run, he gave her instructions to get her mistress to bed as soon as possible and to heat some milk for her to drink.

When she was comfortably settled, he went up to see her and watched her sip her milk. Taking a pill out of a little vial he had in his pocket, he gave it to her. "Here, take this. What you need is a good night's sleep and this will give it to you."

She took it from him without offering any remonstrance and swallowed it. "Good night, Nick," she said faintly. He went to the door and looked back at her. "Good night, my little love," said Nick, but he was careful to shut the door firmly behind him before he uttered the last three words.

Chapter Sixteen

One day late in the fall when Margaret was out driving with friends, the coachman took a short cut through the factory district of the city and they passed a building with a sign over the door, *H. E. Cuyler, Manufacturing.* It was where Jonathan's invention was being made. To Margaret's great surprise there was no evidence that Jonathan had any connection with the firm. She had understood that the firm was to be called *Cuyler and Wellfleet,* and she was disturbed by what she saw.

That evening she waited until the children were safely tucked into bed and the two old servants had retired to the kitchen before she said nonchalantly, "I was driving with Helen Hodge today and we passed the factory."

Jonathan glanced up from the notes he was making in the margin of his Bible. "Did you? That is a rather odd neighborhood for an elegant carriage such as the Hodge's."

"The coachman was trying to find a short cut to Taffy Mill's. There was what looked like a brand new sign on the building but our name was not on it."

Jonathan closed his book, using his finger as a marker, and his eyes were troubled. "I know."

"Why didn't you tell me?"

"I didn't want to trouble you and I am afraid that now that you know, I can give you only bad news."

Margaret went taut in a moment. "What do you mean?"

"I am afraid that we have all the money that we are going to get out of the invention."

"But you told me that there was a fortune in it."

"There is, but it looks as if Cuyler was planning to keep it all for himself."

Margaret was indignant. "How can that be? It is your invention, isn't it?"

"Yes, but he has it and I didn't have enough sense to get it patented."

Margaret did not attempt to keep the edge out of her voice, "Why not, in heaven's name?"

"Because Cuyler is a Christian and I trusted him."

"Well, I hope that this will teach you a lesson. Have you talked to him about it?"

"Of course, and I could get nothing out of him. For a long time he avoided seeing me, but when I finally cornered him he would give me no satisfaction. He has the invention and he is manufacturing and selling it and there doesn't seem to be anything I can do about it."

"You could mash his face in!" said Margaret angrily.

"Not as a Christian and if I did he would have me arrested. Where would that get us?"

Margaret struck her small hands together furiously. "There must be something we can do! You could sue him, couldn't you?"

"I don't know. I haven't had time this week to go and see a lawyer and I am not sure that it would be the right thing for me to do in any case."

"Why not?" asked Margaret, angrily.

"Because by suing, I would be disobeying God. The Bible definitely forbids Christians to go to law against one another."

"Oh, for heaven's sake," cried Margaret, in exasperation. "Are we living in the Middle Ages?"

"There is no age nor time when Jesus' commands do not apply to believers."

"Well, I'm not a believer and I won't be held down by them. How do you know Cuyler is a Christian anyway? He doesn't seem to be as concerned as you are to follow the commands of Christ."

Jonathan shook his head. "No, but he claims to be a believer and I have no right to doubt it."

Margaret was beside herself, screaming, "Christianity! Christianity! How I hate that word! I'm sick of the sound of it and sick of the sight of it. At every turn in my life it foils me!" Jonathan had grown pale at her furious words, but she was too agitated to notice. "Didn't religion spoil my girlhood? Now it is ruining my adult life. If you don't get any more money from Cuyler we can't move out of this neighborhood for years and I had counted on getting the children away soon. Do you want them to attend the River Street school with foreigners all their life? Well, if you cared anything at all about either them or me you would do something and not just sit back and allow yourself to be fleeced like this."

"It would be better for them to attend the River Street school all their lives than for me to disobey my Lord." His face was white, but his voice was quiet with the deadly determination he could display when it came to matters of his faith.

Tears of fury and bafflement filled Margaret's eyes and overflowed down her flushed cheeks. "Don't you care about me any more or what I want? Doesn't it matter to you that I hate this stupid little house and that I'll never be happy until you get me out of it? Are you trying to deliberately wreck what is left of our marriage?"

He was beside her in a moment. Dropping on his knees, he put his arms around her and cried, "Don't talk like that. You know better than to say such things. I did try to get you the house on the hill, and if my first attempt failed, I'll see to it that my second will not. I invented one thing. I can invent another and next time I'll get a patent. I won't be so trusting a second time. Just give me a little time, darling. I'll make this up to you. Truly, I will."

"I don't want to wait. I want my house *now*, while I'm young enough to enjoy it."

"And I want you to have it and I'll do my best to get it for you. I've several good ideas in mind already. The business is almost paid for and it won't be long before there will be more coming in from that. Don't be discouraged, darling, I won't be any longer about it than I can possibly help."

She found it hard to resist him when he was so close to her. She was almost willing to put her arms about his shoulders and return his embrace, but some seed of stubbornness in her nature made her resist the impulse. "How long does it take to get a patent?"

"Six months or a year, I think."

She stiffened at once. "You see, I'll just have to wait that much longer because you have some crazy notions about not going to law to get what is rightfully yours."

"But it would take as long as that or longer to get a decision from the law courts and if I lost the case I would have to pay the court costs."

Somewhat mollified, she permitted herself to relax against him. She sighed and tears of weakness and exasperation coursed down her pale cheeks.

He took a clean handkerchief out of his pocket and dried her tears. "Don't cry, beloved. You tear me apart when you weep." He picked her up in his strong arms and carried her to the love seat where he settled himself with her in his arms. She wanted to fling out angrily that he was not torn apart enough to do as she wanted, but if she did she would have to leave the comfort of his embrace and that she did not want to do. If she could not feel close to him in any other way, it was heavenly to be close to him physically and since the paths they had started following had led them in different directions, they had been seeing very little of each other. Just to feel him near her was food and drink for her soul, and she didn't need anything else at the moment. To be in his arms rested her as nothing else could; with them about her she felt safe and secure. Arguments were exhausting and depressing and depleted her slender store of strength. When he held her against his heart like this she felt as if she were renewing her strength.

As for him, he brushed his cheek against her hair and his arms caressed her, but even as he did so, his heart longed for a spiritual understanding between them. He wondered if he were going to have to go through life without ever experiencing it.

Chapter Seventeen

It was shortly after the holiday season that Jonathan received a letter from his mother's lawyers informing him that his mother had died and left her estate to her church with the provision that Phoebe should have the use of the house and the income for the duration of her life, providing she made no attempt whatsoever to contact her brother and his wife. This news upset Margaret greatly, not only because had Jonathan had his fair share of the estate they would have been well-off, but because she was unwilling to admit to herself that had she herself not been so spiteful and allowed Jonathan to inform his mother of his conversion as he had wished to do, the money would undoubtedly have been left to him.

Instead of accepting her share of the responsibility for the loss, she became more bitter than ever and her determination to acquire what she wanted was strengthened. Jonathan had gone rather white when he read the letter, but he had not reproached her. She almost wished that he had, for then she could have put into words the torrent of invective abuse with which her soul was seething. Instead of accepting her fair share of blame for their misfortune, her hatred for Christianity increased and she laid all her troubles at its door. She was now no nearer to getting what she wanted than she had been since Jonathan had permitted Mr. Cuyler to steal his invention. The more she thought about it the more resentful she became, and it needed but a mere trifle to blow the top off the boiling cauldron of her emotions.

Among the women whom she now counted as her intimate friends was one whose husband owned a large brewery and several saloons in the city. Because of her friendship for Margaret, Mrs. Tredway persuaded her husband to replace the ancient wooden awnings on his properties with canvas ones and to give the order to Jonathan. Margaret was delighted because of the size of the order and because she had been able to procure it through her social connections. She could hardly wait to tell Jonathan about it. However, his reaction to such a stroke of good fortune was entirely different than hers.

"Isn't that the Tredway who owns the brewery?" he asked her.

"Yes, he is." Something in the way he asked the question warned Margaret of impending disaster. "What of it? Doesn't he need awnings as much as anybody else?"

"I suppose so, but I can't take an order from a saloon-keeper."

Margaret was furious, "He isn't a saloon-keeper!"

"He's worse. He is a brewer and supplies the stuff to the saloons. Because of his business, children go hungry and cold and untold numbers of people suffer."

"It isn't his fault that some men drink too much."

"It may not be his fault, but it is his responsibility as long as he makes the stuff."

"If he didn't, somebody else would."

"Without a doubt, but I wouldn't take an order from that person either." He leaned toward her and his eyes begged for understanding, but his square jaw was set. "Don't look at me so, darling. If you had seen the results of liquor as I have seen it this winter down at the Mission, you would agree with me, I know you would." It was the first time he had mentioned the Mission, which had been established in the south end of the city. "Besides, how could I tell Mike O'Reilly that he must give up drink and then make money on an order from a brewer? I don't happen to care for liquor but Mike did and I have no right to ask him to give up something from which I benefit financially. Mike hasn't touched a drop since I took him on and he is turning into one of the best workmen in the shop. What do you think he would think of me if I were willing to profit from the very thing that I have been warning him against?"

When Margaret answered him, her voice was very bitter. "I suppose that it is more important to you to please an Irish bum whom you picked up on the streets than it is to please me, your wife." As he made no immediate reply to her accusation, she went on passionately, "Can't you see what it will mean to you in a business way if you take this offer? Mr. Tredway has many interests in the city and he can throw lots of orders your way. He is interested in politics and there is no telling what he might not do for you, if he were pleased with this order, but if you offend him by turning him down and make an enemy of him there is no telling how much harm he might do you."

"All I can say is what the Psalmist said long ago, 'I will trust in the Lord and not fear what man can do to me!' "

"Don't you go quoting Scripture to me or I'll scream!"

He turned away from her and a shadow crossed his face but he made no comment. Picking up his Bible, he opened it and commenced to read to himself, but she would not leave him in peace. She had all she could do not to snatch the book from him and fling it on the floor.

"Can't you see why I want you to do this?" she cried indignantly. "It's because it may be the means of getting what I want most in the world: a house on the hill!"

He looked across at her with a deep sadness in his eyes. "And what I want most in the world is to serve my Lord. We have become a house divided against itself."

Ignoring his last remark, she returned to her attack. "You cannot *afford* to turn down this offer. Can't you see that?"

"Neither can I afford to go contrary to God's will. You are reasoning from a human viewpoint and I am reasoning from a divine one. I am willing to trust God for our prosperity and if you will only be patient I know that it will come. The business is improving all the time and will continue to do so if I obey and trust Him. The Bible says that no good thing will He withhold from them that walk uprightly. You won't always have to live on River

Street, although for myself," his voice was wistful as he finished, "I shall be sorry to leave this little house. It was our first home."

The next morning, Margaret was finishing a late breakfast when Sarah brought in the morning paper. She had slept poorly and when she awoke unrefreshed and unrested, the same problems with which she had wrestled during the night were waiting to confront her. She seethed with indignation at the prospect of Jonathan turning down Mr. Tredway's offer. If he would only be diplomatic about turning it down, it would not be so bad, but it would be just like him to tell Mr. Tredway exactly why he was refusing it. That could not fail but anger the tycoon and without a doubt he would go straight home and tell his wife and then there would be no more invitations for Margaret from the Tredways. After all the trouble she had taken on Margaret's behalf, Muriel Tredway would be wild. She belonged to the charmed inner circle in which Margaret had only recently been included, and if she decided to turn the other women against her, Margaret would be excluded in the future from the intimate little parties which she so loved to attend.

"If only there were something I could do," she thought frantically as she pushed the tray away from her and picked up the morning paper. The first thing which struck her eye was the announcement of the death of the owner of the house just up the hill from Nick's. It was a house on which she had had her eye for some time and now that it would be thrown on the market she had no money to buy it. In desperation and fury she turned to another sheet of the paper only to see a picture of one of the handsomest houses on the hill. An article accompanying it stated that it had been purchased recently by Mr. and Mrs. H. E. Cuyler. Margaret tossed her head with rising indignation. *This* was the straw which broke the camel's back! That house, of all the houses on the hill, the one which she would have liked most to own had she been able to afford it, was being bought by the man who had cheated Jonathan. Oh, it was unendurable! She had taken all she could stand! If she could not have the house she wanted, and if

186

the only thing she cared about, her position in society, was to be taken from her as well, she might as well die! She wouldn't stand for it! She would pack up and get out. She would go so far and so fast that Jonathan would never be able to find her! If he came home to find her gone, then perhaps he would come to his senses and realize that he would have to choose between having her and serving God.

She had tried everything she could think of to make him see her point of view but nothing had worked! He would not listen to her or pay any attention to her arguments as long as she was near him. Perhaps if she removed herself, he would be shocked into the realization that she had to have her way once in a while. She refused firmly to contemplate the results of the last time she had had her way with Jonathan, over the writing to his mother, and the more she thought about leaving the more entrancing the idea became. She would teach him a lesson that he would never forget. Reason cautioned her to remember that he would go to great lengths for what he believed, but anger and frustration urged her frantically on. But where to go and what to do? Ideas flitted across her mind like race horses about a track. Ah, she had it! She threw aside the covers and running out into the hall called over the banisters to the woman working in the kitchen. "Sarah, where is Zach? I want him to go up in the attic and get my suitcases. I am going on a trip. Find him at once and tell him to hurry."

The doctor sat slumped forward in his office chair too tired to move. He had had a full office hour and he had been up all night with a difficult delivery. He gave a deep sigh and pulled himself together. He must turn out the lights and get started if he were to finish his work that night. He had only just left his chair when he heard a loud pounding on the office door. His nurse always locked it when she left for the day and he could not help but wonder what the frantic summons could mean.

He had no sooner released the lock than the door was pushed roughly open to reveal Jonathan, his face white and his eyes desperate. Nick reached out and pulled him into the room. "What's the matter, man? You look as if you had seen a ghost." His voice sharpened as Jonathan caught his breath and did not answer immediately. "There is nothing wrong with Margaret, is there?"

Without words Jonathan handed him a note which he had held clutched in his hand and Nick saw that the writing was Margaret's. His eyes ran over the few lines it contained. "So, she has left you."

Jonathan nodded. "She took Timmie with her and left Peggy with me."

"Have you any idea as to where she may have gone?"

"None, and that is what makes it so terrible."

Weariness dropped from the doctor like a cloak slipping from his shoulders and he was all attention. "Has she any money?"

"One hundred dollars which Mr. Stillwell sent her for her birthday."

"That will not last her long."

"No."

"Do you think she may have gone to him?"

"I do not think so. Not with Timmie."

The doctor frowned. "No, I suppose not. Do you want to tell me what happened?"

"She wanted me to fill an order for awnings for Tredway who owns the brewery and I couldn't see my way clear to do it."

"Was there anything else?"

Jonathan took a sheet of the morning paper out of his pocket and handed it to his friend. It was folded to outline the picture of the recently purchased Cuyler house. "I found this on the bed."

The doctor, reading it, began to see the light.

Jonathan slumped down in the nearest chair and said in despair, "It's my fault, I suppose, for not getting her what she wanted, but I have tried. I perfected the invention for her sake and then was fool enough to let Cuyler get away with it, but I still do not see what else I could have done, believing what I do. If your beliefs are not good enough to influence your conduct they are not worth much. Then I made my second mistake by giving in to her about not telling my mother that I had been converted and when she died she cut me off without a dime. If only I had insisted upon doing the Christian thing that time, this would never have happened. We have been divided ever since I got converted. It hasn't been easy to serve God and see her so unhappy and discontented because I did. I have nearly given in to her a dozen times." He covered his eyes with his hands. "At times it has been hell. I don't wonder some people think there is enough hell right on this earth, without having to endure more in the next world!"

Touched in spite of himself the doctor put his hand on his friend's shoulder. "There's no use in crying over spilled milk now, man. What is done, is done, and if it is any help to you to know it, I have admired your strength in doing what you thought was right. The thing now is to consider what to do to get her back. The very thought of her wandering around with Timmie with only one hundred dollars between herself and starvation makes me fairly sick."

Jonathan looked up at him gratefully and nodded, "I know, but even if we succeed in finding her, how can we (unconsciously he spoke in the plural) persuade her to come back? She says in her note that she will never return to the River Street house, and how can I provide any other place for her to live at this time?"

"I don't think that you will have much trouble getting her back if we can only find her. She was angry when she wrote that and by now she has had time to cool off. What time did Sarah say she left?"

"About eleven-thirty. She had Zach drive them to the station."

"What trains leave about then? Do you know?"

"No, Sarah gave me her note as soon as I got home for dinner and I was so upset that it did not occur to me to try and find out. I came right over here with it. She confides in you and I thought that you might have some idea where she went."

Nick wished within his innermost soul that he had and that he was with her that very minute, but he could hardly tell her husband that. He went over to his desk, "Wait a moment. I think I have a timetable here. Yes, here it is." He held it to the light. "We'll soon find out what trains left here about noon. Here's one — the 12:05 to New York."

"But she knows nobody in New York. Why would she want to go there of all places?" asked Jonathan perplexed.

Nick shook his head, then suddenly he remembered something. He was in the dining room of the little house and Margaret was up on a ladder. He remembered lifting her down, and hearing her joyous voice saying, "Nick, do you know what? If I could just do what I want, do you know what I would do? I would . . . . . " Something clicked in his brain and suddenly he knew where she was. Reaching over he took his friend's arm in a grip that made Jonathan wince.

"I think I know where she is and I will undertake to find her and bring her back, provided you will make me a promise. If I persuade her to return with me, you must let me loan you enough money to buy her the house she wants. I cannot have her tearing herself apart emotionally like this. It is extremely bad for her, and as her physician I am warning you that it cannot go on without her having a breakdown and that we should avoid at all costs. You should have come to me with your invention. I have more money than I know what to do with and I would have been glad to have advanced you the money to start manufacturing it, had I only known about it. After all," there was a sardonic twist to his lips as he finished, "if I return your wife to you, you ought to be willing to make some concession."

Jonathan took his friend's hand and there was nothing but gratitude in his eyes as he answered simply, "I'd do anything which is decent and honorable to get her back and if you will loan me the money, I will start paying off the loan the very first minute I can manage it. That should not take too long even without orders from liquor dealers. You are the best friend a man ever had, Nick, and I can't tell you how much I appreciate it. I would go after her myself, but I think that she will be more apt to listen to you. Lately we cannot seem to talk about anything at all without getting on the subject of religion, which ends in a quarrel. When will you leave?"

"At once. I want you to call my nurse and give her a list of these calls. Tell her to have somebody else cover them. She'll know whom to get. If Margaret has done what I think she has, her money will not last long and I had best get to her as soon as possible. I'll telegraph you as soon as I know whether my hunch is correct. I'm going to pack my bag. Don't worry. I'm certain that I am on the right track."

Nick picked up his hat and coat and the two men shook hands. Jonathan said, somewhat huskily, "My prayers will go with you."

Nick grinned, but his mouth twisted as he replied, "I could use them. I'll undoubtedly need them more than you know." And, in his own heart he knew that there was more truth to that statement than Jonathan Wellfleet would ever realize.

He found her exactly where he had expected to find her, at the Waldorf. As she came down the stairs, her head was high and she walked with her usual light grace, but Nick knew the minute he looked into her eyes that she was frightened. She had Timmie by the hand and he was experiencing all the delight and pleasure which the nagging fear at the back of her mind kept her from enjoying. He paced along beside her and many a curious and covert glance was cast by passers-by at the eager child with his magnificent coloring and the small, erect, modishly dressed woman who accompanied him. Margaret's anger had had time to cool, and she was faced with a problem to which there seemed no solution. She had been appalled at the prices the hotel charged, but she had been too proud to turn away. She realized that it would be impossible for her to stay under its roof for long, but she did not know where else to go. When she had left home she had thought vaguely that she had her teaching certificate and she could get a job and take care of Timmie and herself with her earnings, but when she commenced to consider the matter more closely she was forced into the realization that it was the wrong time of year in which to obtain a teaching position, that it would be a good seven months before she could obtain one in all probability and in the meantime she and Timmie must eat.

As she looked up and saw Nick, joy and relief leapt into her eyes. He had to hold on to himself sternly and remind himself of the good resolutions he had made on the train, in order not to take her in his arms then and there. He took charge of her and Timmie at once. Before she fully realized what was happening, he had obtained a hotel maid to give Timmie his supper, put him to bed and sit with him, while he took Margaret out to dinner and it seemed no time at all before they were seated over a glittering restaurant table partaking of a delicious meal. Nothing was said about her running away and she could forget about her troubles for a while and give herself up to thoroughly enjoying the unaccustomed luxury of dining in a world-famous restaurant with a handsome escort, confident that Nick would help her as he had a dozen times before.

When they had finished their meal Nick called a hansom cab and directed the driver to take them through the park. It had been a warm day and it was very plesant driving along the winding roads in the cool of the early evening, the clop-clop of the horse's hooves accentuating the peaceful scenery. A light breeze rustled the foliage and the moon appeared above the horizon. Margaret lay back against the padded seat content to rest and gather her resources for the struggle with Nick which she was sure was to come. She thought she knew why he had followed her to New York and she supposed that he would insist upon her returning, but in spite of her lack of funds she did not intend to give in easily. Maybe, if she was very nice to him, he would loan her enough money to carry her and Timmie awhile. As she was contemplating putting her pride in her pocket and asking him outright for a loan, he called to the cabby to stop the cab and, after helping her to alight, told him to return to the same place for them in an hour's time.

Margaret squared her slight shoulders. "Here it comes," she thought, but Nick made no effort to bring up the subject of her sudden departure. They sauntered slowly along the paths until they found an empty bench in a secluded spot and Nick suggested that they rest for a while. He was having no less of a struggle with himself than she was having with herself, for everything within him cried out that this was the strategic time to try and make her his own. For the first time since he had known her she had become sufficiently angry with her husband to take drastic action, and she need never know that Jonathan had trusted her to him or that in a weak moment he had suggested loaning him the money to get her the house she wanted so much. His thoughts milled about within him in an ever-widening circle.

If he could persuade her to go away with him he could keep her in New York until Jonathan could be persuaded to institute divorce proceedings. Should he refuse there were always ways of getting around such technicalities if one had plenty of money, and when they were able to marry, he would take her to Europe for an indefinite stay. When they returned they could settle in New York or some other metropolitan center where they were not known so that the stigma of being a divorcee need not bother her. His imagination, freed from restraint, galloped away him. Margaret had to put her hand on his arm to draw his attention to herself. "You might as well get started with the lecture, Nick, and get it over with. I don't want to miss the first act."

His thoughts came back reluctantly from afar. "You gave us an awful scare."

She ignored the inclusion of himself in his statement. "Well, Jonathan deserved it," she said and her small mouth tightened.

As he did not answer at once, she went on defensively, "He just wouldn't listen to reason and I had to do something to make him understand that I had come to the end of my rope. Turning down the Tredway order was the straw which broke the camel's back."

"What do you expect him to do now?"

"I want him to get me a decent place to live. I don't care how he does it. He can get what rightfully belongs to him from that wretch, Cuyler, or he can take the Tredway order or do something by which I know that, at last, he is showing some regard for my wishes."

"And supposing he won't?"

Margaret had not let herself consider that aspect of the situation for any length of time. It frightened her too much. She threw up her head with a proud gesture, but her tone wasn't as convincing as she would have liked to have had it as she answered, "Then, I'll stay away until he comes to his senses!"

His keen eyes did not miss her fright nor the defiant front she was making herself put on for his benefit. "How do you propose to support yourself and Timmie in the meantime? There won't be much of your hundred dollars left when you pay your hotel bill."

"I am an accredited teacher. I can get a teaching position in the fall."

"But it is some time until fall. What will you do in the meantime?"

She had removed her hand from his arm when he had started to question her, but now she slipped it through his arm once more and lifted her face to his. "I was hoping that you would loan me enough money to carry me over."

He thought to himself, "Now, when she wants something of me is the time to take her in my arms and kiss her and tell her how much I love her."

Rising, he drew her to her feet. They were standing under an alianthus tree whose big leaves and long fronds sent a pattern of light and shade over her uplifted face. As he raised his arms to draw her to him, a policeman, swinging his billy, rounded the turn in the path. Nick let his arms fall, and turned away slightly. The officer gave them a curious look as he sauntered past, but deciding that they were respectable citizens, went on. Margaret, puzzled and hurt by the thought that Nick's delay in assenting to her request meant that he had not liked her asking such a favor of him and that he was going to refuse it, sat down on the bench once more, trembling with embarrassment. He seated himself beside her, so concerned with the fact that he had had to let a golden opportunity slip through his fingers, that he temporarily forgot the request she had made of him. For a moment neither spoke. Nick sat forward frowning at the path at his feet and Margaret nervously removed her gloves and stuffed them into her bag wishing with all her heart that she had not mentioned the subject of money. It had been hard enough to get up enough courage to ask him without having him act like this. She felt tears smart just beneath her eyelids. Nick straightened at last. The policeman's timely interruption had brought him to his senses. She didn't want him. The man she really wanted was Jonathan. She showed it plainly by every word that she spoke and everything that she did. He turned to her. "I would loan you the money gladly, but that won't be necessary. Jonathan has agreed to let me loan him enough money to get you a house on the hill. He gave me his word before I left."

The strain that Margaret had been under snapped suddenly. She put her two small hands over her eyes and started to sob convulsively. His arms were about her in a moment, but his touch was quite impersonal as he drew her head down on his shoulder. "There, there, Maggie. Don't cry. You can have Jonathan and your house, too. Please, dear, please, stop crying. You'll bring back the policeman and he'll arrest us for disturbing the peace. Here, take my handkerchief and dry your eyes. You haven't a thing in the world to worry about. Everything is going to be all right, I promise."

Margaret took his big handkerchief which smelled faintly of bay rum and wiped her eyes and blew her nose. She leaned against him, emotionally spent and exhausted. "Oh, Nick, I've been so miserable and frightened! I was so angry when I left that I did not realize how much I would miss him. I only thought of getting away because he can talk me into almost anything if he as much as puts his arms about me. Then, when I was on the train, I remembered how stubborn he can be when it comes to matters of religion and I began to be afraid that he never would give in. The thought scared me almost to death and I missed him horribly. When I thought of perhaps having to spend the rest of my life without him, I cried so hard I frightened Timmie." Fresh tears started to her eyes as she talked. He took the handkerchief and gently wiped them away, suddenly intensely thankful that he had been prevented from forcing himself upon her. Had she drawn away from his embrace with distaste it would have been more than he could have borne. Even though he might have suc-ceeded in persuading her to go off with him, he now knew beyond a shadow of a doubt that Jonathan would always have stood be-tween them. If every time he kissed her he realized that she was secretly wishing they were Jonathan's kisses, he could not have endured it.

Her words cut across his forlorn thoughts. "I hate his religion and the silly things it makes him do, but I love him so! I can't seem to help it!" She twisted the fine linen through her fingers. "Sometimes I wonder whether I am not as crazy as he is to feel like this."

He sighed, but the sigh was more resigned than bitter. "No, dear. You cannot help the way you feel about him any more than he can help the way he feels about God."

She leaned her tired head against his shoulder and the weight of her slight body against him was very sweet. He might not mean any more to her than a convenient resting place in time of trouble, but he would rather be that to her than to be the whole world to any other woman. His arm tightened about her and he wished that she would remove her hat so that he might feel her soft hair against his cheek. These few fleeting moments would probably be all he would have to remember in a lifetime. They sat quietly for a few moments until in the distance a clock struck. The steady strokes brought her back to a sense of reality and she sat up and straightened her hat and pulled on her gloves. As she did so they heard the clop-clop of a horse's hooves behind them. The cabby had returned. When she had tidied herself as best she could, Nick helped her to her feet and stood looking down at her. "We'd best send Jonathan a telegram before we go to the theater. We can just about make it." He offered her his arm, but before she took it, she looked up at him gratefully in the dim light and said softly, "You are such a darling, Nick, and so good to me. I wish that I could do as much for you as you have done for me."

Then, without warning, she put her two small hands on his shoulders and lifting herself on her tiptoes, she pressed her soft lips against his cheek. The unexpectedness of her words and gesture took him off guard and the wild beating of his heart ren-dered him incapable of speech, as he helped her into the cab.

Taking his seat beside her, he comforted himself somewhat grimly with the thought that he would have one small shy kiss with which to feed his hungry heart for the rest of his natural life.

Chapter Eighteen

By a queer quirk of what Margaret would have called fate and Jonathan, the hand of God, Margaret did not have to take advantage of Nick's generosity. When she returned home, she found waiting for her a letter from Rosemary Sawyer telling her that her father and stepmother had been burned to death when the farmhouse had caught fire for some unknown reason. Inasmuch as Rosemary remembered Margaret's saying that her father kept his money in the house, she had sent Jim to look over the ruins. He had unearthed a tin box, safely lodged in the brickwork of the chimney, containing nearly twenty-eight thousand dollars, which had been deposited in the bank in her name. They were awaiting instructions from her as to the disposal of the money.

Overjoyed at such good fortune, she did not waste time mourning her father and stepmother but set about house-hunting at once. It was an exhilarating feeling to know that she had money of her own in the bank to spend exactly as she chose. After considerable searching, she decided upon the house next door to the doctor's and when she had purchased it and renovated it, she set about furnishing it. She had acquired expensive tastes during her residence in the Stillwell mansion and she wanted nothing but the best. It did not take long, therefore, for her to come to the end of her inheritance.

The first two years in the new house she was busy entertaining and being entertained and she found plenty to do to amuse herself. What Jonathan had said to Mr. Tredway she never knew, but whatever it was, it did not succeed in alienating Muriel Tredway, much to Margaret's relief. Her life took on a rosy hue and she busied herself so extensively with her own activities that she could ignore Jonathan's. For a while she radiated happiness and contentment and the two men who loved her could bask in the reflected glow of her enthusiasm. But then in the third year of their occupancy of the house on the hill, tragedy struck. Sarah and Zach occupied a small shed room off of the kitchen, heated by a gas heater. One unusually bitter night somehow the fire went out and they were asphyxiated by the gas. Jonathan found them in their bed, stiff and cold, when he went to investigate the reason why no sounds of activity were coming from the kitchen.

With their death, life, which for the past two years had been so easy and pleasant, suddenly began to take on quite another aspect for Margaret. She had lost two competent, reliable, and inexpensive servants and she soon came to realize that she could now afford only one maid. It was far more expensive to run the house on the hill than it had been the small one on River Street and with the rising cost of living, money did not go as far as it had. She began to wish that she had not bought quite so much expensive furniture and had saved a little for emergencies. Everybody else on the hill had a coachman and she wanted one too. Most people had three maids in the house and she began to feel deprived with only one. Her ambitions, which had been anesthetized for awhile, began to come to life once more and she was faced with the same problems she had faced on River Street, only on a larger scale. She wanted to live in the same manner as the people about her and she could not afford to do so.

It was at this time that she began to resent bitterly the amount of money that Jonathan gave away. He insisted upon giving one tenth of his income to some form of religious work and this diverting of money which she considered rightfully hers into other channels infuriated her. She often thought what she could have spent it on had she had it to spend. Her restlessness and dissatisfaction returned fourfold. Her new maid was not an experienced cook and in order to serve meals which were up to her usual standards, Margaret found that she had to spend considerable time in the kitchen. It was not long before she was receiving many compliments for her light tea cakes, muffins, and pastries. She was too proud to admit that they were the products of her own efforts, but her friends' enthusiasm for them gave her an idea which might be the means of getting her out of her difficulties. There had recently been established in the city a Woman's Exchange which sold home-baked goods and needlework at a good profit. One day she was lunching at the Exchange with a group of friends and she heard a clerk tell a customer who was disappointed in finding something she wanted sold out, that they could sell ten times what came in.

She determined at that moment to send them some of her cakes and pastries, but she also determined that they should not know from whom they came, for she was too proud to advertise the fact that she needed money. For some little time her pride was an insurmountable barrier to the success of her scheme, but a solution finally came to her. Several months before their death, Sarah and Zach had made the acquaintance of a family who lived down by the flats. The family was large but very poor. One daughter of about sixteen years of age had helped Sarah with the cleaning once or twice. Margaret sent for her and hired her to deliver the cakes and pastries to the Exchange under an assumed name. She told her she would pay her on the condition that no one ever discovered from whence the baked goods came. The girl jumped at the chance. When Margaret sent her with the first batch of baking, she returned with a promise from the Exchange to take all she could supply. Before six months had passed, Margaret was making enough money to hire a coachman and a second maid. It meant that she had to spend her mornings in the kitchen, but the results were worth the effort. She succeeded in keeping Jonathan in the dark about the matter because he was at the sail loft while she was working, but fooling Nick was another thing entirely. He came and went as he chose and it did not take him long to discover what she was up to.

He remonstrated with her for driving herself so, but she flew into a tantrum so he decided he had best let her alone.

When Jonathan learned what was going on, he was as bothered as the doctor, but Margaret had come to the place where she would brook no interference from anyone and she told him bitterly that the only thing that would make her abandon her project would be for him to give her the money he gave away. This he felt he could not do, so he found himself in just as helpless a position as the doctor.

In a year's time Margaret felt independent enough to raise her prices, but she still was able to get rid of all she managed to produce. Her vaulting ambitions led her into making jams, jellies, preserves, and pickles for sale, too. It seemed that the more money she made the more she wanted. There were so many, many things upon which to spend it. The women with whom she spent much of her time vied with one another in dress and entertainment to see who could outdo the other and Margaret was not willing to be left behind in this race for superiority. She spent her mornings in the kitchen, and then, dressing herself in her latest new ensemble, sallied forth to luncheons or teas or whist parties. Finally her seething ambitions carried her to such lengths that in order to keep her orders filled, she had to work in the kitchen during any free evenings that she had. The doctor learned to watch for the kitchen lights to go on in the house next door and whenever he had some free time he would go through the break in the hedge and do what he could to help her. He became quite expert at pulling taffy and cracking and sorting nuts. Sometimes Jonathan would join them, but he had become interested in establishing a mission work at the flats and he spent many of his evenings there. Margaret never told him when she had an engagement so he had no way of knowing when she was planning to be home. Their interests had become completely divergent and they drifted farther and father apart. He could not give in to her and she would not give in to him.

So matters stood when one evening Nick saw the lights go on in the back of the house next door and went through the gap in the hedge to see what assistance he could give. It was Jonathan's prayer meeting evening so Margaret was alone. They worked together for several hours and then he insisted that she sit by the fire in the back parlour for awhile and rest. But she could not relax. Even though he settled her in her favorite chair, she picked up a bit of sewing. Her needlework sold no less successfully than the products of her culinary skill, and she always had something on which she was working. The doctor wished that she would sit and relax, but he knew that it was worse than useless to tell her so.

The back parlour was a cozy room filled with the warm light from lamps and fireplace. Margaret never bothered to draw the curtains, for that side of her house faced a house occupied by an old woman who lived alone and retired early. There were never any signs of life from it after eight o'clock in the evening. As Margaret commenced to embroider she said, "Nick, do you know how to fight?"

Nick was puzzled. "Fight? What exactly do you mean by that? Protect myself from attack or fight for my rights? You are not by any chance referring to the manly art of self-defense, are you?"

Margaret looked up from her work. "Yes, I am. Wrestling, boxing, fighting, or whatever you call it. Protecting yourself, anyway."

Nick looked thoughtful. "What's on your mind, Maggie?"

Margaret gave him a reproachful look. She had long since learned the futility of reproving him for using that detested nickname. She reached for her sewing box and began to search for some embroidery silk while she kept him waiting for the answer to his question in reproof for his impertinence. When she had cut off a length of thread, threaded her needle, and recommenced her work, she said, "Timmie is."

He picked up a small pincushion from among her sewing equipment and regarded it thoughtfully. It was made in the shape of a small tomato. Holding it by the green cord which was attached to it, he spun it about in his fingers and watched it revolve rapidly. If she could be provoking so could he. Finally he said, "What's the matter with him?"

"Nothing that I can exactly put my finger on, but I am a-fraid that there may be something later on and that is why I want you to teach him to fight."

Nick watched the little cushion reverse itself on its cord and, hitting it with his finger, sent it spinning about once again before he said, "I still do not get your point. You want him to learn to protect himself. Why?"

"Do put that silly thing down," she said crossly. "Because Jonathan is filling him with all kinds of crazy notions, and I don't like it."

"Really? Such as?"

"Last week, Timmie asked his father what he would do if somebody abused him and mistreated him, and Jonathan told him that that would depend upon whether he acted as a man or a Christian. He said that if he were to act as a man he would probably make whoever mistreated him pay for it, but were he to act as a Christian, he would be willing to take a good deal of abuse for Christ's sake. He went on to tell Timmie how much Christ had endured at the hands of men, and I could see that Timmie was impressed. Then he asked Jonathan if Christ ever got angry and Jonathan said yes, but not for His own sake but only for the sake of others and I knew then that Timmie had something on his mind. When next day he came home with mud on his face and his clothes torn, I was sure of what it was all about. He wouldn't talk, but Peggy told me that Buddy Forsythe had called him names and when Tim hadn't answered him, the little bully had thrown mud at him and tripped him so that he fell and tore his trousers. Buddy Forsythe is a nasty, spoiled brat and Tim should have beaten him soundly. His father would have at his age before he went crazy on religion. But instead of standing up for his rights, Timmie comes skulking home with his tail between his legs, so to speak, and won't talk. It made me wild!"

Nick put the pincushion back in the basket, "Hum, I see what you mean. Perhaps I'd better have a talk with Tim!"

Margaret's relief showed in her face, "Oh, I wish you would. He admires his father so that he takes every word he says as law."

The doctor's opportunity to talk to young Tim came the next day. He had to go out into the country on a professional call, after school was out, so he invited the lad to go along. He told Margaret to keep Peggy at home and gave his coachman the afternoon off. To Tim's great delight, Nick let him drive after they had left the crowded thoroughfares. The boy sat up very straight, holding the reins steadily. Nick kept his eye on his pair of matched blacks, for they could be lively upon occasion, but Tim managed them well. He was a sturdy, well-developed lad with his father's keen mind and magnificent coloring but his mother's sensitiveness and highly geared nervous system. As the doctor watched him, he did not wonder that Margaret was proud of him and wanted the very best in life for him. He had realized for some time that she was gradually transferring the ambitions and aspirations she had once had for Jonathan to this small son of hers.

Tim tightened his hold upon the reins when he saw a chicken run across the road ahead of the carriage, and Nick put his hand over the swelling muscles on the lad's arm. "You're developing some muscle, son."

Tim merely glanced at the doctor out of the corner of his eye for a moment then immediately returned his attention to the horses.

Nick continued blandly. "You'll need all the muscle you can acquire if you are going to learn to handle horses." The passion of Timmie's life was a deep and abiding love of horse-flesh in any form or shape. "How would you like to try some boxing lessons with me? That ought to help strengthen your arms."

"I'd like it very much, sir."

"Good, then the sooner we start the better. If you can acquire enough holding power, I might let you try riding Midnight."

Tim's eyes shone. "Oh, would you, Uncle Nick? That would be wonderful!" Midnight was a powerful black stallion that was Nick's own saddle horse.

"But," qualified the doctor, "I would want to be sure that you could handle him. He is a cantankerous brute at times and your mother would never forgive me if he pulled your arms out of their sockets!"

"He wouldn't," said Tim eagerly, "I'm really quite strong, Uncle Nick. Besides, Midnight likes me."

"I'm afraid that that wouldn't make much difference if a dog started to yap at Midnight's heels or a motor car frightened him. I would want to be sure first. How about school?" he continued casually. "Can you take care of yourself there?"

Timmie looked sober. "What do you mean by that, Uncle Nick?"

"Well, when I was a lad there were plenty of fights in the school yard and I don't think that things have changed much."

But Tim refused to rise to the bait. "Some of the fellows fight."

"How about you?"

"I used to."

"But you don't any more?"

"I'm trying not to."

"Want to tell me why?"

"I'd rather not if you don't mind, sir. I — I do not think that you would understand."

The doctor was rather taken aback and his tone had an edge on it as he replied, "Indeed! Why not, if I may be bold enough to inquire?"

Tim's face flushed, but he did not give ground. "Because you and Mommy do not feel the same way about things that Daddy and I do."

Nick considered the matter. "About what, for instance?"

Tim took the horses through a narrow gateway and up a lane without decreasing their speed, his hands firm on the reins. If, as his mother feared, he was showing cowardice among his companions, he certainly displayed none in his handling of horses, and Nick gave him an approving glance. Reaching over, he pulled the horses to a halt. He felt himself at too much of a disadvantage when the lad could not look at him. Perhaps he could get something definite out of Timmie if he made him look him in the eye. "Let's stop here for a few moments so we can talk. We've come at a pretty good clip and we've plenty of time. I don't want to get there until after the patient has had her afternoon nap." The doctor took his big watch out of his pocket and looked at it as an excuse for his delay.

Tim took his attention from the blacks and leaning back turned to Nick. There was a slight frown between his eyes, but he did not evade the doctor's look. "I wish that I could make you understand what I mean, Uncle Nick. I think that it has something to do with getting all lit-up inside. It's — it's what makes people get lit-up, I guess." His look besought the doctor's understanding, but the man beside him gave him no help. He swallowed and continued earnestly, "Mommy gets all lit-up and shiny if she is getting dressed to go to a party, but Daddy gets all lit-up and shiny when he's talking about — about Jesus. It seems to me that I've got to choose what I want to get all lit-up about and — and I have decided to choose Daddy's way."

"What's that got to do with not fighting when a bully trips you and calls you names?" Nick's irritation made him divulge the real reason for his questions, but Timmie didn't notice, so intent was he upon expressing himself in such a way that he would make himself understood without hurting the doctor's feelings.

"Jesus didn't say anything when they plucked the hair off his face, spat upon Him, and called Him names."

Nick frowned, "But, Timmie, that was for a purpose. He was going to the Cross and He knew it."

Tim turned about on the seat so that he was looking directly at the doctor. "If you believe that, Uncle Nick, then why aren't you a Christian?"

Nick was taken aback. Somewhat testily he said, "And how do you know that I am not?"

Tim shook his head, entirely unaware of the reproof the doctor's tone held for his presumption, and with the honesty of childhood said simply, "I often watch your face and Mommy's when we are having prayers and you both have a shut-up look. Your face doesn't get as closed as Mommy's, but it isn't joyful either, like Daddy's is. Daddy's face just shines and I think he gets that shining look because he loves and obeys God, so that is what I want to do, too." He leaned back against the side of the carriage, glad that it was out at last.

Nick felt himself to be slightly beyond his depth. "But you say your mother has a shining look, too, upon occasions. They are just caused by different things, Tim."

The child shook his handsome head. "But Daddy's never completely goes away. Even when he is not reading from the Bible, his face has a happy look. When Mommy isn't all lighted up inside, she doesn't look happy, the way Daddy does. I guess," he finished somewhat lamely, "that is why Daddy isn't cross and impatient with us the way Mommy is."

Receiving no comment from the doctor, who had been given more to think about than he cared to admit, Timmie went on hesitatingly. "I — I asked him once what made him look like that and he said that it was because he loved God so much. Afterwards he told me that if you loved God, you had to obey Him and he taught me a verse: 'To obey is better than sacrifice and to hearken than the fat of rams.' I asked him what hearken meant and he said it meant to listen when God tried to tell you something, and that God was trying to tell people that in His sight obedience was better than anything else. Last week he read us about Jesus saying that we should take up our cross and follow Him and I made up my mind to do it."

"But what has all this to do with not protecting yourself when somebody attacks you?" Nick could not keep the irritation out of his voice. Perhaps there was more to be said for Margaret's side of this thing than he had fully appreciated up until now.

"Jesus didn't defend Himself when they abused Him. He could have destroyed his enemies with a word, but He did not do it."

There seemed to be no answer to this. At last Nick said, "You have undertaken to do a hard thing, Timmie."

Timmie sighed, "I guess so, sir. I sure would have liked to knock Bud down when he tripped me. I could have given him a good thrashing, too. He's bigger'n me, but he's fat and slow on his feet!"

Nick said somewhat testily, "If you had, you probably would have had no more trouble with him, but now he will think he can do anything he likes to you and get away with it. That may give the other boys ideas, too, and you may have still more trouble."

Timmie nodded his head, "Daddy says that it is always harder to act Christlike than to be yourself, but he says that it is more worthwhile in the end."

Nick made no answer to this and the boy, putting his hand on his arm and looking up into his face, said beseechingly, "I can't know about that unless I try his way first, can I, Uncle Nick?"

The doctor shook his head, won in spite of himself. "I suppose not, but I wish that you would promise me one thing."

Relieved that the doctor's frown had vanished, the lad said eagerly, "Anything that I can, sir."

"I want you to learn to protect yourself with your fists, just in case you should ever have cause to change your mind. Besides," he continued, "there is Midnight, you know."

After a minute's reflection, Timmie nodded and Nick handed him back the reins, deciding that he would have to be content with a partial victory and wondering in his own mind just how much of this enlightening conversation it would be wise to repeat to the child's mother.

Timmie proved himself to be an apt pupil and Nick got as much pleasure out of the boxing lessons as the lad did. Margaret was delighted when the doctor reported on Timmie's rapid progress in the art of fisticuffs and she bided her time in the hopes that Buddy would one day overreach himself and then Tim would be forced into displaying his new-found prowess. Nick had not given Margaret an account of his conversation with the lad. He had told himself that she had enough to upset her without his adding to her difficulties. As for Jonathan, when he discovered what was going on, he held his peace although he had a very good idea of what was behind it. The lad would have to make his own choice. He would not coerce him in any way. He wanted his son to serve God willingly from his heart, not from any compulsion. The choice must be left entirely to him.

He knew that Margaret was doing her best to see that Timmie go in her direction, but that did not trouble him too much. If Timmie wanted to learn to fight, well and good. The important thing was to be able, but not be willing; to possess strength, but not to exercise it in the wrong way. He watched the lad closely, as did the other adults who loved him, to see what he was going to do with what he was being taught, but for awhile, nothing happened. Buddy Forsythe contented himself in tormenting others and let Timmie alone until one day Tim inadvertently roused his ire by besting him in a spelling match and once more the bully concentrated his attention upon the Wellfleet children.

Nick was just closing his office when he received a frantic call from Margaret. Buddy Forsythe had pushed Peggy and she had fallen down and cut her lips on a sharp stone. Timmie had brought her home with her dress torn and her face dripping blood and he had not done a thing to Buddy. Margaret was almost sobbing with nervous excitement and anger. Nick rushed to the house and found that her alarm was somewhat warranted for he had to put three stitches into the small upper lip and he put the child to bed with a sedative to quiet her. Timmie held his sister's hand while the doctor was working on her, but when it was over he crept away from his mother's angry torrent of words and Nick found him later out in the barn sitting gloomily by Midnight's stall, his head in his hands. He was obviously having a struggle with himself and the doctor did not interfere. He would have to work this out for himself. He was perfectly capable of administering punishment to Buddy, and for his own and his mother's sake, Nick hoped that he would do so. There was more involved here than just a children's quarrel and he begged Mar-

207

garet to hold her hand for a few days until they saw what would come of it.

The next morning Timmie started for school alone. Peggy's injuries were not alarming, but she cried at the very idea of having to go to school, so Nick told Margaret to keep her at home for a day or two. Watching the sturdy young figure trudge down the hill all by himself, he determined to look in at the school yard about noon, but that morning a farmer was gored by a bull and Timmie and the school yard went completely out of the doctor's mind. He was late for his office hours and the office was full, so that it was well after five before his office nurse said, "Just one more, doctor."

The doctor sighed with weariness. He wanted a hot bath and his dinner. He had had a devilish time sewing up the tendons of the farmer's hand and he felt that he deserved a little rest. He turned to his nurse, "Can't you persuade him to come back to-morrow?"

The nurse smiled somewhat dryly, "I think you will want to see this patient, doctor."

She opened the door and said to the unseen person, "The doctor will see you now."

Nick frowned. He usually trusted Miss Frost's judgment, but tonight he resented her overriding him this way. He was about to protest when a small boy's face with a shock of matted and disordered dark red hair appeared in the doorway. One eye was a deep and angry purple and rapidly swelling shut. Several scratches flamed across one cheek and a hanging tooth protruded through a cut and swollen lip. The lad advanced into the doctor's office somewhat shamefacedly and managed to mumble, "I thought I'd better come see you before I went home."

Setting himself to repair the damage as best he could, Nick asked, "Buddy?"

Tim nodded. "I couldn't let him hurt Peggy without doing something about it. I told him he better never do that again and he said to try — ouch — to stop him, so I did."

"Did you succeed?"

Timmie grinned up at the doctor and a trickle of blood dripped down his chin. "Yes, sir. He looks worse than me. I had to keep pounding him 'til he promised not to hurt Peggy any more."

Nick said simply, "Stout fella! I'm proud of you."

Timmie winced at the application of an antiseptic, but his brow did not clear when the smarting ceased. "I hope," he said wistfully, "that Daddy will understand why I did it. He said that Jesus always protected the small and the weak."

"I'm sure he will," the doctor assured him heartily. "Something had to be done to protect Peggy. He'll be as proud of you, as I am."

The lad leaned against the doctor's shoulder. "You know what, Uncle Nick?"

Nick smiled and put his arm about him. "No, what?" he asked earnestly.

"Daddy was right. It was much easier to fight, once I got started, than not to fight."

The doctor considered the matter as he measured off a piece of court plaster. He nodded his head, "I can see that it might be."

"Which just shows," said Timmie through his swollen lips, "that what Daddy said is true. It's harder to be Christlike than to do as you want. When I thought about Peggy's crying over the stitches you took in her lip, it felt awful good to punch Buddy in the nose."

The doctor finished his work and handed his tray of equipment to the nurse. He ignored the last remark. "There, at least we got the dirt out of your wounds. Now, you had better let me take you home. The sooner we get some raw beef on that eye, the better. I think that your mother is going to be awfully proud of you in spite of your scars."

Tim seized the doctor's hand, "But what about Daddy?"

"Daddy, too," insisted the doctor, as they started down the stairs. "You just wait and see."

Chapter Nineteen

As time passed, Margaret's secret enterprise grew into a thriving business. She could have expanded it and hired several people to help her but she could not bring herself to reveal her work. She knew that her fashionable friends had enough to say behind their gloved hands about the oddities of her husband, and she did not intend to add fuel to the fire. That what they whispered about Jonathan was less damning than what they said about the husbands of others in the group did not in any way console Margaret. There were many evening affairs planned for couples in which she might have been included had Jonathan not had such strict ideas, and she resented bitterly being excluded from them for lack of an escort. She refused to acknowledge that Jonathan naturally had no taste for cards and dancing and pinned his refusal to attend the social gatherings upon the strictness of the church which he had joined. No matter from which point her thoughts commenced, they always gravitated eventually to religion and the way in which it dogged her steps and limited her activities. She loved to dance and she hated having to refuse the many balls and parties to which she was invited.

Once or twice she had asked Nick to take her, but he had told her brusquely that he was too tired at night for such shenanigans. She was so cross with him about it that she didn't speak to him for days, for she did not see why if he could spend time with her in the kitchen in the evening, he could not take her to a ball. Pulling taffy wasn't exactly a restful occupation, but for once he would not listen to her blandishments and she could do nothing with him.

As for Nick, his refusal hurt him more than it did her, but he knew perfectly well what a hornet's nest of gossip would be down about their ears were he to grant her request. He told her crossly that she would have to restrict her social activities to day time functions and evening affairs given for ladies only. As it was, he did not approve of her running about even that much, and he did not hesitate to say so.

So she worked and acquired possessions and money, but the more she had, the less pleasure she seemed to get out of what she gained. She kept pace with her fashionable friends and sometimes outdistanced them, but her success did not give her the satisfaction she desired. Where once a new piece of furniture or a new gown would please her for days, she now seemed to tire very quickly of the new things she was able to procure. She went blindly on, however, unwilling to acknowledge to herself that her ambition had become a relentless taskmaster with an appetite which only increased the more she fed it.

One thing seemed to lead to another. When she got a new carriage, she then needed new horses and the coachman needed new uniforms. There seemed to be no end to it, so she drove herself on and on until the two men who loved her began to feel the strain nearly as heavily as she did. They both gave up trying to remonstrate with her, for she only flew into tantrums. Jonathan increased her household allowance, but it still was not enough to cover the lavish entertaining that she insisted she had to do. The doctor sometimes thought to himself wearily, "Well, at least I'll be here when the crash comes, to do what I can for her." Jonathan prayed that she might come to see how foolishly she was wasting her energies and frittering away her time, but if he so much as mentioned the subject, she flew at him and told him that she would never give up her manner of living unless he gave up his. So they always arrived at the same impasse.

One Wednesday evening when Jonathan was at prayer meeting, Margaret collected her candy-making paraphernalia and set to work. Peggy was in bed and Tim was studying in his room with instructions to retire at nine o'clock. As Margaret worked, her thoughts milled about within her head. One satisfactory thing about Tim was that he could be depended upon to obey even if he were not watched. Peggy was not so dependable. She had to admit to herself that everything the child did and said annoyed her to a greater or lesser degree. When Peggy sat at the table she often fiddled with her napkin ring, making a small scraping noise which got on her mother's nerves, or she slid her shoes along the rung of her chair until she had to be sent away from the table. She was never tidy. Her shoe laces came undone or her stockings came down on her thin legs or her hair ribbon dangled. She was continually asking the silliest questions which Margaret had neither the time nor inclination to answer.

As Margaret stirred up the fire she wished for the thousandth time that Peggy were more like Timmie. Margaret had never even tried to achieve Nick's tolerance for human foibles. She was not willing to allow people to be themselves if their personalities did not fit her expectations and ideals. Her young daughter's silliness and shallowness certainly did not! The child had none of Tim's poise in public and she was almost ill from shyness when her mother, upon occasion, tried to show her off. How Margaret was ever going to get her ready to take her place in society she did not know! As time went by this caused her considerable concern and a great deal of irritation.

Tim was entirely different. He was utterly self-possessed and it was a joy to present him to her friends. Already they were exclaiming about his manners and poise, and Margaret was centering all her hopes on him. He must enter Harvard and then he must go on a world tour. Perhaps she could go with him. Her thoughts pleased her as she considered the matter. She had just put her candy on to boil when she heard the three light taps on the back door that was Nick's signal for admittance. She went to admit him with pleasure. If he helped her, she could get through sooner and then perhaps she could finish the dressing sack which she was embroidering. The doctor hung his hat and coat on a familiar peg and sat down at the table. "What's the program for tonight?" he asked.

"Two pans of fudge and some popcorn balls."

"Sounds good. I'm ready."

"You can start cracking those nuts."

"No sooner said than done. Where's the nutcracker?"

"Right beside you. If it was a bear it would bite you!"

The doctor grinned, but he did not take his eyes off of Margaret's face as he felt for the nutcracker. She did not look any more weary than usual, he reassured himself. "What makes you so solemn tonight?"

"Peggy's been provoking and Jonathan's acting up."

"Let's take Peggy first. What has she done?"

"Last night when I went to a whist party she got into my jewel case and tried on all my things. I have expressly forbidden her to touch them because she is so heedless. Of course, she broke a string of beads."

"Don't you think you are a little hard on the child? She likes pretty things as much as you do and takes pleasure in handling them."

Margaret scowled, "You and Jonathan are entirely too lenient with her. She has her own simple locket and chain and the bracelet you gave her. She should be content with those and not play with mine. They are entirely unsuited to a child of her age."

"She is growing up. After all she is a female of the species. It's too bad she had to be caught. I'm sure she was having a wonderful time."

"Oh, Nick, you are impossible!" exclaimed Margaret, provoked.

Nick said nothing. He had wanted to talk to Margaret for some time about her treatment of her young daughter, but this was no time to start an argument. He did not believe she realized how impatient she was with the child nor to what extent the characteristics which so annoyed her in Peggy were magnified by her own impatience and irritability in dealing with her. Margaret was driving herself at too swift a pace and her nerves were on edge most of the time as a result. Peggy was so afraid of upsetting her mother and bringing down wrath upon her defenseless head that she was even more clumsy and awkward than a child of her age needed to be. She never acted entirely natural in her mother's presence. Mother and child acted as counter-irritants to one another, but Nick's heart failed him when it came to telling Margaret that much of the situation which she so deplored was her own fault.

Margaret went to the stove and tested her candy. Finding that it was not yet ready, she swiftly collected her pans and began to grease them. Nick watched the small fingers as they worked so quickly and skillfully. He knew that she wore herself out by the very rapidity with which she worked, but he also knew that it was useless to tell her so. She would only reply that she had to work fast in order to get the work done. He decided to change the subject. "And what has Jonathan been doing to displease your highness?"

"He's had some old bum sleeping in the shed room again." There was concentrated bitterness in her tones. Unfortunately, the maids had somehow discovered that two people had died in the small shed room off the kitchen and they had refused to sleep in it, so Margaret had had to go to the expense of having two rooms finished in the attic for them. This annoyed her extremely but it annoyed her even more to have any portion of her house used by people she called tramps.

"Who was it this time?"

"Oh, some old bum who he picked up at the Mission, I suppose. I didn't see him. He got up and went off before I came down, but the girls told me about it."

"Then why does it bother you so much?"

"Because Jonathan did not lock the door into the kitchen. Some night we'll all be murdered in our beds."

Nick gathered together the nut shells which he had scattered about on the table and put them in a bag. He rose and going to the stove lifted one of the covers and thrust it inside. When he returned to the table he seated himself and started to pick over the nut meats. "I do not think that you need worry about that. There isn't a person down on the flats who does not love and admire Jonathan. They wouldn't hurt him or any member of his family."

Margaret lifted her fudge off the stove and set it in the sink. "How do you know so much about the way they feel about Jonathan?" she asked over her shoulder.

The doctor did not look up from his task. "Oh, they tell me."

Margaret returned to the table and sat down beside him. "So he's got you going down there, too. I don't suppose that you get paid a penny for it, either."

"A doctor always does a certain amount of free work," Nick defended himself, not looking at her.

Margaret made no attempt to hide her annoyance. "You are as bad as Jonathan. The way he coddles and encourages those people is a crime. They are a dirty, lazy, shiftless lot. They make him think they are interested in his religion so they can use him. If he continues to bring them home and give them a clean bed and a hot meal they will soon come to the conclusion that we are running a free hotel. I told him the last time he did this that if he insisted upon having them here, he would have to wash the bed linen himself, for I won't have it mixed up with ours. Why, we might get something."

"What did he say to that?"

"Oh, you know Jonathan! He said he would, of course, rather than turn them out. He will do anything for any down-and-outer that comes his way. I'm sure that they have a way of identifying him."

"He's done a lot of good down there." He did not remind her that inasmuch as it was she who kept him from doing mission work on a foreign field, it was not fair to complain because he had located some nearer home.

"Persuaded a few drunks to stop beating their worthless wives and go to work, maybe, but how long will it last?"

"Some of it has lasted quite a while. He has done more to clean up the flats than anyone else ever succeeded in doing."

"Well, let him keep his work down there and not bring it into my house. I don't want that riffraff here. It is bad enough for him to give away all he does, without his housing and feeding them, too." This was a shot in the dark, but when she saw Nick flush, she knew that her surmise that he was helping Jonathan with his work was correct. She pressed her advantage. "Another thing that makes me furious is that he spends so much time on that sort of work that he has had no time to perfect any other inventions. If he would only give one-half the time and a third of the effort that he expends down there, to making money we would be rich."

In spite of himself, Nick found himself defending Jonathan. "Money isn't everything in the world, Margaret. No one will ever be able to measure the amount of good he is doing down there and after all, you are not poverty stricken, you know!"

Margaret flung up her head and her eyes snapped. "No, but in order to get the things I want, I have to earn money and work hard to do it. If that worthless lot of no-accounts down at the flats worked one-half as hard, they would not need to go to Jonathan for a handout. It makes me boil every time I think about it, and how much good does it do? He goes right on doing it. Do you know old Tom Short?"

The doctor nodded.

"How many times do you suppose Jonathan has sobered him up, straightened him out, and found him a job? About twenty. The children call him 'the fallen man' because as soon as Jonathan gets him on his feet, he falls down again. He simply cannot keep away from the bottle."

"But on the other hand, there is Mike O'Reilly who has never touched a drop since he was converted. You have to admit that he is a credit to Jonathan and so are many other cases I know about. I think that perhaps poor old Tom Short has a weak heart and suffers a good deal of pain and it is then that he takes a drink to tide him over, but unfortunately he never stops with one."

With a sigh, Margaret gave Nick the pan of fudge to beat. "There is just no use in discussing it. I should know by now that no matter how I feel about it, Jonathan will continue to give any old reprobate who comes along a clean bed and a hot meal and there is nothing I can do about it unless I get up and leave him as I did before."

Nick's hand slowed its rythmic beating. "You are not thinking of repeating that performance, are you?"

Margaret shook her head. "No, although he deserves it. He is the most sweetly persistent person when he thinks he is right that I ever saw. No, I learned the folly of that the last time. I was more unhappy without him than I am with him, in spite of his crazy religious notions."

Nick handed her the fudge and she added the nuts and poured it. When she had completed her task she looked up at him as he stood beside her, with her whole heart in her eyes. "Nick, you're a doctor. You ought to know the answer. Why is it I love him so much physically when I cannot agree with him at all mentally? It seems that I cannot live with him and I cannot live without him. What is the matter with me?"

The doctor looked down at her and his eyes were full of pain. "If I knew the answer to that one, I'd be the first to do something about it, but I have to confess that I don't. It humiliates me to admit it, but it is the truth." To ease his inward hurt, he turned from the sublime to the ridiculous. "How about giving me the pan to scrape?"

The twins' fourteenth birthday was drawing near and the time had come to consider the matter of presents. Margaret was not greatly concerned with Peggy's gift, but she wanted Tim to have exactly what he wanted most. When she asked him what that might be, he hesitated to tell her, but Peggy blurted out that he wanted a horse of his own. Margaret was somewhat taken aback by the size of the gift and the expense involved, but from the moment she knew what he wanted, she determined to get it for him. Unfortunately, she had just invested all her spare cash in a sealskin coat and she had none left to buy a horse. She would just have to make some extra batches of marmalade for the Exchange and see if she couldn't build up her bank account again. It was when she was absorbed in her tenth batch of marmalade that the accident happened. In her weariness and haste she reached across the stove, upsetting a kettle of the boiling liquid over her feet. Her wild scream brought Nick and Jonathan rushing in from the garden where they had been discussing moving the hedge between their properties.

Fortunately, she had on fairly heavy house slippers and black cotton stockings which she wore in the kitchen in order to economize, but her slim ankles and the upper part of her feet were burned sufficiently to cause her much pain. They got her to her room and the doctor dressed the burns at once, but her shuddering and sobbing did not cease for some time. It was when Jonathan began to plead with her to try and control herself that she turned on him and screamed that if he had done what he should she wouldn't have needed to burn herself in order to get Timmie the horse that he wanted for his birthday. Jonathan turned as white as a sheet at her wild accusations, and Nick, unable to stand her sobbing and shrieking any longer, administered a sedative that put her out of her misery for a while. It was necessary for her to spend several weeks in bed, but she could get no rest worrying about how she could get together enough money to get that horse. She was in considerable pain when the blisters broke and in more agitation of mind when she thought of the unfilled orders which were piling up for her at the Woman's Exchange. She made no effort to apologize to Jonathan for the bitter and unjust things she had screamed at him at the time of the accident, and he went about looking pale and drawn. When the pain eased, she had an impulse to tell him that she hadn't really meant what she had said, but some imp of perverseness within her made her want him to suffer as she was suffering and kept her quiet. The one satisfaction she had was that her friends rallied around her and filled her room with flowers and small gifts and delicacies. The doctor would not allow her to see the ladies, but it flattered her that they missed her and remembered her.

Her recovery was slow, but eventually the day came when she could once more walk around. Nothing more had been said about the horse for Timmie, but when the children's birthday finally dawned bright and clear, Jonathan, who had left the house early and without an explanation as to where he was going, was seen walking up the hill, leading a strange horse by the bridle. They all left the breakfast table and Jonathan gravely presented the animal to his son as a birthday gift. Peggy danced about and uttered squeals of delight, but Timmie could hardly believe his eyes. So much fuss had been made about his mother's illness that he had thought his father had forgotten all about his birthday. Margaret felt a deep shame and regret in her heart for the cutting things she had said to her husband. He tried her to the very end of her endurance and then he turned about and did a thing like this just to please her and she could not help but feel ashamed of herself. She wondered where he had obtained the money for the horse, for she knew that at the time of her accident he had been short of funds. When she asked him point blank he told her that he had been able to collect a debt long overdue. He did not seem to want to talk about it, so she let the matter drop.

The children were walking the horse up and down the drive under the coachman's watchful eye, when Nick came out of his house and came through the hedge to see what all the agitation was about. He had already arranged for the purchase of a horse for Timmie himself and he was surprised and disappointed to discover that Jonathan had succeeded in getting ahead of him. He joined Jonathan where he stood watching the children. Nick was an expert judge of horseflesh and when he looked the animal over he did not like its looks. "Where did you get that brute?" he asked his friend. "He has a mean eye and I do not think that he will be easy to handle."

Jonathan answered him brusquely, "He was all I could afford," and, turning on his heel, when into the house. Nick was chagrined. If he had only known what Jonathan had in mind he would have insisted upon loaning him the money to get a safe horse and have gone with him while he chose it. Jonathan knew less about horses than the doctor did about navigating and he had a sneaking suspicion that in this instance he had been unmercifully cheated. If that beast did not have an ugly streak in him he was a poor judge of horseflesh, but there was nothing he could do. Jonathan had left for the sail loft and Margaret didn't seem to want to discuss the matter. He went on about his work but his mind was distraught, and it was with relief that he saw the two children watching the Wellfleet coachman rub down the animal when he returned for lunch. Perhaps he had been unduly alarmed. The brute seemed quiet enough now, and it was obvious that Tim already adored the animal. That might go far toward controlling him.

As for Margaret, she felt happier than she had for days. Jonathan could not be utterly calloused and indifferent to her wishes when he would do a thing like this, just to please her. She was not quite so pleased when he presented Peggy with a pearl and amethyst ring, but she had to reluctantly admit to herself that it was only fair. After all, it was her birthday, too, and horses cost a good deal of money. That afternoon she watched Tim ride off up the hill with a light heart as she dressed herself to attend a whist party. It was the first time that Nick had permitted her to attend a party since her accident and she was looking forward to it with great pleasure. The ladies she knew had begun to play for money and if she had any luck at all she might earn a neat sum, for she had become proficient at cards. The idea stimulated her and she hummed a little tune as she pinned her elaborate new hat on her high pompadour. She stood before the mirror regarding her reflection with pleasure. Her hair was so heavy and thick that she could obtain an enormous roll without the aid of stuffing, to which most of her friends had to resort. This was a great source of satisfaction to her as was anything in which she excelled. It was balm to the wounds her vanity had received in her youth.

The party was very gay and everybody made much of her. She had a wonderful time and made twenty-three dollars which pleased her. Her costume was much admired and the refreshments, she noted with satisfaction, were no more elaborate nor extensive than the ones she had served at her last party. As she stood in the hall, bidding her hostess good-by and waiting for her carriage to be called, she felt that the afternoon had been eminently satisfactory, from every point of view. She would hardly feel like eating much of the birthday dinner she had ordered, but probably nobody would notice but Nick and she would squelch him if he so much as opened his mouth. She was glad that she had not listened to Peggy's plea for a party. Had she done so she would have missed a great deal of pleasure and satisfaction that afternoon and after all, she told herself, there was plenty of time for Peggy to have parties. The child was young enough; she could have a party next year.

When her carriage was called she went out under the porte-cochere to find her coachman standing beside the carriage, holding the door open for her. As he handed her into the carriage, she felt the hand on her elbow tremble and she looked at him sharply. His face was red and his eyes swollen and she wondered crossly if he had been drinking. If he had, Jonathan would be sure to insist that she get someone else and she didn't want to go to the bother. She must speak to him about it, but just now, she was too weary. Of late, the inevitable aftermath of a crowded party was to leave her feeling unutterably exhausted and oddly depressed. Perhaps, she thought, Nick is right and I try to do too much. She wished that she could go to bed when she got home and have what dinner she wanted on a tray and not have to bother with the children's festivities. As these thoughts milled about in her tired brain, the coachman touched his whip to the horses and they were off at a sharp clip. Margaret frowned at his back. They almost grazed the pillar of the porte-cochere. It was not like Harry to be so careless. He must have been drinking, although she had never known him to do such a thing before. "Harry," she called out sharply, "what is the matter with you? Do be more careful."

The man nodded his head in its tall silk hat, but he didn't turn and it was not until they rounded a corner that Margaret observed a tear steal down his cheek. Why, the man was crying! He must be drunk! Alarmed, Margaret sat forward in her seat. In spite of her protest, Harry had not decreased the horses' speed and it was not long before they were turning into their own drive. He drew up by the front porch, but his usual flourish was missing. As he helped Margaret to alight, she looked at him keenly and

220

snapped, "Harry, have you been drinking?" The man shook his head without speaking and she saw that his pale blue eyes were swimming with tears.

Baffled and vaguely alarmed, Margaret ascended the steps. Ellen, the second maid, opened the door for her. Her usually high color was gone and she looked pale and frightened. At the sound of the opening of the heavy front door, Jonathan appeared from the back parlor. He, too, looked queer, almost as if he had seen a ghost. There was a taut whiteness about his face and a drawn expression about his mouth. For a fleeting moment she thought that he might have had some trouble at his church, but that would not concern Harry and Ellen, and they looked as odd as he did. What was the matter with her household all of a sudden? Even as the question crossed her mind she could hear Peggy sobbing somewhere at the back of the house. She's hurt herself and is making a great fuss about it, she thought crossly. Gently Jonathan unpinned her hat and helping her out of her jacket, laid it carefully on a chair. He evidently had something to tell her but did not know how to go about it. If it were only Peggy she could stand it; it was Tim about whom she would be really concerned, in case anything had happened. Out of her weariness and fear of the unknown, she cried out to him sharply, "In heaven's name what has come over everybody? You'd think there had been a funeral in the family! What did Peggy do to herself?"

He drew her tenderly to him and, looking down at her with eyes full of love and pity, said gently, "It's not Peggy, Margaret. It's Tim. The horse I bought him threw him this afternoon." He swallowed and could not finish.

Margaret clutched at him with frantic hands. Somehow she managed to articulate the awful words, "He isn't dead?"

Jonathan nodded, his arms closing more tightly around her to try to ward off some of the shock. "He-he died of a broken neck, an hour ago."

Chapter Twenty

From the very first, Margaret did not shed a tear. There was something tight inside of her which forbade her to weep. She went through the motions of living, like a sleepwalker. Even when they brought Timmie's body home in a coffin, she did not shed a tear although she winced at the bruises on his face which even the undertaker's art had not entirely concealed. All the outward signs of irritability and sharpness which had grown in her so steadily over a period of years were in abeyance. When Peggy's muffled sobbing came to her ears, she merely requested with a deadly patience that the child be taken to where she could not hear her. She refused to eat, but she drank whatever they put before her. She would not leave the side of the casket even to sleep and the only rest she had was produced by the drugs that the doctor slipped into her coffee.

While Tim's body was in the house she sat quietly without speaking or showing any sign of emotion. She had no words for anybody, even her husband, and paid no attention to anything that went on about her. She was like a woman turned to stone. Jonathan stayed with her as much as he could, but she seemed unaware of his presence. Nick's troubled eyes watched her intently and he said to Jonathan, "This can't go on. If she could only be made to break down and weep, it would relieve the tension. If she doesn't, something is going to snap."

Jonathan answered him sadly, his eyes on the beloved face, "Perhaps she will cry at the funeral. If she would only weep, I might be able to comfort her, but as it is she hardly knows I'm alive. She stares through me as if I were a perfect stranger."

But she did not break down at the funeral. She stood erect and dry-eyed at the grave's edge and did not even listen to the comforting words of the funeral service. Her only reaction was to be thankful within herself that the weather was good, for she felt that she would never have been able to leave that once warm and vibrant young body lying in the cold ground in sleet and snow.

Nothing reached her apathy. She did not even notice that the funeral was attended by everybody of any status in the city. There were so many floral tributes that it took six carriages to carry them from the house to the cemetery, but she looked at the elaborate pieces with eyes that did not see them, and for once, a lavish display found no pleasurable response within her soul. She helped Jonathan choose the grave stone without a tremor and when he told her that he would like to have the words Job uttered when his children were taken from him engaved upon it she made no objection although the sentiment was not hers. The magnificent sentence did not even rouse her as she looked at it. "The Lord hath given and the Lord hath taken away; blessed be the name of the Lord!" Jonathan had had the word *blessed* underlined and there had been a time when the very sight of that line underscoring such a word in such a connection would have sent her into a tantrum, but now it seemed to have no meaning for her. It was as though her ability to feel and react had completely atrophied.

When it was all over, they took her home and for the first time since Timmie's death, she expressed a wish. She wanted the curtains left drawn and the furniture shrouded and his room left exactly as he had left it. She thought numbly that if he could not see the sunshine and the flowers, she did not want to see them, either. Sitting alone in his shuttered room in the dark, she felt closer to him than in any other way. She would see no one and go nowhere. Day merged into night and night into day and she scarcely noticed. Finally in desperation, Nick persuaded her to go to the cemetery, hoping that the sight of the new grave would break the dam within her, but she merely sat down on the ground and gently stroked the tender new grass which was already trying to hide the earth's scar.

It helped her to some extent, however, for after that she had Harry drive her there every day and the doctor encouraged it, for at least it got her out of doors for a little while. As time went on she spent more and more hours at the cemetery and one day Jonathan, concerned for her after a particularly protracted absence, found her face down on the sod with her face buried in the short grass, but as dry-eyed as ever. He lifted her gently to her feet and carried her to the carriage, and when he spoke to her, his voice was tender, but determined, "My darling, you cannot go on this way. There is no use coming out here. Timmie isn't here. He is with God and is happy. He had accepted Jesus Christ as his personal Saviour and for him all troubles are over." But she merely looked at him dully as if he were speaking to her in some foreign language which she could not understand.

By fall, Nick and Jonathan decided to send Peggy away to boarding school. The atmosphere of the house was not suitable for an adolescent girl and there seemed to be nothing that they could do to change it for the better. Margaret had forgotten all about her business and even about her hard-fought-for place in society. She made no effort whatsoever to see her friends although many of them called to express their sympathy. In spite of Jonathan's remonstrances she continued to go to the cemetery daily and spend long hours there. Even bad weather did not stop her. If it rained, she just sat in the carriage and looked at the grave. The two men who loved her were helpless and their very helplessness made them frantic. Jonathan had tried everything he knew of to reach her, but nothing had prevailed. If only he could arouse her old spirit. Even her antagonism against his religion was better than this cold, stolid indifference. He and Nick discussed the matter but they could see no solution for the problem. Nick was more worried than Jonathan, for he knew that this sort of thing could not go on indefinitely. She needed a shock of some kind to get her out of herself, but when it came, it unfortunately was not the kind he would have chosen.

She was returning from the cemetery one afternoon and Harry was helping her to alight when the front door opened and one of her erstwhile friends fluttered down the steps. Margaret would have turned aside, but there was no way of evading the encounter without a direct cut, so she stood frozen, her foot on the bottom step. Her friend gushed up to her and enveloped her in laces and ribbons and the ends of a feather boa, exclaiming, "Oh, you poor, poor, dear. You look simply awful and I don't wonder!" Then, as Margaret stood silent, looking at her with what the woman later described as "a wild look," she rushed heedlessly on. "It would have been bad enough to have had him killed outright, but to know that his brains were slowly bashed out on the cobblestones as the horse dragged him must be just too awful."

At that juncture, Harry who had been standing by, a helpless and distressed listener, intervened with the suggestion that he drive the lady home. Margaret merely nodded her assent and proceeded into the house in a stupor. Ellen was waiting for her and took her hat and jacket. Instead of going directly to Timmie's room as was her usual custom, she turned into the front parlor and seated herself by the empty fireplace. There was something she had to think about before she went upstairs. Ellen looked surprised, but she made no comment.

As Margaret sat straight and stiff in her chair, her back not touching the cushion, her small hands clutched in her lap, all the stolidness of the past months broke its hold upon her, and her emotions tore through the dam she had erected inside herself like flood water cascading over a spillway. So that was why they had not let her see him for two days! That was why they had told her that his neck had been broken — because they wanted her to believe Timmie had died quickly and painlessly. This accounted for the queer angle in which they had placed his head in the coffin. This accounted for the fright on the maid's face when she had overheard them whisper that his foot had been caught in the stirrup. He must have been dragged helplessly down the cobblestone hill while his skull was bashed in bit by bit. The horror of it engulfed her.

Suddenly everything in her rose up in bitter rebellion and deep resentment. This tragedy need never have happened. Had Jonathan listened to her, he would have had enough money to purchase a safe horse for Timmie. Had he sued Mr. Cuyler as she wanted him to and obtained what was his by right, he would have had it. Or had he taken the offer from Mr. Tredway, her friend, the improvement in his business would certainly have provided the money. It was all the fault of religion, all of it: his tithing, his principles, and his mother's spite. There would have been no necessity of getting a bargain in horseflesh had there been more money in the bank. Suddenly, it seemed to her as if religion was a great monster which had pursued her and thwarted her at every turn, until some unseen power had succeeded in torturing to death her precious son. That an all-powerful, loving God should have allowed this to happen to Timmie who tried so hard to serve Him and do His bidding was more than she could imagine. Burning resentment boiled up within her soul and she gave a moan like an animal in pain.

The front door opened and she heard Jonathan and Nick enter the house. She rose with a speed that she had not shown since Timmie's death and moved swiftly out into the hall. At sight of her face, the doctor stopped short, but Jonathan went to her at once, his arms out and his deep concern on his face. She looked up at him wildly as his arms closed about her. All of a sudden she forgot that this was the man whom she loved and who loved her. Before her very eyes he turned into the monster who had haunted her and hurt her and deprived her of all she wanted and cherished most in life. She wanted to kill him slowly, making him suffer as poor Timmie had suffered when he had been dragged down the long hill. She gave a wild sob and, throwing his arms from her, lurched at him, raking his face with her sharp nails and sinking her teeth into his arm, kicking and screaming. Something burst in her brain and suddenly bereft of strength, she felt herself, still struggling feebly, sinking into a black, bottomless pit.

The late October sunshine filtered softly through the partly drawn blinds and lay in narrow bands across the covers of the bed. The room was very quiet, with a quietness which in itself carried a healing quality. The bed felt soft and easy under Margaret's body in a way it had not felt for many weeks. She lay limp and exhausted against her pillows, dimly aware that for the first time in a long, long while she was not bound to the bed by heavy restraining bands. She experimented weakly and found that she could move her arms and legs without interference. Her head felt singularly light and she raised a limp hand to feel her hair. The great thick ropes of which she had been so proud were gone. Tears filled her eyes, for beneath her weakly experimenting fingers her hair felt harsh and coarse where it had been cropped. She turned her head on the pillows and the tears trickled down her neck, but she was too exhausted to wipe them away. She closed her heavy eyes and lay sunk in a stupor of weariness. Someone bent over her and gently sponged her face with cool water, and she opened her eyes to see Nick beside her, his keen eyes searching hers. Feebly she smiled at him to let him know that his presence was reassuring and drifted off into the first relaxed and dreamless slumber she had known for many weeks.

When she awoke hours later he was still there. As she opened her eyes once more he said softly, "Hello, dear, you are much better," and added under his breath, "thank God!" Her keen hearing had not been affected by her illness and she heard him perfectly, although she did not let on that she had done so. Her brain was quite clear at last, but she knew that many dark waters had passed over her soul since the day she had learned how Timmie had died. As she lay there, she was thankful that at last she could think about it without horror, but she had no desire to talk about it.

For the next few weeks of her life she was content to just rest and allow herself to be tended lovingly. She ate a little and slept and opened her eyes to eat a little more and drifted off again into restful and healing slumber. No one came to her room but Nick and the nurses who cared for her and she did not ask to see anyone else. Her mind was not entirely clear as to just what had happened and she wanted to straighten events out in her own thinking before she saw her husband. When she felt equal to it, she would ask Nick about it, but just now she did not feel up to making the effort to recall that grim scene.

Slowly, and bit by bit as her body rested, matters clarified themselves and fell into their proper places in her mind. The terrible vacant emptiness which had kept her numb for so long was gone and she was now able to face what lay behind her. There were still a few things that she did not understand, but she knew that Nick would straighten them out for her when she felt like discussing them with him. So she rested and bided her time.

One evening when Nick was sitting with her until the night nurse came in, she approached the subject timidly. He had dismissed the day nurse early and had fed her her supper himself. Cold fall rains had streamed down all day. It was very pleasant to lie in a soft bed, watch the fire glowing in the grate, listen to the rain pelting down on the roof and dripping off the gutters, and to feel safe and warm and secure. It was wonderful to be no longer haunted by what had been, to feel some degree of resignation creeping over her and to realize that her hurt was slowly healing. She could even think of Timmie now without too much pain.

Nick finished spooning soft custard into her mouth and put the dish back on the tray. "That's a good girl," he said approvingly, "you are now eating about half what you should to get well. If you keep this up we may get you out of bed by Christmas."

Margaret put out a hand to him. "Nick?"

"Yes, dear."

"I want to ask you some questions."

Nick sighed, "I supposed you would, sooner or later."

"What has been the matter with me?"

"You have had a very serious attack of brain fever."

For a moment she digested this in silence. Then she asked simply and without emotion, "Is that a polite way of saying that I went crazy?"

The doctor would not look her in the eye. He took out his watch and wound it carefully before he put it back in his pocket. When he could find no further excuse for delay, he said, "You were rather violent for a time."

"Did I hurt Jonathan?"

The doctor fitted the tips of his big fingers together precisely before he replied. "So, you remember that?"

"Faintly, and it makes me rather ashamed of myself."

"You needn't be. He knew that you did not really mean to hurt him. Your emotions had been dammed up too long, that was all. They were bound to spill over sometime and he just happened to be there when they did."

"Why hasn't he been in to see me?"

"Because I asked him to stay away."

Margaret considered this. "Then I did try to kill him and you thought the sight of him would upset me."

228

The doctor nodded miserably, refusing to meet her inquiring eyes.

Margaret continued inexorably, "And, you cut off my hair to keep me from tearing it out by the roots?" He still would not look directly at her, but she was relentless. "Nick, if I was that bad, what brought me out of it?"

He shook his head at her reprovingly and she noticed for the first time that the thick hair over his temples was quite white. "Can't we talk about something else?"

"Not until you tell me what I want to know," she said firmly.

"There never was any use in trying to hide things from you, Margaret," he said resignedly, "but, I wish we could talk about this later when you feel stronger."

"I feel strong enough to get an answer to my question right now," she said, with a return of her old spirit.

He looked down at his big hands clenched on his knees, uncertain of just how to proceed. There was no use in trying to tell her anything else but the truth, for she would learn it herself sooner or later, but he had hoped to avoid it until she had regained enough of her mental balance to receive it without undue emotion.

"Well," she prompted him persistently.

His eyes were still on his hands as he tried to tell her. "You were quite violent for a time and I despaired of your life, let alone your sanity." He closed his eyes as if to shut away from his vision the sight of her as she had been at her worst. "There was nothing I could do and I knew it."

She put her hand on his arm comfortingly. "Poor Nick. I put you through a bad time, didn't I? But I did come through it. I wonder why?"

He took the thin little hand between both his own and stroked it gently as he talked. "I honestly don't know. I only know that I was at the end of my rope, and when I told Jonathan, he got a delegation from his church to come here and pray for you. They prayed all night and in the morning your fever broke and your brain cleared." His keen eyes searched hers to see what effect this revelation was going to have upon her, but she took it quietly enough and made no comment. "No matter what you may think of Jonathan's religion, dear, you should remember in the future that you owe your very life to it, for I have never had a patient as sick as you were who did not end his life in an institution."

For a long moment there was silence between them. At last she spoke and when she did, he was relieved to see that her mind was not dwelling upon what he had told her. "Does Jonathan want to see me?"

"Of course, but I only let him look at you when you are asleep."

"Don't you think you could let me see him now?" For the first time her eyes were eager.

"Yes, if you are sure that you want to see him."

"Oh, I do, I do!" exclaimed Margaret, weak tears filling her eyes and spilling down her pale cheeks. "I want to tell him that I love him and how sorry I am!"

The nurse was preparing Margaret for the night and the doctor and Jonathan were sitting in the back parlour over a glowing fire waiting for her summons.

Nick filled his pipe and leaned back in his chair, "There is something I want to talk to you about before you see Margaret, Jonathan."

Jonathan looked over at his friend and there was affection and respect in his eyes. "Yes?"

"Now that Margaret has been given back to us," he used the plural unconsciously, "she has got to be treated very gently for a while."

Jonathan smiled in spite of himself, "Do you think you need to tell me that? I love her."

Nick shook his head, "I don't mean in the way you think, but in another. The mind is a very delicate organ and Margaret's mind has been very sick. I do not need to tell you, for you saw her at her worst, that she was a raving maniac. We know that the break finally came because of Timmie, but a sound mind does not usually give way just because of one incident. There was more behind this than appeared upon the surface; something of long duration, which broke only when Timmie's death was added to it. I think I know what that strain was and I would not be your friend, let alone a competent doctor, if I did not warn you that in the future you must be extremely careful to avoid that particular thing." As Jonathan made no audible reply but sat gazing into the fire, the doctor continued, "I think you know I mean your religion."

Jonathan took his hand down and turned to his friend. "You are using the wrong word, Nick, what you mean is my Christianity." .

The doctor frowned. He had hoped that his friend was not going to be difficult about this matter, for it was one that he wanted settled before he allowed him to see his wife. "What do you mean?"

"Simply this. there are many religions in the world but only one Christianity. Christianity is not a religion. It is knowledge of and obedience to the living Christ. Terrible things have been done in the name of religion. You know that. It is religion which makes an Indian woman throw her child into the Ganges River to appease the river god, but that is not Christianity. Christ would never want such a thing. If you are going to talk about what I believe, at least call it by its right name. I serve a God of love and it is not likely that I would, because of that very thing, knowingly bring harm to my beloved."

The doctor moved restlessly in his chair. "Not on purpose, I know. But there is one thing you must face. Margaret's constant antagonism to what you believe has been a contributary cause for her illness and from now on I want you to promise me to make a concerted effort to keep it out of her life. Oh, I don't mean that you should abandon your beliefs," as he saw the expression on his friend's face, "but that you might arrange your life so that what you believe interferes with her as little as possible. She is going to be a semi-invalid for a long time so it shouldn't be too hard."

"Just precisely what do you want me to do?"

"Give up saying prayers and grace at the table for a time and cease to make any reference whatsoever to what you believe. If you have to read your Bible, don't do it in her presence. In fact, avoid all reference to the strain that helped bring on this break in the first place. If you don't, I cannot promise that it will not be repeated."

For a long moment Jonathan was silent. Then he asked the doctor a question, "What do you suppose brought on her terrible resistance to the truth, Nick?"

"As far as I can make out it started when she was very young and thought that God failed to help her when she asked help of Him. From that time on she feels somebody else's beliefs have always stood in the way of her getting what she wanted for herself. You must remember that when she met you, you felt much the same way she did."

"I know," said Jonathan and sighed. "That is the tragedy. I have come to believe the truth, but she won't let herself. It is really quite unreasonable of her to expect God to give her everything she asked and yet to ignore what He asks of her. After all, He has infinite wisdom and is able to recognize that what she wanted may not have been good for her.

"But she got it anyway and she thinks that it was the best thing in the world for her which, in her thinking, immediately puts God in the wrong.

"God is never wrong, and if her experience has made her believe any such thing, it is proof that what she got was very bad for her, indeed."

The time was getting short and the doctor was growing impatient. "There is nothing we can do about that now. We are helpless and all we can do is to avoid the tension which brought this thing on. Will you give me your word to do this?"

"If that is what you wish. I respect your judgment, but you are quite wrong in believing that we are helpless. I can still pray and prayer is a mighty powerful weapon. When the day comes when my prayer is answered and she comes to see things God's way, she will be well."

Christmas came and went and still Margaret made no effort to get out of bed. Peggy had received an invitation to visit one of her classmates and the doctor urged Jonathan to let her accept it, for he was anxious that no undue nervous strain be brought to bear on Margaret for as long a time as possible, and that Peggy got on her nerves was undeniable. Jonathan had turned one of the upstairs bedrooms into a sitting room for Margaret's use. It was a sunny room on the corner of the back of the house, entirely free of street noises and other distractions, and Margaret spent her days there. Her strength returned very slowly and she was content to just lie quietly and rest. After awhile the night nurse was dismissed, but the day nurse stayed on, for the doctor did not want his patient left alone for a minute, and she was not strong enough for the stimulus of outside visitors.

Margaret retreated into a little world of her own where nothing was allowed to disturb her. Her room was always full of flowers and books and every week the doctor brought her a new puzzle. Many of them were large enough to cover a card table and were so exquisitely fitted together that they could almost be picked up in one piece when completed. Jonathan had made her a table on rollers which fitted over her bed and which could be drawn toward her or pushed away with equal ease and on this she kept a puzzle ready to be worked at any time.

When the nurse left for the day, either Jonathan or Nick was in attendance. At Christmas time the doctor had presented her with a gramophone and she derived endless pleasure and amusement from the records which he brought her. Jonathan did as he had promised: religion was never mentioned. He did not read his Bible in her presence and he abandoned his evening meetings altogether, unless he was certain Nick could be with her. She had nothing to trouble her and nothing to annoy her, and bit by bit her strength gradually returned. When spring came she was still content to just lie in her room in the sun or amuse herself in her sitting room with her simple pleasures. As summer approached, the doctor saw to it that Peggy was sent to a girl's camp so that her presence about the house might not be a disturbing element. Margaret never wrote the child and thought of her as seldom as she possibly could.

A second Christmas had come and gone before she showed any signs of wanting to see her friends. It was very nice to have Jonathan's full attention centered upon herself once more, and she was loathe to relinquish it. Sometimes she mused within herself that she had had to go crazy to get him to do what she wanted, but somehow the thought was not very pleasing. It had been a high price to pay.

When the doctor allowed visitors to see her, her friends crowded around her. They were all very curious to see how she looked, for there had been many wild rumors about her condition, and they were anxious to verify them. To their surprise she acted quite normal and looked quite charming with her clipped hair soft and pretty about her face. She was ·soon swamped with invitations, for she could be a gay and charming companion when she chose, and they had missed her. The doctor

233

and Jonathan talked about the matter and Nick persuaded Jonathan to give her an allowance large enough to prevent her going back to her cooking business. If she wanted to go to parties in the afternoons, he insisted that she stay in bed until noon.

Nick offered to loan Jonathan the money, but he refused the loan courteously, and if it took every cent he made to pay Peggy's heavy expenses and keep things going the way Margaret wanted them at home, he told no one, and never mentioned the fact that he had had to abandon the idea of purchasing some new machinery for the sail loft, now turned factory.

Chapter Twenty-one

It was a broiling day in early August, 1914. Margaret had established herself in a hammock which Harry had strung between two trees in the back yard, in the hopes that it would be cooler there, but not a breath of air stirred the leaves which formed a canopy over her head and the small breeze she produced by swinging the hammock was hardly worth the effort. Nick came into the yard next door waving a newspaper at her, then came through the hole in the hedge, "See, what did I tell you? Germany marched into Belgium, just as I was afraid she would. Britain will be in it before morning. Where is Jonathan? He will want to know about this!"

But Margaret was not concerned with Belgium nor Britain, nor at the moment with Jonathan. She was concerned because she knew that if there were a war, Nick would be determined to·get in it. He had received part of his education in Paris and he felt a responsibility to help the French. She did not want him to leave her, for she had grown to depend greatly upon him and his ability to keep Jonathan walking the way she wanted him to go.

"He will be home to lunch in a few minutes. Hasn't Belgium an army? Can't she do something to stop them?"

The doctor groaned. "I doubt if anything will stop them. They have been preparing for this for years. The Serbian affair was only an excuse for them to get going."

Jonathan appeared in the doorway and Ellen rang the bell for lunch. Nick waved his paper at his friend and Margaret covered up her anxiety by suggesting that the doctor join them.

Full of news, Nick followed her into the house, stopping only to show Jonathan the headlines of the New York paper which he held. The two men spread the paper out on the table and eagerly read the scanty news it contained.

Jonathan straightened and took his place at the table opposite Margaret. "This is sad news."

Nick nodded. "Yes, and there is no telling how much blood will be shed before it is over."

Jonathan bowed his head in silent grace. He had not offered grace aloud at the table since Margaret's illness, but he would not eat his food without returning thanks to God and somehow the doctor did not have the heart to suggest that he abandon the simple and reverent gesture. He raised his head and said sadly, "Men cannot get away from blood. The world will not accept the shed blood of Jesus Christ, but they accept the blood of war."

Margaret looked uneasy and the doctor raised his eyebrows. It was the first time that Jonathan had broken his promise to the doctor not to mention his religious convictions in front of Margaret. Margaret hoped fervently that the war wasn't going to start him up again and the doctor said hastily, "This may involve us eventually if Britain is dragged into it, for she is pledged to protect Belgium's borders."

Margaret stirred her iced tea impatiently. "Oh, Nick, we are too far away. Why should we be concerned anyway? It isn't our fight!" Within herself she was thinking how unfortunate the whole war situation was, for it was disrupting and disturbing her tranquil life.

Nick put down his knife and fork. "You forget that I spent several summers in Germany when I was in school and I understand the German character. They are very persistent and very thorough. If they sweep through Belgium and France falls, there

236

is no end to where their lust for conquest may take them."

Margaret looked at him in surprise. "You don't think that they actually have some chance of success?" She was startled, for she had thought that at best this war would be of short duration and of little consequence.

Nick nodded gloomily and Jonathan, seeing the amazed expression on her face, said gently. "I wouldn't worry too much, darling. God is still in His Heaven and He still rules over the destinies of the nations."

Nick and Margaret made no reply, but there was something subtly comforting in the positiveness of his assurance. For the first time in her married life, Margaret began to realize that there were times when what Jonathan believed could be a comfort and solace.

She found that there was no getting away from the war. It was a topic on everybody's lips, and Nick in particular could not seem to forget it. He had a large scale map on which he followed every movement of the troops that was reported in the papers and the nearer the Germans got to Paris, the more tense he got. He wanted dreadfully to be over there helping in the fight, but he could not quite bring himself to abandon Margaret, and the struggle between his desire and his conscience made him irritable. It was not, however, until the battle of Ypres in April, 1915, when the Germans used poison gas, that the restlessness which was seething within him came to a head.

The weather was beautiful and the earth clothed in the gay garments of spring. An unprecendented hot spell had brought everybody out of doors in their light clothes and it seemed incredible that a few thousand miles away men were bleeding and dying. Margaret was in the garden with Harry, supervising some planting. When she saw Nick come through the hedge, she left Harry and went with him to a stone bench which stood at the foot of the garden. Seating herself, she looked up at him and knew from his expression that the news was not good.

He put one foot on the bench and stood staring gloomily down at the earth under his feet. He seemed to have forgotten for the moment that she was there. She put her hand on his knee, "What is it, Nick? You might as well tell me."

"The Boche have started to use poison gas!"

"But that is inhuman!"

"It is not only inhuman, it is diabolical and devilish."

"I thought that there was some kind of an agreement forbidding its use."

"There was. The Geneva Pact. But that has proven only to be another scrap of paper to the Boche. When I read about this in the morning paper, I was inclined to agree with Jonathan that the whole human race must have been born children of the devil!" The words were out before he thought and he glanced down at her uneasily to see how she would take them, but she was watching a fat robin pecking worms and she appeared not to have heard him. To cover his uneasiness, he sat down beside her. "I feel that I must get over there and do something to help."

This remark brought her attention to him at once. "Oh, no, Nick!" and at his look, she pleaded. "After all, it isn't our war, and what would I ever do without you? Why, I just couldn't go on living."

His keen eyes went swiftly over her face. "You are all right now. You don't need me any longer."

She clutched his arm. "But I do! I do! It is you who has kept Jonathan in order these last few years and made him act more reasonably. You didn't think I knew that, did you? But I did. If you leave, he will probably go back to his meetings and leave me alone night after night." Then, as she saw no softening of the determination in his face, she added, "Supposing that I had another," she hesitated for the right word, "attack?"

"You won't," he said almost harshly, trying to hide his keen disappointment that her need of him was purely professional. "You are as right as rain if only you use a little sense."

"But, Nick, I'm never sure." The idea had just occurred to her and seeing from the expression in his eyes that it had weight with him she emphasized it. "With you near, I do not worry about it; but if you went away, I would be afraid. It happened once and it might happen again." Tears filled her eyes and her lower lip trembled.

Nick covered her hand with his, all the bitterness gone out of him at the sight of her tears. "Don't cry, dear. I cannot bear it and I have enough on my mind as it is. I will never leave you, while you need me, unless. . . " he hesitated and did not find the words with which to continue.

"Unless what?" she prompted.

"Unless," and he looked at her out of the corner of his eye to see how she was going to take it, "we are drawn into it. In that case I would have to help my country in anyway I could."

"Oh!" exclaimed Margaret with a sigh of relief. "Then I won't worry!"

It was a cold Sunday afternoon in March, 1917. Torrents of rain had fallen all day and washed the remnants of the dirty snow into the gutters. It was a disagreeable cold rain driven with the full force of the March wind behind it, and late in the afternoon the dropping temperature was turning it into icy fingers of sleet which tapped sharply against the window panes and made the warm fire and the soft lights seem all the more cozy and comforting. Nick and Jonathan sat in front of the fire discussing the latest war news. Margaret was asleep, for the doctor still insisted that she take a long nap. Because of the coldness and darkness of the day she had slept later than usual and the two men were enjoying a big pot of fragrant coffee and a thick pile of cinnamon toast which Ellen had prepared for them.

Nick handed his empty cup to Jonathan to be refilled. "If this unrestricted submarine warfare goes on much longer, it won't be long before we get in it."

Jonathan handed him back his full cup and picked up his own. "And then you'll be off."

The doctor nodded. "I have felt guilty about staying out of it this long." He did not divulge his reasons for doing so and his friend did not ask for them.

Jonathan added some hot coffee to his cup and said thoughtfully between sips, "Tim would have been just the right age to have gone, had he lived."

The doctor nodded.

Tim's father stirred his coffee thoughtfully. "I have come to realize these last few years that it was the goodness of God that took Tim suddenly, for I believe that Margaret would have broken mentally under the strain of his going off to war if he were alive now."

"But, why did Tim have to die at all? Couldn't God have kept him from that accident and through the war years as well?"

"Of course. But I am afraid that the reason God took him was because Margaret had come to worship him instead of worshiping God, and that He could not allow."

"It was rather hard on you who did worship God in what you call the right way."

"Yes, it was hard, but not crushing as it was for Margaret, who has refused stubbornly to acknowledge Him. It is unreasonable to expect God to deal anything but judgment to a persistent unbeliever. That is the way we treat those who break our laws and we consider it just and reasonable. Why should not the same rule apply to those who persist in unbelief, which is breaking God's commandment: you shall love the Lord your God with all your heart. If people will not accept God's love, they must expect His judgment."

"Why should a loving God want to send anybody to hell?" Nick's tone was truculent.

For the first time a little impatience crept into Jonathan's voice. "Who said He did? The Bible says: 'God is not willing that *any* should perish, but that *all* should come to repentence.' Oh, Nick, can't you see at what a great cost He provided a way back to fellowship with Himself? Think of His standing back and permitting men to torture His only Son the way they did, without any interference upon His part. It is far easier for a loving parent to suffer pain himself than to stand back and watch His child die, yet that is exactly what God did to procure our salvation. When He paid the price of His Son's blood to keep men *out* of hell, how can you talk about His sending them *to* hell?"

For a moment when Jonathan ceased speaking there was silence. Both men, concerned with their own private thoughts, had their eyes on the fire. The mantle clock slowly chimed the hour and the coals fell together in the grate. Nick looked up. "You are always talking about blood. Why is that so important?"

"Because without blood there is no life; a bloodless body is a dead body. Physically there can be no life without the shedding of blood. I remember well your concern for Margaret when the twins were born, lest she bleed to death. One thing you should know is that it was not the twins' blood that was shed at their birth, but the blood of their mother. In spiritual birth, the same thing holds true. It is not the blood of the one being born again that is shed; it is the blood of another: Jesus Christ. The same principle holds true for both physical birth and spiritual birth. Why are you willing to accept it on the physical plane, but not on the spiritual?"

The doctor's eyes had not left his friend's face. "You are very persuasive at times, Jonathan." And as he spoke the words, the thought went through his mind that whether what Jonathan believed was right or not, it had certainly helped him to meet the troubles of life with courage and fortitude, while Margaret, who had flouted Christianity, had broken under the same strain. the thought was disturbing.

Once more silence reigned in the warm room. The house was so quiet that they could hear Margaret walking softly along the upper hall, and in a moment she appeared in the doorway, her hair in lovely disorder and her face flushed from sleep. Both men rose, their hearts in their eyes at the sight of her, and the doctor drew her favorite chair up to the fire. She thanked him with a nod and seated herself, but her smile was directed toward her husband.

Jonathan was in his office going over a long list of figures and had become so absorbed that he looked up with a start when Nick suddenly appeared from nowhere and impetuously flung the door open without the preliminary courtesy of knocking. Nick never visited him in his office and for a second, a stab of alarm went through Jonathan, to be quickly allayed by the sight of the glaring headlines on the newspaper the doctor carried.

"It's war?"

"Yes. I am leaving on the noon train. I have been ready for this for weeks."

"Where are you going?"

"To Washington. There are some strings that I can pull and I want to get across as soon as possible."

"We will miss you."

The doctor brushed that aside. "Probably not half as much as I shall miss you, but there is something that I've got to say before I leave. It's about Margaret."

"Yes?"

"You've been awfully good about following my instructions about not talking about religion and I want you to continue to do so while I'm gone. Another thing I want you to make sure of is that she doesn't go back to working for the Exchange. She hasn't the stamina for that kind of thing anymore." He hesitated a moment and then continued. "I don't know just how to say this, Jonathan, but I've got more money that I know what to do with and I've arranged with the bank for you to draw against my account if you need to. You may call it a loan if you like."

For a long moment Jonathan stared down at the papers in his hands without seeing them. Then he said quietly, "I am not sure that what you are asking of me is the wisest thing to do, but you have been so good to us that it is hard for me to refuse you. I'll continue to do as you want, but as far as the money goes, I'm sure I won't need it. If I get that army contract for tents, I'll be all set."

"But I'll feel better if I know it is there to be used just in case of necessity," the doctor insisted.

"Oh, very well," conceded Jonathan and the doctor sighed with relief.

"One more thing. Keep Peggy away from her mother as much as possible. Oh, I know," he continued as he caught Jonathan's expression, "it is hard to understand why a mother should feel about her own child as Margaret does, but just because a woman carries a child in her own body for nine months does not necessarily mean that she will have a close affinity for it when it is born. I do not know exactly what causes the friction, but you must admit that it is there and it has been heightened by Peggy's being Tim's twin. Will you do as I want about this, too? I know I'm right about it."

Again Jonathan nodded his assent. "Good!" exclaimed the doctor. "Now, I can go off with a quiet mind."

Jonathan looked up at his friend. "There is one thing I want you to realize, however. In promising not to let my beliefs annoy Margaret, I do so only because I am trusting God to reach her somehow, sometime. That she will someday come to believe, I know, for God has promised believers the salvation of their house and Margaret is a member of my house. I may not live to see her a believer, but God will not fail to fulfill His word because I trust Him." Jonathan rose and held out his hand with a smile. "Goodby and thanks for all you have done. The only way I know of to repay you is to pray for you and my prayers will follow you whereever you go."

The doctor's voice held an unaccustomed note of huskiness as he replied, "Good. I'll count on that. I once heard you read these words from the Bible and I have never forgotten them: 'The effectual fervent prayer of a righteous man availeth much.' At the time, you said that to be righteous meant to be right with God. I want you to know, just in case we don't meet again, that I consider you the most righteous man I have ever known and I wish I had what you've got. Good-by and may your God bless you and yours."

It was a bitterly cold winter day toward the final year of the war. The yards and lawns were buried deep under several feet of well-packed snow. Icicles several feet long hung from the eaves of the houses. Margaret had spent the morning at the Red Cross headquarters rolling bandages and the afternoon at a bridge party, only to return home, eat her dinner, and go out to another party. As she prepared herself for bed, she admitted to herself that she had been foolish to do so much. Ellen had opened her bed and placed a hot water bottle between the sheets, but even as she crawled into the warm bed and relaxed against the pillows she realized that she was too weary to sleep. She lay there watching the fire in the grate and wishing that Jonathan were home. The nights he knew she was to be out, he went out himself. She never inquired where it was he went, but she supposed that it was to the Mission. She had had the carriage so he was afoot and she lay listening for the crunch of his footsteps on the drive.

Since Nick had gone off to war she had come to depend more than ever on her husband. In about a half hour she heard a carriage stop in front of the house. Somebody must have brought him home. She heard him stamp the snow off his boots and shut the front door. Then all was quiet. She could not help but wonder what he was doing. He had gone back to the kitchen. Perhaps he was hungry and was getting himself something to eat, but he was taking a long time about it. It was all of twenty minutes before he came upstairs.

When he opened the door softly, she said querulously, "What in heaven's name have you been doing down there? I thought you'd never come up."

He entered the room and taking off his coat, hung it over the back of a chair. "I brought home an occupant for the shed room and I was getting him settled."

"Who is it this time? The 'fallen man' once again?"

He nodded, somewhat shamefacedly.

"I suppose he is drunk."

"He isn't now, but I am afraid that he has been quite recently. He lost his job again, of course, and spent all his money and he didn't have any place to go. I didn't have the heart not to take him in on a night like this."

Margaret sighed, "I suppose not. You are a terribly easy mark. I should think that you would realize by now that you can never get him to remain sober for any length of time."

"I cannot turn him down just because he is weak. Is there anything I can get you, darling, before I come to bed?"

"Yes, I would like some hot milk. Perhaps it would make me sleep."

"I'll get it for you right away."

"And, Jonathan?"

He turned with his hand on the door know. "Yes?"

"Please lock the door to the shed room. I don't want the 'fallen man' wandering about in his sleep."

"But, Margaret, it seems unkind to lock the poor wretch in as if we were afraid that he would contaminate us."

"Well, maybe you are not afraid of him, but I am, and I'm too tired tonight to worry about him. Lock it, Jonathan, please. Promise me."

For a long moment Jonathan hesitated, but as he looked across at her and noted the black circles under her eyes and her air of evident weariness, he remembered Nick's final admonitions and nodded his head in agreement. "Very well. I'll do it if you wish, but I hate to. I'll bring the hot milk in a few minutes."

The occupant of the shed room, comfortably established in the old double bed, fell into a light doze. He had fully intended to blow out the oil lamp before he went to sleep, but he hated the dark and so he drifted into slumber with it still lit, standing on the small table beside the bed. Sometime after midnight he was rudely awakened by sharp pains in his chest. He raised himself on his elbow and leaned against the back of the bed. As the minutes

244

passed, his breathing grew more and more labored and he became frightened. He had no whiskey to help him endure the pain; he must have help. Managing to swing his feet over the edge of the bed, he staggered to the door. He turned the knob and realized to his horror that it was locked. Leaning against the door, he wondered with mounting panic what he was going to do when all of a sudden a wave of blackness swirled around him. He reached for the bed post, missed, and fell forward, knocking the lighted lamp onto the middle of the bed. It ignited instantly and the flames leapt up about him, but he was already unconscious.

Upstairs, Margaret moved restlessly in her sleep. Jonathan roused sufficiently to ease her into a more comfortable position against his shoulder and then dozed off again. Sometime later he was awakened by a peculiar and unfamiliar crackling sound. Margaret had at last fallen into a heavy slumber and it was not until he had eased his shoulder cautiously from under her head that he was able to sit up and listen. What he heard sent him to the door in a rush, but even as he put his hand on the panel he could feel the intense heat on the outside. He was back at the bed in a bound and he thanked God in his heart that he had had a telephone installed in the bedroom for Margaret's convenience. After he had called the fire department he ran to the closet and procured the heaviest garment of Margaret's that he could find. As he wakened her rudely and forced her arms into it, he could see small tongues of flame licking under the door. Running to the window he opened it wide. Returning to the bed he wrapped his wife in the blankets and picking her up in his arms ran with her to the window. "The house is on fire and I am going to throw you out into the snow. Go next door to Mrs. Fairchild's and pound on the door until you rouse somebody."

Without giving her a chance to protest he lifted her sideways through the window and tossed her as far as he could. Leaning over the sill he watched the small dark bundle plummet into the snow-laden bushes near the house, and waited until he saw Margaret stagger to her feet before he went through the bathroom to Peggy's room to see if he could gain access to the third floor where the maids were sleeping. Then he must somehow reach the shed room and extricate the old man.

Realizing that he was dressed only in his pajamas and had no shoes on his feet, he turned back into the room to fetch a coat and shoes, but the curtains were already in flames and he had to abandon the effort. Closing the doors between the rooms he cautiously crossed Peggy's room and felt the door into the hall. It was as hot as the one in the front of the house. The fire must have come up the back stairs as well as the front. He must cross the upper hall to reach the third floor staircase. Turning back into the bathroom he started both faucets running in the basin and splashed the water liberally over his pajamas. Then, throwing a towel into the basin he soaked it thoroughly and, covering his head with it, took a long breath and opened the door into the hall.

Margaret sat by the big bed in Mrs. Fairchild's guest room and listened to Jonathan's labored breathing. His head, with its twisted mass of dark red hair, moved restlessly on the pillow. His face was an angry red and his hands and arms were bound with soft rags saturated with ointment. From where Margaret sat she could look out of the window and see the ruins of their home. There was nothing left but piles of scarred bricks. The cold had been so intense that the water the firemen pumped into the flames had frozen as soon as it contacted the walls. They had been unable to save a thing. Everything that they owned in the world lay in that pile of black rubble. The very clothes on her back belonged to someone else, but for once she was not concerned with her possessions. Jonathan had pneumonia and that his condition was serious she knew, more from what the doctor did not say than by what he did. Her main concern was that he should live. She longed for Nick. She did not know the doctor who had been treating Jonathan and she would have felt much better if Nick had been there to lean on.

The door behind her opened softly and the doctor entered the room. He went to the other side of the bed, and bent over the sick man. Margaret rose and went to the window where she stood with her eyes shut, the doctor straightened and, going to Margaret, led her out of the room. Closing the door softly behind him, he faced her and she knew from his expression that his news was not good. She held herself steady, but her voice shook as she articulated her words. "He is dying." It was more a statement than a question.

The doctor nodded his head.

"I may stay with him until the end?"

"If you wish, but it is rather foolish. I doubt if he will come out of his coma sufficiently to recognize you."

"I intend to stay."

The doctor was too tired and too busy to argue. "As you wish."

Margaret fought to steady her voice. "How long?"

"An hour or two, maybe less."

"Thank you," she managed to say with dignity, and going back into the room, she shut the door behind her. There was no noise in the quiet room but the painful drawing in and letting out of labored breath. It made Margaret's chest feel sore just to listen to it. She wished that she could hold his hand, but even that was impossible, for his hands were bandaged and the pressure would cause him pain. She sat with her hands folded in her lap, her thoughts pricking her like the stings of a swarm of hornets. This then was the end of their love. She went back over the years in her mind and reviewed his tenderness, consideration, and kindness. He had been very good to her, very good and loving. Again and again her mind's eye saw the sad and pained expression that her rantings against his religion had brought to that beloved countenance. She wished that she could tell him she was truly sorry, but he was beyond apologies now. If he would only recognize her just once more so that she could tell him that she loved him. He turned his head restlessly on the pillow and opened his eyes, but there was no recognition in his glance. Her hand flew to her mouth to smother a sob. He turned from her to gaze steadily at the foot of the bed. As she watched him breathlessly, his eyes seemed to clear. Love and recognition shone in them, but not for her. Without warning he sat up with raised arms and held them out to some unseen presence, saying distinctly in a tone of ineffable love, "Jesus, my Lord and my God, I am coming home!" Before Margaret could move to catch him, he had fallen back on the pillow, dead.

Chapter Twenty-two

For the second time in her life, Margaret donned black garments, and she sat silently by a casket which contained all that was left of one she had loved. For the second time she followed the hearse to the graveyard and listened to the magnificent words, "I am the resurrection and the life; he that believeth on Me, though he were dead, yet shall he live, and whosoever liveth and believeth on Me shall never die." They had no meaning for her. She moved as if in a dream, but she did not dare to let herself go, for she knew there was no one to lean on. Tim was gone; Jonathan was gone; and Nick was far away. She was alone in the world. She had a child to support, but her resources were very limited, and she could not afford to sit down and indulge herself in sorrow.

She had sat on the landing of the staircase where she could watch, without being seen, the stream of people who came to view the remains of Jonathan Wellfleet. She was astonished and overwhelmed, not only by the numbers who respectfully requested admittance, but at the deep sorrow they showed so obviously. She had never seen most of them before and she did not know who they were. They came from all walks of life, although poor people made up the majority of the crowd. They came silently and they left silently, but the shine of tears was on many faces. One young lad sobbed convulsively as he gazed at the handsome face in the coffin. An old man knelt beside it to pray and one toil-worn woman dressed in shabby garments bent and reverently kissed the peaceful forehead. The mayor came and stood, respectfully holding his hat by the casket, making the remark as he left that Jonathan Wellfleet had done more for the community than any man of his time. A group of businessmen came, shook their heads sadly and went quietly away overcome by emotion. The president of the bank where Jonathan had done his business came to pay his respects. The room could not hold all the floral offerings which arrived. None of these people asked for the widow, all they were concerned with was the man lying in state in the simple coffin. Margaret would have liked to put on an expensive funeral but she did not dare to do so. All she owned in the world was the lot on which their house had stood and the business and she had no idea how much money she could realize from either.

As soon as the funeral was over, she set to work to straighten out her affairs. She had notified Peggy's school of her father's death, but she had requested that they should not let the child attend the funeral, so she was not bothered with her. She was still staying at Mrs. Fairchild's. She did not feel that she was welcome there, but none of her friends had offered to have her and she did not know where else to go. It humiliated her to have to accept hospitality from a woman whom she scarcely knew and whom she suspected disliked her, but she could do nothing else for the time. She put the house lot and the business up for sale and decided that she would write to Mr. Stillwell asking if she could get her old job back. Knowing that he could not attend the funeral she had not notified him of Jonathan's death. Now she sat down and wrote him a long letter telling him what had happened. In the meantime, there was nothing to do but wait for an answer.

This was where matters stood three weeks after the funeral. She and her unwilling hostess were seated over a fire in the cluttered back parlor when the doorbell rang and the surly old housekeeper stumped in with a telegram for Margaret. Margaret's thoughts flew to Nick and she opened the yellow envelope with trembling fingers. The telegram was from Michael and announced briefly, "Mr. Stillwell died at ten o'clock this morning."

Margaret sat staring blindly into the fire. It certainly never rained but it poured, she thought grimly. The only place of refuge that she thought might be open to her was gone. She had no place to go and no one to depend on. Everything for which she had struggled so hard was gone. She wished dully that she was dead.

Old Mrs. Fairchild peered at her curiously over her spectacles. She was a shrewd old woman who knew a great deal more about Margaret's affairs than Margaret realized. When she saw the despondent expression on the younger woman's face, she was alarmed. That was just the way she had looked when she had sat around and moped until she had finally gone crazy. Mrs. Fairchild straightened her plump shoulders and thought to herself that it was about time someone took a hand. If she thought that she could sit around her house and mope until her mind cracked a second time, she had another guess coming to her. It was about time somebody told her the truth about herself and made her realize her selfishness. Mrs. Fairchild had not spent many evenings peering down into the lighted windows of the Wellfleet's house for nothing.

"Bad news?" she asked briskly.

Margaret surrendered her bleak thoughts with a start. "Yes, I am afraid so. It is about the death of a dear friend of mine. I had hoped that he would be able to help me."

Another infatuated male, thought the acid old woman, I wonder how she does it. Aloud, she said, "What will you do now?"

"I don't know," said Margaret and lapsed again into gazing blindly into the fire.

But her hostess gave her no peace. "You have to do something. You have a child to support."

"Yes, I suppose so."

Mrs. Fairchild's temper flared. "Well, it's about time."

Margaret looked up, unable to ignore the open hostility in her hostess's voice. The old woman continued acidly, "Oh, don't look at me like that. You've had everything your own way for a long time now, with a doting husband at your beck and call and that infatuated doctor watching every breath you drew. You've had your share of the good things of life. Is there any reason why you shouldn't have your share of the bad, like everybody else?"

Margaret looked up and her face flushed. She was speechless before the audacity of this harsh old woman. No one had talked to her like this for a long time. Mrs. Fairchild continued brusquely, glad to see that she had drawn blood, "I used to sit in my bedroom window and watch you and your husband. I often wondered at the inequalities of life. Why should you have a man like that, while I had a good-for-nothing philanderer? You never appreciated him; all you thought of was yourself."

She saw resentment and anger gather in Margaret's gray eyes and she thought to herself, "Good, this will make her forget her troubles and leave off her self pity! Make her buck up and do something!" Outloud she continued pitilessly, "Do you know the reason your house burned down? Because you made your husband lock the door on that poor old man he had in the shed room. Oh, don't deny it," she snapped as Margaret started to protest, "I saw the whole thing. When you are immersing yourself in self-pity, just think what you did to him."

Unable to defend herself, Margaret said icily, "You seem to know a good deal about my affairs."

The old lady snorted through her nose. "There isn't much about you I don't know. I know that you had a thriving business once and that what you did once, you can do again."

At that, Margaret cried out furiously. "Do you think that I could stay in this town and do that?"

Mrs. Fairchild picked up her knitting and settled back in her chair. "No," she said evenly, "I don't suppose you could put your pride in your pocket sufficiently to admit to all your friends that you used to work for all your fripperies. But you will have to do something. Nicholas Thorpe is somewhere in France and can't come running if you send for him, although I've no doubt he would if he could, for I've never seen a man with a worse case on a woman than he had for you."

Glancing over at her guest, the old lady saw that Margaret was fairly boiling with anger and she knew that she had accomplished what she had set out to do. That young woman wouldn't sit and mope; she would get up and go to work and that was what she needed.

Margaret rose with what dignity she could muster and her eyes were blazing with fury. "I had no idea that I had provided you with so much amusement for so long. I can see that my presence here is unwelcome. You may be assured that I will remove myself from your house at the earliest possible moment. I am going to my room now to pack what little I have and it will not take me long to get out. Good evening." She turned and left the room and the old woman watched her go without making a move to stop her.

"I certainly got her started!" She chuckled to herself with satisfaction as she turned the heel of the sock she was knitting.

When Margaret left the city which had been her home for so long, she purchased a ticket for New York. She did not know exactly why she did so, except that she had been there once and so was somewhat familiar with it. During the long trip she had plenty of time to think and to speculate upon her future. She had enough money to carry her until she could get a teaching position, but somehow she no longer had any desire to teach. Her ideas had changed radically since the days when her heart's desire had been to become a teacher, and with them her values had altered. She now knew that what she wanted from life she would never attain in the teaching profession. It might be a means of earning a living, but it would not pay enough to suit her present tastes and it therefore no longer appealed to her. But what else could she do? That was the question. How else could she make enough money to live as she liked? When the train pulled into Grand Central station she was no nearer the solution to her problem than she had been when she started.

The porter carrying her suitcase hustled into the waiting room and asked her where she was going. She stuttered that she did not know, and he left her unceremoniously. She sat down on a low bench and watched the hurrying crowds. Everybody seemed to have a destination. The woman sitting next to her was absorbed in a newspaper. As she turned the sheet, a large picture of the nation's capitol building caught Margaret's eye. "That," she thought to herself, "is something that I have always wanted to see. Well, why not? I might as well make a new start there as anywhere else." On the impulse of the moment she arose and, lifting her suitcase, went to the ticket window and bought a ticket for Washington.

When she arrived at Union station she decided that her impulse had not been such a good one, for wartime Washington was packed with crowds of soldiers and civilians. Seeing a Traveler's Aid desk, she approached the clerk and requested help. The motherly woman in charge looked at her deep mourning and her pale, tired face. Concluding that she was a war widow, the clerk went into a conference with her assistant and finally produced an address where she was told she could find a room. The room was not in a very good neighborhood, but it was clean and cheap and Margaret rented it for a week. The next day she bought all the morning papers and looked over the ads, but there was nothing that appealed to her. There were plenty of jobs, but what she wanted was a *position.*

It was not until the fourth day that she came across an ad which caught her attention and held it. Sitting on the side of her narrow bed, she read it carefully. "Wanted: woman of refinement to act as housekeeper for large establishment. Would have complete supervision of eight servants and must be able to act as hostess upon occasion. Applicant please apply in person." She cut out the ad and put it in her bag.

Taking a taxi to the address given, which was in a good part of the city, she knocked at the door of a large house. It was opened by a butler. She squared her small, black-clad shoulders and handed him the ad. "I have come in answer to that." He nodded and, opening the door further, motioned her to follow him along a spacious hall and up a short flight of white marble stairs. There was a small reception room to the right into which he showed her and announced in stentorian tones that he would inform the lady of the house that she was there.

What Margaret had been able to see of the house as she passed swiftly through the hall took her breath away. It had a magnificience even surpassing the Stillwell's. For a moment she wondered if she would be equal to the task of housekeeper. She had no time, however, to ponder the matter, for the butler returned and requested her to follow him. They crossed a hall where a small elevator was waiting, its door open. They entered and it shot them up two floors before the butler again opened the sliding door. He then led her along a corridor to the back of the house and tapped softly on a white-paneled door. A trained nurse opened it and he motioned her to enter.

The room in which she found herself was enormous, running across the back of the house. The nurse led her silently across the room and motioned her to be seated in a chair next to a great canopied bed, so placed that its occupant had an uninterrupted view of a wide balcony with trees beyond.

"Here she is, madam," the nurse said softly and retired to her place at the other side of the bed. Margaret found herself gazing into a pair of keen, but kindly, brown eyes. The eyes smiled at her and a cultured voice said, "I am Mrs. Wilcox. You came about the position as housekeeper?"

Margaret nodded. "Yes, I saw your advertisement in the paper."

"Have you had any experience with this kind of work?"

Margaret had expected this and was prepared for it. "I have never had more than four servants to manage, but I am sure I could handle more."

The woman on the bed nodded her head. "Four would be enough to give you the experience you need. Tell me something about yourself."

"I am a widow. My husband died suddenly, leaving me very little. I must support myself. I have a daughter, but aside from her I am quite alone in the world."

"When could you come?"

"Anytime you wish."

Mrs. Wilcox smiled. "This is better and better. For my purposes, I mean." She turned to the nurse. "We must tell Dana that I was right about advertising after all. See what luck I've had already. It does my soul good to prove him wrong once in a while. In fact," she turned from the nurse to Margaret, "it does all men good to be put in their place every so often, as I am sure you know. Tell me your name."

On her way to the interview, Margaret had decided to use her maiden name and then if she did not like what she found she could extricate herself without the people knowing who she was. She replied, "Mrs. McAskie."

The sick woman closed her eyes for a minute with a grimace as pain overwhelmed her. The nurse was beside her swiftly with a glass of cloudy liquid in her hands. After she had taken it, she was able to continue. "I will tell you precisely what I want. I'll tell you plainly: I am dying." She spoke as if death were as matter of fact as the ordering of the day's groceries. "I need someone to take my place and manage my household. My son, Dana, is in politics and he needs a woman who can be trusted to keep things running smoothly here and act as his official hostess upon occasion. His father has a sister who would dearly love to fill the place, but he cannot abide her and so, in order to save hurt feelings all around, the simplest thing to do seemed to be to hire an outsider, but I hardly hoped for success so soon. I can see from your appearance and manner that you are a lady and I would like to have you start immediately, so that by the time I am not here," her voice did not falter, "you will be able to manage alone. You may have your own apartment: a sitting room, bedroom, and bath. Your duties should not be too onerous for a while. Except for ordering meals, keeping track of the linen, china, and silver, and supervising the servants, your time is your own. Because of my illness, we are doing almost no entertaining in the house and my son dines out five nights a week. Do you think that you would be interested?"

Margaret's hands were clenched nervously in her lap, but her voice was steady as she replied, "I most certainly am, if you think that I can manage."

"Fine. I'll take the chance. Would you be willing to come tomorrow? I want to give you as much assistance as I can and I haven't much time. Oh, I almost forgot to tell you the salary." She named a figure which was higher than Margaret had hoped she might get. "Is that satisfactory with you?"

"Quite," replied Margaret and rose to leave before Mrs. Wilcox had time to change her mind.

Life in the Wilcox mansion soon settled into a regular routine for Margaret. She was afraid of the servants, especially Jenkins the butler, but she was wise enough not to let them know it, and it was not long before they came to realize that there was not much which went on below stairs that missed the new housekeeper's eye. She had not been there a week before she had checked every piece of china, linen, and silver against a list given her by Mrs. Wilcox and demanded to know where the missing pieces had gone. She kept track of the larder, too, and checked the bills herself so the padding which had been going on had to stop. Two of the servants gave notice, but the rest stayed, for the wages were high and the table better than in most places. It was not long before she had replaced those who left and had the entire situation under control.

The only thing which bothered her was the entertaining that she would eventually have to undertake. By adroitly questioning her employer she was able to learn what she needed to know. It was not long before she and Mrs. Wilcox became fast friends and she was frequently summoned to the sick room when there were visitors. "I want my friends to get used to seeing you around," she told Margaret easily. "And, I have told the right ones that you are the daughter of an old friend who has consented to help me out. They will get the information to my sister-in-law so when the time comes for me to go, there will be no gossip about Dana's not bringing his aunt here to live. That will save family friction, which is a necessity in this case, I assure you."

Mr. Dana Wilcox proved to be a mild-looking, rather reserved, bespectacled, middle-aged gentleman with none of his mother's charm, but much of her kindness. He treated Margaret with courtesy and consideration, but as his official duties kept him away from home a great deal, she saw little of him. She had dropped into the habit of taking most of her meals with the invalid, at her request, and she discovered her to be a delightful woman whose personality, even on her death bed, sparkled with wit and humor. Here was a person who had no religion who was not afraid to die. She summed up her philosophy to Margaret one afternoon over tea. "I'm an old woman and I've lived a long time. I've had a good life, with a full share of trouble and sorrow, enough to make me have no regret that I will soon rest peacefully in my grave. My only regret is that Dana never married. He will come into a great deal of money when I'm gone and I'll have to trust you to see that some fortune hunter doesn't get her clutches on him. But, as I have nothing more to experience, I must face the inevitable."

Something within Margaret wanted to cry out that she did not know of a certainty that there would be peace for everyone in the grave, but she smothered it in disgust at herself for having thought it.

Spring came much earlier to Washington than to the part of the country where Margaret had lived formerly. The trees outside the sick room were lacy with tender new leaves when the end came, quietly and without any fuss. Mrs. Wilcox looked slightly more drawn and weary one evening when Margaret bade her good night, and in the morning the night nurse gave the announcement that their employer had passed away quietly in her sleep.

Margaret set about making the necessary arrangements at once for the funeral. She had her hands full for sometime after the funeral also, getting the big house to rights again. After it was all over, Mr. Wilcox told her that he would be pleased if she would dine with him in the dining room whenever he was home and she readily agreed. He had decided not to open the house at Bar Harbor, Maine, for the summer. There was much to be done in Washington that last summer of the war, and he would be very busy. During the summer months social events were at a minimum and he was home more often. She was glad of his company, for she missed his mother more than she was willing to admit. She had experienced a good deal of death in the past year; the inevitable reaction had set in, and she was lonely. She could busy herself about the house during the day, but the evenings were long. On the whole, her life satisfied her well. She had only one worry. She had written Nick about what she was doing, but she had never heard from him. This bothered her and she wrote again, but she got no reply. She was beginning to wonder if he, too, were dead, when something happened which drove him and everything else out of her mind.

She was in the dining room with Mr. Wilcox sitting companionably eating their dessert, discussing one of the vital issues of the day when the butler announced a visitor to see her. Margaret had just succeeded with her usual finesse in getting Mr. Wilcox to express himself at length. He had been enjoying himself and he looked up with a frown at the interruption. Margaret could scarcely believe her ears. She knew nobody in Washington well enough for them to call upon her at this unconventional hour. Whoever it was would give no name. Hurrying out into the hall her dinner napkin still in her hand, she found Peggy, ill at ease on one of the straight hall chairs. Resentment and indignation at the impromptu manner in which her daughter had put in her appearance made Margaret ask sharply, "What are you doing here?"

Peggy rose awkwardly and Margaret saw with surprise that she had grown into quite a pretty girl, in spite of her lack of poise. Her eyes begged her mother's forgiveness. "There was an epidemic of influenza and they closed the school. I didn't know what else to do, so I came here."

Margaret was exasperated. Just as she was getting along so nicely in her position, she had to have this great gawky girl thrown on her hands. What in heaven's name was she to do with her? As she stood staring at her daughter, uncertain as to what to do next, Mr. Wilcox came out into the hall and inquired courteously, "Nothing wrong, I hope." There was nothing to do but introduce them.

He was kindness itself and insisted upon taking Peggy back to the table and giving her some dinner. Margaret sat in tight-lipped silence at the head of the table, but no one noticed, for Mr. Wilcox was questioning Peggy and she was answering him timidly. When he learned about the closing of the school, he insisted upon her staying with her mother until it opened again. That certainly was a solution to the problem, but not one which pleased Margaret. The last thing in the world she wanted was to have Peggy underfoot, but Mr. Wilcox seemed delighted with the idea. He had an engagement for that evening, but he expressed the hope that he might be able to find something to do to amuse the young lady.

He was as good as his word and undertook to show Peggy the sights of Washington, although Margaret would have gladly spared him the trouble. For the next few weeks he and Peggy spent much time together. Peggy's unease and timidity seemed to fall away when she was in his presence and Margaret was increasingly surprised at the interest he took in her.

One morning at the breakfast table he announced that he had to drive south of the city on business and would be gone most of the day. He would appreciate company on the long ride and would Miss Peggy care to go along? Miss Peggy most decidedly would. In fact, her mother was ashamed of the shameless pleasure she displayed over the proposal. "The little silly should not be so eager," she thought to herself indignantly.

It was ten o'clock in the evening when they returned. Mr. Wilcox, beaming behind his thick glasses and looking extraordinarily pleased with himself, and Peggy, radiating happiness, announced that they had been married that afternoon in Gretna Green, Maryland.

While the newly-weds were on their honeymoon, Margaret had plenty of time to ponder on the situation. It did not take her long to realize that she had a far superior position in the household as a relative than she had as a housekeeper. Of course, the marriage was entirely unsuitable, for Dana Wilcox was nearer her age than her daughter's and her daughter was too young to be married; but on the other hand, there were distinct advantages, too. Her new son-in-law had told her before they left that now he would need her more than ever. She realized that more than he, for Peggy was not only too much of a flutterbudget to manage such a big establishment, but she had had no experience.

Margaret sighed as she contemplated Peggy's awkwardness, ineptness, and gaucheness. All this would have to be trained out of her before she could be presented to Washington society. Margaret was thankful that it was summer and wartime, for there was practically no entertaining going on so she would have a little time to groom her daughter.

Peggy returned from her honeymoon pregnant and it was immediately apparent that she was going to be very ill. Her mother thought with contempt that this was just another sign of Peggy's weakness. As it was, she did not quarrel with the fact that her illness would postpone the time when she could take her place publicly as Dana Wilcox's wife, and in the meantime, her mother could continue to act as hostess. This suited Margaret perfectly. By fall it became apparent even to Margaret that Peggy's sickness was not imaginary. The doctors called it pernicious vomiting and took her to the hospital where she stayed for nearly three months. When they brought her home she was a mere shadow of her former self and she had to be kept in bed for the duration of her pregnancy. Her husband was devoted to her and he spent every minute he could spare in her company. But there was still much time that Margaret had to spend with her daughter and this she did not enjoy. They had nothing whatsoever to say to one another, and it was painful for them both. Peggy's habit of reading her Bible quite openly was a further source of annoyance to her mother.

Early in March, Peggy prematurely gave birth to triplets. In so doing, she lost her life. For a while her husband was inconsolable and the entire responsibility for the household rested on Margaret, including the welfare of the two little girls and the little boy who were her grandchildren. She was very busy, but happier than she had been in years, for although the two little girls were dark and as alike as two peas in a pod, the tiny lad's head was covered with a fine reddish fuzz, just as Tim's had been when he was born. For the first time in years, Margaret had something beside herself on which to fasten her devotion. She haunted the nursery and tormented the nurses with her supervision and once again she began to plan and dream. Here was a boy whose life she could mold exactly as she chose. He would have all the advantages which Jonathan had spurned and which Timmie had missed. There seemed to be nothing to interfere with her plans because religion had been put forever out of her life, and she could do as she pleased. Everyday the boy grew to look more like his grandfather, who had been the most charming man she had ever known. All Margaret had to do now was to make sure that Dana Wilcox did not marry again, thus giving young Dana a stepmother. To this end, she endeavored to make him so comfortable in his own home that the idea of taking a wife would not occur to him.

Peace had been declared the previous November, but the armistice had been only a passing incident in her busy life, involved as she was with her complicated household. She still had heard nothing from Nick which was a nagging worry until after the triplets were born. From that time on, however, it gradually faded from her mind, except when she saw a uniform and was reminded that the war had ended. Her life was very full. At long last she was leading the kind of a life she liked, in the midst of surroundings she enjoyed, and there was in the center of her affection a small red-haired boy.

Chapter Twenty-three

Dr. Nicholas Thorpe stood at the rail of the troop ship and watched the tugs nose the big vessel into the wharf. It was a lengthy job and he felt he could not stand it if they did not hurry. The war had been over for a year, but he had had to stay with the army of occupation because they had discovered that he spoke both French and German fluently. He had not heard from Margaret since she had sent him the barest outline of Jonathan's death, although he had written her frequently. He had been moved about so much that a lot of his mail had been lost, but after the armistice he had sent her an address in Paris, and then had been sick with worry when no letters arrived. He had written his lawyer to look her up, but all he could learn was that she had sold the awning business and had left town. He wrote to Mrs. Fairchild and received a reply stating that she did not know where Margaret had gone and cared less. He had finally contacted the school where Peggy had last been enrolled and been informed that Peggy had gone to Washington to her mother when an epidemic of influenza had broken out in the school, and had never returned. He had written to ask where in Washington, but they did not know.

Why Washington, of all places? There was no answer that he knew of and he was anxious to go himself and look. Nothing would stop him if only he could get off this ship!

Somehow, he got through the discharge procedure and without even changing his clothes he entrained for Washington. He had learned from the president of his bank that Margaret had deposited her money in a savings bank in Washington. He went directly to that bank and demanded to see the president, and by sheer force of will and the fact that he was still in uniform, succeeded in obtaining the information that the money had been deposited sometime ago and that no withdrawals had been made against the account.

He went to the address Margaret had given the bank, but no one in the second-rate boarding house had heard of her. Either Margaret was dead or she was well enough off to get along without the money in the savings account. Nick's emotions fluctuated between despair and elation when he thought about it. If she were alive he would find her somehow. If she were dead — he refused to allow his thoughts to travel in that direction.

He put the case in the hands of a competent detective agency and walked the streets of Washington for days peering at every woman he passed who was of Margaret's height and build.

Before leaving Germany he had tried to contact Mr. Stillwell, only to be informed by his lawyers that they were as anxious to find the lady as he was, for their client had left her his entire fortune. When he thought of the pleasure it would give him to be able to tell her that at last she could have anything she wanted, he could hardly stand it. But he had to find her first, and he could not. When he realized that policemen were watching him as he followed any small woman he saw on the streets until he could get a glimpse of her face, he decided that madness lay in that direction and he must find something to do to stay sane.

He was too restless to try to establish a practice in Washington, but he had better fill his time with something which would keep his mind off Margaret. The only thing in which he was interested in studying was psychology and the only place he could get what he wanted was abroad, so he arranged for a weekly report from the detective agency and departed for Europe, having done all he could.

After several years of study his nerves were steadier and he felt equal to establishing a practice in Washington. As long as it was in Washington that Margaret had disappeared, it was in Washington that he would stay until he was certain she could not be found.

It was a beautiful spring day and the cherry trees along the tidal basin had clothed themselves in glorious color. Nick sat on a park bench and admired their beauty, but as he filled his eyes with the beautiful sight, he wished in his heart that Margaret was beside him. The faint sense of loss that he could never quite eliminate took the keen edge off his pleasure. He never listened to great music, saw great beauty, or tasted delicious food without thinking that anything which pleased him would give him twice the pleasure were she only at his side to share it. He sometimes thought that it would not be so bad if he knew positively that she were dead. Then at least she would be enshrined in his heart forever. But not knowing that, he could not help but hope, and hope was a pain in itself.

It was after five o'clock and the usual crowd of sightseers, who during the afternoon hours had swarmed about the basin, had departed. Here and there a few stragglers were wandering along the paths or occupying the benches. As he lounged on the bench, his thoughts on the woman he had never ceased to love, he was rudely recalled to reality by a rubber ball bouncing off his chest. He looked up quickly. An English nursemaid was occupying the next bench keeping an eye on three children who were playing in front of her. Two little girls were swinging a jump rope and a sturdy red-headed lad was bouncing a ball. The ball had escaped his clutches and hit the occupant of the adjoining bench squarely on the chest. The little girls let out a shriek and the lad ran to retrieve the ball, an apology on his lips. As he stood looking up at Nick, his hand out for his ball, something vaguely familiar in the color and shape of the eyes rang a bell in the man's heart. Those eyes were Jonathan Wellfleet's. Handing the child the ball, he asked, "What is your name, son?"

"Dana Wilcox, sir," answered the child, "I hope I didn't hurt you."

Nick shook his head, a wave of disappointment going over him. Even if this boy were Peggy's son, he doubted if she would have named him for anybody but her beloved twin. Still, her husband might want his son named after him. Nick sat up with a shrug. He mustn't let his imagination run away from him because of a chance resemblance.

Suddenly, the children sprinted down the path toward a small dark-haired woman, calling joyously, "Gram! Gram!"

Following them with his eyes, Nick saw the woman gather the little boy into her arms. When she raised her head and approached the bench where the nurse had risen respectfully, the children dancing about her, Nick got a good look at her face. With a glad cry he leaped to his feet. It was Margaret. Margaret, alive and well! He had found his love at last!

Nick, resplendent in evening clothes, sat in the lobby of the Waldorf Astoria waiting for Margaret to descend in the elevator. She and the children had just returned from a summer in Europe, and he was going to celebrate her return. They were going to the theater. They had finished dining and Margaret had gone upstairs to have a look at the children before they left the hotel. Nanny was perfectly capable of looking after them, but Margaret always made a ritual of bidding young Dana good night and she let nothing interfere with it. The doctor frowned when he thought of Dana. Fond as he was of the child, he realized fully that he was the reason that he and Margaret had not married. Her complete absorption in the boy overshadowed everything else in her life. Soon after he had found her again, he came to the realization that this small grandson of hers constituted the center and the circumference of her existence. She worshiped him and her whole life was planned about him. He even took precedence over her social engagements. Nick thought the matter over carefully and as a doctor feared the psychological effect of trying to separate her from the child. His father could not be expected to let the boy go with his grandmother if she were to marry.

As he had become a part of Margaret's life again, he saw that she had an overriding fear: that Dana Wilcox would marry again and give the child a stepmother who would want to take him away from her. So Nick had allowed things to slide along without bringing them to an issue. Perhaps he was a coward, but he felt that if he forced the issue and she refused him on account of the child, he would be worse off than he already was. He saw her frequently and had the pleasure of her society and when she was happy she was a lovely person to be with. Nearly four years had passed since he had found her, and Dana was now eight years old. The boy would grow up, go off to school, and then Nick could step in to fill the vacancy his leaving would produce in Margaret's life.

As he mentally reached this conclusion, the elevator door opened and Margaret stepped out into the foyer. She saw, rising to meet her, a distinguished looking man with an erect carriage and iron gray hair, and she went toward him smiling. All Nick's discontent and frustration vanished into thin air when he saw her and he forgot everything but that they were together once more.

When they arrived at the theater she slipped the wrap which she had kept about her at dinner off her shoulders and he suddenly realized that she had lost considerable weight. Her shoulder blades stood out sharply and her slender arms were like pipe stems. He frowned. "What have you been doing to yourself?" he asked gruffly. "You look as if you had dropped fifteen pounds and I know you couldn't afford to lose an ounce."

"I have lost a little, but not that much, Nick. I've been having some trouble with my stomach."

"Did you see anybody over there about it?"

"No, I wanted to wait to get home to you. I don't like going to other doctors."

In spite of the pleasure her remark gave him, he could not forbear to question her further. "How long has this been going on?"

"Soon after we left. It started in Paris and at first I thought it was only indigestion, but the attacks have persisted all summer."

He groaned silently. "I'll take you to a stomach specialist and we will find out what this is all about. It is not something to fool about with."

She smiled and slipped a small hand into his. "It's wonderful to have you to take care of me," she whispered as the curtain went up, and he sat and watched the stage in a daze of happiness with eyes that did not see.

He insisted that she see the specialist at once, but the reports were far from encouraging. The doctor thought an immediate operation advisable and agreed to perform it in a Washington hospital if the patient wished. The patient most certainly did. She could not keep Dana in New York indefinitely. So Margaret returned home, made arrangements, and entered the hospital. She had done her best to pump Nick as to her condition, but she could get nothing out of him except that the operation would be the answer to their questions. He assured her that he would stay with her throughout the ordeal and with this she had to be content. As long as he was with her she knew no fear and the last thing she remembered as they put the ether cone gently over her face, was the reassuring pressure of his hand. He was sitting beside her when she came out of the ether and it was he who wet her lips with a piece of cracked ice to relieve their dryness. Although she was kept under opiates for the next few days he never left her side except to eat and change clothes, and when she finally came out of the merciful fog in which she had been drifting, it was to find him seated beside her. From that time on he was her constant companion except when she slept and he promised her that he would get her home to Dana at the earliest possible moment. She was fairly comfortable and quite free from pain, so she did not concern herself for the moment with what had been the matter with her. They took her home in an ambulance as soon as she could be safely moved and placed her in the big bed in Mrs. Wilcox's room looking out over the tree tops. The day after her return the awful gripping pains seized her once again and then she knew. She gave herself a little time to face her knowledge and then she spoke to Nick about it.

He was sitting beside her in the late afternoon sunshine, and for the first time she noticed how gray and haggard he looked. His big hand lay on the outside of the covers and she slipped her small one under it. "Nick."

He turned to her as though coming from a long distance. "Yes, dear?"

"It's cancer, isn't it?"

His tortured eyes met hers and he nodded his head. "Yes."

"And nothing can be done about it."

This time he shook his head but he would not look at her, and she saw a tear tremble on his lashes. He shook his head im-

266

patiently once more and the tear dropped on the counterpane. He managed somehow to mutter, "I won't let you suffer too much."

Her hand tightened in his. "How long have I?"

"Three months at most. Probably less."

She digested this in silence, and then said, "I am glad to know. It is better that way."

He slipped out of his chair to the floor and buried his head in her pillows, dry sobs shaking his big body. Her hand went to his hair and she stroked the thick gray locks softly. "Poor Nick. You've always been so good to me and I've been such an ungrateful wretch. I've known that you loved me for a long time. Mrs. Fairchild told me, but I wouldn't let you tell me for fear of losing Dana. I should have married you and tried to repay you for all your love and loyalty, but I was too selfish and now I shall have to leave Dana anyway and it is too late to do anything about our getting married. Can you ever forgive me?"

He raised his head and looked deep into her eyes, unashamed of his tears. "There can never be any talk of forgiveness between you and me, my beloved," he said softly, and gathering her up in his arms kissed her gently, full upon the lips.

Margaret had been hoarding her steadily diminishing store of strength for days. There was something she must say to Nick, and some instructions she must give him, for in her innermost soul she knew that the end was not far off. She had chosen a time when they could be alone and free from outside interference. The trees outside the big sheet of glass were entirely bare now, but they were silhouetted against a magnificent sunset. Nick had fed her an early supper. It did not take long, for she ate very little. Now she lay back against her heap of pillows, her hand in his and together they watched the gorgeous color slowly fade out of the darkening sky. At last she whispered, "Nick, dear."

He turned to her at once. "Yes, beloved?"

"I have something to say to you and I want you to help me say it. It is about Dana." He saw her hesitation and so he came to her aid.

"Something you want to leave him?"

"Yes, something I want to leave him. Something I want you to give him for me."

267

"You know that I will do anything you want."

Once more she hesitated, uncertain of how to continue. What she had to say was not easy to put into words. Finally, she said softly, "When I am gone, I want you to tell Dana the story of my life. I want you to tell him how all my life I have hated religion and fought against God, but that when I came to die, I could not die without Him. Tell him that I felt capable of managing my own life so I did, but that when I got what I thought I wanted, it was all dust and ashes. Tell him, that in getting it I became small and irritable, hateful and mean. Then tell him about Jonathan." Her voice softened as she spoke the beloved name. "And, tell him how he gave God a chance in his life and how that made him considerate of others and kind and patient and loving, and how when he came to die the whole city mourned his passing, but that when I came to die there was only you, my dear and faithful friend to sincerely grieve over my going."

He started to protest, but she silenced him with a shake of her head. "Oh, I know that both big and little Dana will miss me for a time, but not in the way those people I saw mourning over Jonathan's coffin missed him. I have lived too selfish and self-centered a life to make myself that necessary to anyone. I have had a lot of time to think as I have lain here waiting for the angel of death to claim me, and at last I have had to be honest with myself. I wanted too much to have what I called the finer things of life: culture and social position and money, but in my mad scramble to attain them I completely lost sight of the most important thing of all, the condition of my soul and my relation to my creator. Make Dana understand that no matter what else he has, if he does not know God in the way his grandfather did, he has nothing. Everything in the world fades away and in the end there is only the soul and God. Tell him how his grandfather could face life with courage and fortitude and with his head high because he had a real and vital faith in God, but how I went crazy because I didn't." As Nick once more started to make a protest, she stopped him. "Yes, tell him just that. Oh, Nick, I see it all so clearly now that it is too late to do anything about it. I was abominably selfish and inconsiderate of others. Jonathan gave up a great deal for me, yet I wasn't willing to give up anything for him. I didn't even try to see things his way."

Nick could not stand to hear her flagellate herself. "He always loved you with all his heart and it is easy to be good to one we love."

Margaret sighed and tears of weakness filled her eyes and flowed down over her pale and sunken cheeks. "Yes, and I never deserved it. That was just another way in which God blessed me far beyond my due. I had Jonathan and I had you." She raised his hand to her face and rested her thin cheek against it. "And, I never deserved either of you. I had so much love poured into my life I should have been grateful enough to let God's love into my heart."

Nick could not speak and for a long moment there was silence. Then Margaret once more garnered her failing resources and continued. "I see now how my rebellion against God brought harm to myself. Jonathan tried to tell me once that God may have refused to save my lamb in order to prevent me from getting something which might be harmful to me and now I see that he was right. For it was when I got away from the farm that I acquired tastes and ideas which I was not willing to relinquish. He tried to make me see that God might have given me my heart's desire if I had put Him first in my life, but I never gave Him a chance. It was my fault that we were always pinched for money because I was not satisfied with the things we had. I had to go on acquiring more things than we could possibly use, but I found when I got them they did not satisfy me, so I went blindly on and on refusing to learn from my mistakes.

"I know now that you can't go through life thinking of nobody but yourself and have anything but yourself left in the end. It was my fault that Tim was killed. If I hadn't wasted so much money we would have had enough to buy a good horse. It isn't easy . . . " Fresh tears trickled down her face and dampened Nick's fingers. "It isn't easy to have to face that fact. What a fool I have been. Oh, what a fool!"

Nick said brokenly, "Margaret, my darling, you must not eat out your heart with regret. We all have things to regret when we come to die."

She turned her face toward him and pressed the fingers she still held against her cheek. "I'm not eating my heart out with regret, Nick. I am merely confessing my sins and it is said that confession is good for the soul. As I have been thinking about these things, portions of the Bible that I had to memorize in my youth have been coming back to me and one of the sweetest is this: 'If we confess our sins, He (God) is faithful and just to forgive us our sins and to cleanse us from all unrighteousness.' I have confessed to God and now I am confessing to you, and I have to believe that what the Bible says is true, that God is forgiving me."

A spasm of pain seized her and her hand tightened on his as she closed her eyes and gritted her teeth to endure it. Nick groaned within himself. Her tolerance for narcotics was now very narrow and there was nothing he could do to help her. When the spasm had passed she opened her eyes and smiled into his.

Nick slipped to his knees by the side of the bed and gathered her up in his strong arms. Resting against his shoulder, her face close to his, she put up a small hand and gently stroked his cheek. "I kept you from believing, Nick. I know I did. Jonathan had you almost convinced more than once. I do not want you to suffer for my folly. That is the reason I had to tell you all this. I don't want you kept out of the Kingdom of Heaven on my account."

Nick shook his head, unashamed that tears were blinding his dark eyes. Margaret reached for her handkerchief and wiped his eyes tenderly as he had hers so many times in the past, and he managed to say huskily, "Where you are going I must follow and you are right, I have wanted to believe. Only heaven would not have been heaven to me if you were not there, and I couldn't bring myself to a decision for God because you were so much against Him."

"Oh, I am so glad. I have been like the man in the First Psalm who stood in the way of sinners. I stood in your light, but I don't want to anymore, Nick. You won't let me, will you?"

Again, he shook his head without words, and she murmured gladly, "Then we'll see each other in heaven."

Unable to speak, he held her to him, his cheek against her soft hair. She rested against him for a few moments before she continued, "But, I don't want Dana to get into heaven by the skin of his teeth, as I am doing. I want him to be like Jonathan, strong in the Lord. And, Nick," her voice grew wistful as it grew weaker. "Tell big Dana and the girls, too, to believe on the Lord Jesus Christ and be saved! I want all my family with me in Heaven!" She smiled a small twisted smile. "Selfish to the last, you see!"

Her voice trailed off into stillness and she lay back exhausted, but her face shone with a light not of this earth. Nick hardly dared to breathe for fear of startling her. In spite of the pain she was in, the face that she lifted to his was radiant and as she began to speak once more, he realized that she was quoting from the Scriptures.

"For this is the victory which overcometh the world, even our faith!"

Her eyes smiled up at him for the last time and then went past him to a presence he could not see. "Oh, thanks be to God, who gives us the victory through our Lord Jesus Christ!" With a supreme effort she raised her arms and held them out toward the unseen person. "Jonathan, my beloved, at last I, too, have come home!"